# "Lame Deer Is
# a Magnificent American . . .

He has demolished so much misinformation and so
many stereotypes about Indians and their values and
ways of life that we should be ashamed of how little we
have actually known of all that he has to tell us. As an
individual and as a representative of his people, he is
someone whom all readers should get to know—not
just those who are interested in Indians, but every
American. The book is destined to become a classic. It
will be read, and reread, and quoted from through the
years. Personally, I am enormously enriched by it."

—Alvin M. Josephy, Jr.,
author of *Indian Heritage of America*

"A FASCINATING STORY."　　　　*—Library Journal*

---

This Enriched Classics edition is introduced and
edited by Dr. Ruth Rosenberg, a longtime teacher of
Native American literature at both the high school
and college levels. Her work on *LAME DEER, SEEK-
ER OF VISIONS* was completed with the help of a
grant from the New York State English Council.

## Titles available in the
## ENRICHED CLASSICS SERIES

# Lame Deer
# Seeker of Visions

## John (Fire) Lame Deer
## and
## Richard Erdoes

WASHINGTON SQUARE PRESS
PUBLISHED BY POCKET BOOKS
New York   London   Toronto   Sydney   Tokyo   Singapore

**WSP**

A Washington Square Press Publication of
POCKET BOOKS, a division of Simon & Schuster Inc.
1230 Avenue of the Americas, New York, NY 10020

Introduction and supplementary materials copyright © 1994 by Pocket Books, a division of Simon & Schuster, Inc.
Copyright © 1972 by John (Fire) Lame Deer and Richard Erdoes

All rights reserved, including the right to reproduce this book or portions thereof in any form whatsoever. For information address Washington Square Press, 1230 Avenue of the Americas, New York, NY 10020

ISBN: 0-671-88802-1

First Washington Square Press printing April 1976
First printing of this revised edition October 1994

10  9  8  7  6  5  4

WASHINGTON SQUARE PRESS and colophon are registered trademarks of Simon & Schuster Inc.

Cover art by Pamela Patrick

Printed in the U.S.A.

THIS BOOK IS DEDICATED TO:

Frank Fools Crow
Pete Catches
George Eagle Elk
Bill Schweigman
Leonard Crow Dog
Wallace Black Elk
John Strike
Raymond Hunts Horse
Charles Kills Enemy
Godfrey Chips

*and all the other medicine men
of the Sioux Nation*

# CONTENTS

# Contents

# INTRODUCTION

Lame Deer and Richard Erdoes first met in the 1960s. Erdoes came to America in 1940 when he was twenty-eight years old. Of Jewish and Catholic descent, he escaped from Vienna during World War II. Trained as an artist in Berlin and Paris, he found work as a freelance illustrator and graphic artist in New York. He married Jean Sternbergh, an art director at *Time*. Their three children traveled with them when Erdoes was on assignment in the West. When *Life* magazine sent him to do a photo essay on Indian reservations, he was befriended "by an old and almost totally illiterate Sioux medicine man." This was Lame Deer.

In 1967, Lame Deer took a delegation of fifteen Sioux to Martin Luther King, Jr.'s peace march in New York City. Afterward, they had dinner at Erdoes's apartment, where Lame Deer sang the Sioux national anthem and accompanied himself on his drum. Little did Erdoes expect what was to come. As he later wrote:

> John reappeared a few weeks later, Indian style—unannounced and uninvited, ringing our doorbell, standing there with a cardboard box containing his worldly possessions, saying with a broad grin: "I liked you. I think I'll stay for a while." He stayed about two months that time.

Lame Deer wanted Erdoes to write his life story. Although the artist protested that he was not a writer, he finally yielded to Lame Deer's insistence, "and so began the strangest of collaborations. What made it work was that we both had a sense of humor." The book they produced together changed both of their lives. *Lame Deer, Seeker of Visions* went on to be translated into seven languages, including German, French, Dutch, Japanese, and Norwegian, and made Lame Deer a well-known personality.

After *Lame Deer, Seeker of Visions,* Richard Erdoes went on to publish many more books on Native American subjects. He also became increasingly involved with Native American civil rights issues. In November 1972, the Erdoes family participated in the Trail of Broken Treaties and the occupation of the Bureau of Indian Affairs building in Washington, D.C. Richard and Jean became heads of the defense committee for Leonard Crow Dog, who was convicted in three trials and sent to Lewisburg Penitentiary in Pennsylvania—1,800 miles away from the Rosebud Reservation in South Dakota. The Erdoes family invited Leonard Crow Dog's wife and son to stay at their apartment so that she could visit him in prison. During the year that Mary Crow Dog lived with them, Erdoes taped and transcribed her story, which became *Lakota Woman,* winner of the American Book Award in 1991.

Erdoes gives credit to Lame Deer's powerful "medicine" for having turned him into an author of more than a dozen books, saying that "it was John who actually made me a writer, orginally almost against my will." It was also Lame Deer's influence that led to his involvement with Native American causes, giving his life purpose and motivating his move to the West, away from the pressures of metropolitan existence. "But for Lame Deer," he said, "I might still be designing graphics for advertising campaigns."

\* \* \*

Lame Deer and Richard Erdoes worked together for four years, exchanging visits, consulting other medicine men, taping and transcribing dialogue. Much of that conversational texture is retained. Erdoes relates how he was surprised to be invited to attend a sundance organized by Lame Deer in the town of Winner, South Dakota, since the ceremony had been so long outlawed that he thought it extinct. The story of the sundance is so awesome that Lame Deer feels "uneasy" telling it. In ancient times this could only be done "when twelve old and wise men were present to make sure that what was told was right, with nothing added and nothing left out."

We feel privileged to share in the orchestration of this complex event through Lame Deer's words. Perhaps we may even be moved to undergo similar disciplines of self-sacrifice for the sake of the earth. It is ironic that there is no word for "religion" in any Native American language, since their entire existence was permeated with it. It is even more ironic that we sought to ban the ecological awareness they practiced as "pagan" when the very future of the planet may depend upon our learning it from them.

Through *Lame Deer, Seeker of Visions,* we are taught by an uneducated old man in a patched and faded shirt, with a hearing aid whistling in his ear. And there is much to learn. Lame Deer's memoirs had a groundbreaking impact upon the depiction of Native Americans.

Although the book was all but ignored by literary critics, it achieved its immense popularity because of its humor. Before the publication of this funny book, Indians were shown as tragic. Their role in thousands of Hollywood westerns was to die with solemn dignity. In Leslie Marmon Silko's novels, they are wounded and inarticulate. In N. Scott Momaday's, they are elegiacally grieving. John Neihardt, the epic poet of

Nebraska, removed all of Black Elk's *heyoka* wit from *Black Elk Speaks* for the sake of propriety. Raymond DeMallie's transcripts show how much the original diction was heightened into biblical cadences. Dee Brown's *Bury My Heart at Wounded Knee* sentimentalized and romanticized its warriors. Not until Lame Deer's teasing, ridicule, and satirical mockery reached print could anyone suspect how much Indians like to laugh. Erdoes himself admitted that it was not until he met Lame Deer that his "ideas about frowning, stoic, deadpan Indians were thoroughly shattered."

The joking banter in this book opened up a new field of investigation. After its publication, the role of "survival humor" was explored by Joseph Bruchac, by Laura Coltelli, and by Kenneth Lincoln. Louise Erdrich's novels were suffused with comedy. Michael Dorris, who claims never to have met an Indian who did not have a sense of humor, worked to undo the stereotype of grim-visaged tribal people.

Lame Deer said that as a child, "The only way one could get me to sit still was to tell me a story." His favorite stories were of the wily stratagems of the tribal trickster, Iktome. As a young man, he worked as a rodeo clown, to lure, with his antics, a bull bent on goring a downed rider. As an elder, he understood the capers of the *heyoka* as diverting destruction from his tribe. "When we were dying like flies from the white man's diseases, when we were driven into reservations, when the government rations did not arrive and we were starving, at such times, watching the pranks of a *heyoka* must have been a blessing."

Because Erdoes faithfully recorded the tone and register of Lame Deer's speech, it feels authentic. Since a prophet must win credence, especially if he is urging us to acknowledge our kinship with stones and insects, it is crucial that his voice be humanized. As charismatic raconteur, Lame Deer compels us to recognize how in "fooling around, a clown is really performing a spiritual ceremony."

As Kenneth Lincoln wrote, "John . . . cared little about propriety; he drew gossip like fleas to a hound. From national talk shows to Dakota sweat lodges, he went everywhere, did everything, said anything." Lame Deer flaunts his improprieties for two reasons. First, a respectable medicine man will be ineffective. Unless he himself experienced all the pain and degradation endured by his people, he will lack the compassion to heal their suffering. "You can't be so stuck up, so inhuman, that you want to be pure, your soul wrapped in a plastic bag." Second, having been both lawman and outlaw, he understands the fallacy of such dichotomies. God and nature are both "good and bad." Humans are also. We often can learn more from the bad than from the good. Not until Lame Deer served a sentence in the Chillicothe penitentiary did he discover that he had an aptitude for math, that he could not only learn to write, but could even earn a living painting signs. By embodying contradictions, the *heyoka* liberates.

Lame Deer challenges our storytelling conventions. The hero is not one who overcomes all obstacles to win status or treasure. True heroism, according to Lame Deer, is communal, not individual. The welfare of the group takes precedence over a single person's desires. For example, nothing but bones remained of the man who wanted to possess White Buffalo Woman. As Lame Deer tells it:

> Desire killed that man, as desire has killed many before and after him. If this earth should ever be destroyed, it will be by desire, by the lust of pleasure and self-gratification, by greed.

The way to power is by giving, not by taking. Therefore, a good medicine man is lean and poor, because he heals and "asks nothing in return"; all food must be shared, else the spirits in it will leave; the discipline of fasting and abstaining from water opens up space for the *nagi,* "the spirit," to enter; giving away all one's possessions is empowering; and the offering of one's own pain, as one's flesh is pierced in the sundance, renews the world. Stories that ennoble the ambitions of a solitary protagonist are viewed as destructive. Valid stories can only be told by a chorus of elders who have attained the wisdom of generosity that ensures the continuance of the earth.

Lame Deer's most subversive jokes in his book consist of a running attack on our educational institutions. Leonard Crow Dog was rescued from "book learning" by his father's brandishing a shotgun at the truant officers. "He didn't want a white school spoiling me for becoming a medicine man." When Godfrey Chips showed signs of being spiritually gifted, he was forcibly kept out of school. According to our definition of a good education, students are trained to think analytically. Analysis fragments learning into discrete subjects; it encourages narrow specialization in a single field. In Native American culture, by contrast, they study the interconnections of the entire ecosystem. "Seeing in a sacred manner" means perceiving interspecies links. The word for "prayer" in Lakota is *wacekiye,* which means "to claim relationship with" or "to seek connection to." To the Lakota people, the cosmos is one family. To live well within the cosmos, one must assume responsibility for everything with which one shares the universe. There are familial obligations toward water, plants, minerals. Any harm done to the slightest of these relatives has devastating consequences for the whole ecosystem. Therefore, they monitor their surroundings attentively for the slightest change in the environment. The merest hint suffices as a warning of eco-cataclysm.

We are blinded to these subtle signs by having been taught that matter is dead and inert. Considering it inanimate makes it available for exploitation as a resource. Lame Deer insists that "the earth, the rocks, the minerals, all of which you call 'dead,' are very much alive." He implores us to "talk to the rivers, to the lakes, to the winds as to our relatives."

Lame Deer says that the whole history of his people is enclosed in the pipe he describes in his first and last chapters. As he descends into the vision pit, he "sensed that my forefathers who had once smoked this pipe were with me." The ancestors from whom he inherited it had used that same place on the hill for vision-seeking for two hundred years, "ever since the day they had crossed the Missouri." In the winter of 1776, the Lakota people were driven out of the woodlands by their Ojibwa enemies, who called them by the derogatory name of "Sioux." The tribes who stayed in the East a century longer now collectively call themselves "Dakota." They were the Keepers of the Sacred Red Pipestone Quarry in southwestern Minnesota.

> It is now a national monument, but we Indians can still go there and dig out the red rock from which we make our pipe bowls. The quarry is right in the heart of the old Sioux country. Our eastern tribes —the Wahpeton, Sissetons and Wahpekute—held this land until 1851, when they were forced to give it up to the whites.

Lame Deer's wife, Ida, is from one of these Dakota tribes orginally called "Santee Sioux." He stems from the Teton "Plains Dwellers" led toward the Black Hills by Standing Bull. This migration was depicted on a buffalo hide known as a "wintercount," which recorded the most significant event of each year of the

Lakota people's history. The word "Teton" is from *tintatunwan* ("prairie" + "village"). There were seven divisions, or bands (called "campfires"), of the Teton. People mentioned by Lame Deer are listed below each.

## BRULÉ or SICANGU

Conquering Bear
Spotted Tail
Horn Chips
Godfrey Chips
Henry Crow Dog
Leonard Crow Dog
Bill Schweigman

(Rosebud Reservation)

## HUNKPAPA

Sitting Bull
Gall

(Standing Rock Reservation)

## SIHASAPA or BLACK FOOT

John Grass
Kill Eagle

(Standing Rock Reservation)

## ITAZIPCO (Sans Arc)

Stanley Looking Horse
Orval Looking Horse
Mrs. Elk Head
the two men who met White Calf Buffalo
  Woman

(Cheyenne River Reservation)

OGLALA

Black Elk
Crazy Horse
Pete Catches
Frank Fools Crow

(Pine Ridge Reservation)

MNIKOWOJU or MINNECONJOU

Tahca Ushte
Cante Witko
Big Foot
Kicking Bear
Hump
Iron Star

(Cheyenne River Reservation)

OOHENUNPA or TWO KETTLE

(Cheyenne River Reservation)

The pipe bundles, tended for nineteen generations by the Itazipco, are tied up in seven rawhides so that they are the size of a man bound up in sinews for the *yuwipi* ceremony. When Lame Deer was given the privilege of unwrapping these, he "felt a power surging from them into his whole body." The bands of his people who had been forcibly isolated from each other on distant reservations in order to destroy their sociocultural integrity were reunited through smoking the peace pipe together.

It belongs to the Without Bows people . . . to the Hunkpapa at Standing Rock . . . the people of Sitting Bull, and to the Oglalas at Pine Ridge, Crazy Horse's tribe. It belongs to the Oohenunpa

—the Two Kettles—who share our reservation with us and who got their name when, starving and near death, they found a rawhide bundle full of meat, enough for "two kettles." It belongs to the Sihasapa—the Sioux Blackfeet—who got their moccasins blackened a long time ago when they had to walk over miles of earth charred by prairie fires. It belongs to the Sicangu—the Burned Thigh people of Rosebud—who had their legs scorched by flames when Pawnee enemies fired the grass around their campsite. It belongs to my own people, the Mnikowoju—the Planters by the Water. And in a larger sense, it belongs to all Indians.

The pipe symbolizes such a pan-tribal confederation. What Lame Deer felt was the peak moment of his life was the sunrise ceremony at which he passed his pipe among people from fifty-four different tribes. "I lit it for them, and 161 people smoked my pipe and it never went out. It kept on glowing all through the ceremony. . . . That pipe gave us common language and a common mind." The prayers ascending in all those different languages were unified in the rising smoke, binding the entire cosmos into one being. Lame Deer's motivation in undertaking this book was to fortify his people, through preserving the seven sacred rites first taught to them for their preservation by the being who brought them the pipe and then transformed herself into a white buffalo. His hope is that all humanity will learn from the pipe to leave the paths of self-destruction and enter the sacred hoop.

The ordeal of the vision quest lasts four days because all things are enumerated in series of fours. There are four cardinal directions to which the peace pipe is extended. There are four elements combined in the *inipi* purification that precedes each ritual: fire, rock, water, air.

The sweat lodge is a microcosm of the cosmic cycles: the fire-heated rocks are sprinkled with water, which evaporates into steam to revivify the humans who inhale it from the air. This symbolizes the constant changes in the pyrosphere, the lithosphere, the hydrosphere, and the atmosphere. The pyrosphere is the earth's fiery core, which periodically erupts in volcanoes; the lithosphere is the earth's crust, which constantly erodes into rock and soil; the hydrosphere, in which tons of water are lifted daily by solar energy; and the atmosphere, whose oxygen is the life-giving breath "exhaled" by trees.

A *synecdoche* is a figure of speech meaning "a small part which represents a whole." The contents of the medicine bag are synecdoches, as Lame Deer explains:

> . . . the down of the swan stood for all the fowls, a tuft of buffalo hair symbolized the four-legged animals, grass stood for all the herbs, bark and roots for the trees. The bundle contained four kinds of skins from the birds, four kinds of fur from the animals, four kinds of plants, four kinds of rocks and stones.

There are four time four things, each representing part of the sacred circle that is the whole universe. Lame Deer says that his people "do everything by fours" because "four is the number that is most *wakan,* most 'sacred.'" Therefore, "we pour water four times over the hot rocks in the sweat lodge. For four nights we seek a vision during a *hanblechia."* Four scouts seek out the sacred cottonwood for the sundance; four virgins strike it four times; four medicine men paint it vermilion; four strips of colored cloth signify the four corners of the earth; the sacred pole is raised in four stages; the dancers hang suspended for four days.

It becomes profoundly important to note that this book's sixteen chapters are four sets of four. Lame Deer's avowed intention is to make his traditions "stay alive." The force that animates all things in the universe is called Takuskanska, the moving spirit, the energy of natural processes. To be in harmony with these natural motions, to synchronize oneself with the rhythms of these cosmic cycles, is the purpose of the ceremonies. Lame Deer's purpose is to make "our old beliefs as pure, as clear and true as I possibly can." His aim is not only to fortify his own people, but to persuade all people on this spinning earth that life depends upon perpetual recycling of all its elements. His reinterpretation of the Ghost Dance is an ecological message—we are all "endangered species" now. We must listen to our environment.

The first chapter serves as a prologue, in which the sixteen-year-old boy earns a man's name, and flows into the epilogue, in which Erdoes earns a Lakota name. Within this circumference are circles within circles, each chapter orbiting around one aspect of Lakota culture. The first set of four chapters (2 through 5) deals with personal and tribal disruption —through war, through the imposition of capitalistic economy, through the introduction of alcohol, and through the destruction of the Black Hills. The next set of four chapters (6 through 9) presents the traditions that maintained the cultural coherence of the people. Their extraordinary resilience was due to a shared symbolism, an ability to communicate with nature, a strong sense of family, and an astounding knowledge of every herb, shrub, weed, and wild plant that grew on the plains. In the last set of chapters, the importance of fours yields to that of sevens. Each of the final chapters presents one of the seven rituals brought to the Lakota by their founding figure. She gave them a round red stone inscribed with seven circles signifying the seven ceremonies that had been given to the seven campfires.

The events that Lame Deer relates about the past in the first four chapters can be corroborated in history books. First, the demand for furs and hides by traders decimated the wild animal populations. The successive waves of epidemics introduced—smallpox, influenza, diphtheria, typhus, cholera, and scarlet fever—were interpreted by the Lakota as a consequence of having broken the compact with the animals. Entrepreneurs like John Jacob Astor gained enormous wealth; by 1820, his American Fur Company made him the richest man in America, with profits of half-a-million dollars a year. The cost was a 90 percent decline, from disease, in the Native American population by the year 1900.

Roads through the buffalo's grazing grounds posed another threat. In 1842, eighteen wagon trains carved deep ruts in the grounds, initiating the Oregon Trail. By 1869, 350,000 settlers had come through. Prairie schooners, manufactured by Henry Wells and William Fargo from 1852 on, conveyed the settlers westward. Next, the Mormons traversed Lakota lands, following Brigham Young to Utah. Then, over 170,000 gold-crazed prospectors trampled through the rangelands, gouging trails when gold was found in California in 1849, in Colorado in 1859, and in Montana in 1861.

Lame Deer knows the history of his people, especially the relentless campaign of reprisals led by Red Cloud against the incursion of roads he called. "Thieves' Highways." The abandoned fur-trading posts became army stockades. At Fort Laramie, one such military fortification, an eighteen-day council was convened to ask for safe passage; the federal government asked for permission to construct roads and military posts. The Fort Laramie Treaty of 1851 formally defined Sioux territory as extending from the

Missouri River on the east to beyond the Black Hills in the west—a dominion of 60,000,000 acres.

A disagreement broke out over a cow in August 1854 in the Brulé camp. The compensation offered by Conquering Bear was refused by Lieutenant John Grattan; in the ensuing altercation, Conquering Bear was killed. To avenge the death of their chief, his warriors killed thirty of Grattan's men. In return, on September 3, 1855, Colonel William Harney slaughtered an entire Brulé village with a force of 1,300 soldiers. It is ironic that Harney Peak, the highest and one of the holiest spots in the Black Hills, where Black Elk had his great vision, is named after this man.

After the slaughter, in the summer of 1857, a grand council of 6,000 tribes was assembled at Bear Butte. This stark volcanic outcrop at the northeast end of the Black Hills was called Mato Paha and was considered the place where spiritual power was most intense. Called The Sacred Mountain by the Cheyenne, it is so revered that all the tribal buildings on their reservation at Lame Deer, Montana, face it. Tradition says that once in every generation a holy man must receive a vision there. Sweet Medicine, Erect Horns, and Frank Fools Crow did. The greatest leaders all attended this council: Crazy Horse, then 16; Sitting Bull, then 26; and Red Cloud, then 35. All pledged to halt further encroachment.

This pledge was undermined by the 1862 Homestead Act which unleashed a flood of settlers, and by the Santee war in Minnesota, which began on August 18, 1862. Survivors fled to North Dakota to take refuge with their Teton kinsmen. They were pursued by General Henry Hastings Sibley and, in 1864, by General Alfred Sully until 90 percent of the Santee, and many of the Teton who had sheltered them, were either dead or imprisoned. Sioux scalps sold for $200 in Yankton. Sully adorned the city with a pair of Teton skulls mounted on poles.

In the 1868 Treaty of Fort Laramie, the government agreed to withdraw from the military garrisons protecting the roads. Lame Deer's great-grandfather, Tahca Ushte, affixed his mark and his thumbprint on this document. All land west of the Missouri River was given as "A Great Sioux Reservation." Further, North Dakota, Montana, and one-third of Wyoming were considered their territory. The entire state of Nebraska was reserved as Sioux hunting grounds.

The most important provision, that military force would be exercised against any trespasser on Lakota ground, was soon violated. General George Armstrong Custer broke these terms on July 1, 1874, when he led an expedition of a thousand into the Paha Sapa, the "heart of all that is," the Lakota's most sacred site. When Custer cabled he had found gold, the government tried to buy the Black Hills, but was informed that this was holy ground and not for sale. Then initiatives to provoke a war so that the Black Hills could be seized by force were set in motion.

An ultimatum was issued. Any Lakota found off the reservation after January 1875 would be considered hostile. Two battles were won. Crazy Horse defeated Crook on June 17, 1876. Days later, Crazy Horse and Gall annihilated Custer's troops at Little Bighorn, on June 25. In a third campaign, however, most of the Lakota were forced to surrender. Only the Hunkpapa, under Sitting Bull, and the Minneconjou, Cheyenne, and Oglala under Crazy Horse were undefeated.

Lame Deer's great-grandfather was tracked down in his Montana hunting grounds at Wolf Mountain. General Nelson A. Miles led a cavalry charge at dawn on May 7, 1877. While shaking hands under a flag of truce, Tahca Ushte was shot. His son, Cante Witko, escaped to elude the soldiers all summer. He was finally forced to surrender and settle on the Cheyenne River Reservation. The Minneconjou lived there until their chief, Big Foot, was killed on December 29,

1890. His few surviving followers took refuge at Pine Ridge.

According to Archie Lame Deer, John Lame Deer's son, Tahca Ushte was scalped and stripped. His gun, warshirt, and feather bonnet were kept as souvenirs by Miles and his officers. It is this gun that Lame Deer refers to, in chapter 2, as being on display in the museum.

On September 5, 1877, Crazy Horse was assassinated. He had been the last remaining obstacle to federal seizure of the Black Hills. The Great Sioux Nation was robbed of its 134 million acres. The tribes were confined on small reservations, isolated from one another. Their total holdings had been reduced to less than 15 million acres. Under the Allotment Act of 1889, they were deprived of 7 million more. The census in Rosebud, at which Lame Deer's father was given the name Silas Fire, was the initial step in the allotment procedure. Every man had to be enrolled in order to get a plot of 160 acres. All undeeded land was declared surplus and sold to whites.

Sitting Bull, who had taken refuge in Canada, led his starving followers back to Standing Rock to surrender. On October 9, 1890, he was visited there by two Minneconjou. Short Bear and his brother-in-law, Kicking Bull, brought news from the prophet Wovoka in Nevada. They had learned from him of a Ghost Dance that would "roll up the world." All the white man's things would disappear, and the buffalo would return to a green prairie. Even though Sitting Bull did not participate in this apocalyptic movement, it was used as a pretext for arresting him. He was assassinated on December 15, 1890. General Miles dispatched the 7th Cavalry, Custer's old regiment, to Wounded Knee: On December 29, 1890, over 300 Ghost Dancers were gunned down. A grateful administration awarded twenty Congressional Medals of Honor, since now gold-rich Paha Sapa could be taken.

Lame Deer's grandfather, Good Fox, suffered severe post-traumatic distress after this massacre. The sounds of women screaming would trigger flashbacks.

George Hearst opened the largest gold mine in the country in the northern Black Hills; with the proceeds, his descendants founded the Hearst newspaper and magazine empire. His Homestake mine had extracted eighteen billion dollars' worth of gold by 1992.

Vast seams of coal were strip-mined by the Peabody, AMAX, and Consolidation Coal companies. This Fort Union Coal Deposit is estimated at 1.5 trillion tons. In 1951, geologists found oil. Thirty petroleum companies began exploratory drilling. An energy consortium plans the building of huge generating plants to export electricity to cities. They argue that the country's power needs justify making the Black Hills "a national energy sacrifice area." Lame Deer, whose dilapidated shack was never electrified, told Erdoes: "Us, making this book" will stop the electric light. "There is a Light Man coming" who'll know "how to shut off all electricity," he warned.

The most pernicious find was that of uranium, in 1951, near Edgemont. Kerr-McGee and twenty-four other colossal corporations proposed construction of twenty-five nuclear reactors. Union Carbide dug six thousand test holes in the Black Hills. They anticipated a return of five billion dollars' worth of uranium. They left nearly four million tons of radioactive debris to be dispersed by winds and to seep into the groundwater. This project could turn the region into a desert. To dig a single two-thousand-foot shaft, 675 gallons per minute must be pumped up from the Ogallala aquifer. This ancient underground reservoir, left over from the melting of glaciers ten thousand years ago, is already sinking so perilously that it is expected to run dry within fifty years. It is the only source of water in this arid region of scanty rain.

As Lame Deer is planting his red and black staff on top of Mount Rushmore to reclaim it, the conversation turns to the Gunnery Range. "The federal government took 200,000 acres from us to build a gunnery range. They didn't return it as promised. We've been waiting twenty-six years. And now the Secretary of the Interior has made a statement that he's going to turn it into a national park." The Air Force "borrowed" this area from the Pine Ridge Reservation. It was to have been returned at the end of World War II. Local residents have sighted large containers of high-level military nuclear waste being flown in by helicopter. William Janklow, former governor of South Dakota, advocated this dump site as a "boon to a depressed economy." On June 11, 1962, two hundred tons of radioactive wastes spilled into the drinking water of the Oglala on Pine Ridge. The tribal president's request for uncontaminated water was refused. An alarming increase in cancer deaths there has been reported.

The coming Indian wars will be over water. Vine DeLoria Jr. became a lawyer because he foresaw these court battles. Under the policy of eminent domain, governments can take water from reservations, impound it in enormous dams, and pipe it to cities far away. The Bureau of Reclamation has turned the West into a vast plumbing system. Hydrological engineering has devastated the continental ecosystem. By 1979, the following had been constructed: 14,590 miles of canals, 990 miles of pipelines, 230 miles of tunnels, 35,160 miles of laterals, 15,750 miles of project drains, 345 diversion dams, and 50 hydropower facilities with a generating capacity of 12 million kilowatts.

Floods resulted from the 107 dams along the Missouri River in 1944, 1947, and 1952. Near Lame Deer, the Rapid City Canyon Dam burst, killing 238 people. West of Wolf Point, near Tahca Ushte's favorite hunting ground, rises Fort Peck Dam, impounding an artificial lake of 1,600 miles. A ruined spillway is all that is left of the Teton Dam, which blew out in 1976 while it was being filled for the first time. In North Dakota, the massive Garrison Dam barricades a 368,000-acre lake.

The diversion projects are showing their disastrous impact in Nebraska. The Platte River is nothing but a slowly oozing, muddy trickle. The marshes and wetlands left behind by retreating glaciers have dried up. Three-quarters of the world's sandhill cranes used to perform their graceful courtship dances there on their annual migrations north. There are no nesting, spawning, or brooding sites left. The Lakota, who are so sensitive to dynamic flows of energy that they named their creator Takuskanska ("that which moves"), have warned against blocking circulation: whatever is stopped from moving dies. Dammed-up water stagnates, breeds algae, drops silt, and is poisoned.

A massive complex of 107 dams have been built on Lakota land. They lost 350,000 acres of homes, sacred sites, and ancestral burial grounds. The social trauma caused was even worse than the economic impoverishment they suffered. Five different reservations were partially flooded. More than a third of these tribal people were forced to relocate. Nearly 90 percent of the timberland and 75 percent of the wild game were destroyed.

The dams are so heavy that they cause the earth to sink. The pumping of underground water has resulted in drops of as much as thirty feet in the land above where the suction pumps operate. This is called subsidence. When the earth's crust collapses as the water that had been holding it up is removed, earthquakes can be triggered.

Lame Deer concludes that "We must try to save the white man from himself. This can be done only if all of us can once again see ourselves as part of this earth. We cannot harm any part of her without hurting ourselves."

The desecration of the Black Hills, described in chapter 5 by the protesters who ascended Mount Rushmore in 1970, culminates the military history recounted in the preceding four chapters. In the four that follow, the radiating consequences are traced. For the Lakota, kept from fulfilling their custodial obligations to the most ancient manifestation of Tunkan (the rock power) on the continent, the results were dire. These were philosophical (chapter 6), biological (chapter 7), sociological (chapter 8), and medical (chapter 9). Maps confirm the heart shape of the Black Hills the Lakota called "the heart of all that is." Here were underground springs, mountain streams, wildlife, medicinal herbs, and slopes so dense with pine trees that they actually looked black from a distance. As the source of all well-being, its loss could not be compensated. Therefore, the $106 million awarded by the Supreme Court in 1980 was rejected.

The rest of the book tells the people to endure by returning to their traditional forms of worship. Against the presidential monuments dynamited into Mount Rushmore to attract tourists, they have the *inipi* (chapter 10). The fragile hut of willow twigs into which they crawl to remind themselves of their humility is ephemeral. Against the energy consortia, they have "the little lights" of chapter 11, the "sparks" of spirit. Against the barren ground, plowed until it blew away as dust, they have their solstice festival of chapter 12, in which they dance "the renewal of life." Chapter 13 is their response to the missionaries who imposed alien religions: the Native American Church synthesized Christianity with traditio    forms. Chapter 14 recapitulates the 1890 Ghos  ance. In 1990, the Lakota reconstituted their identity by re-enacting the ride from Pine Ridge to Wounded Knee, to release the spirits of their ancestors and to mend the sacred hoop. Chapter 15 tells how the *heyoka* is used by the *wakinyan* (the thunderbirds whose nest is in the Black Hills) to bring prophecies to the people. When, in their soaring over the world, they detect impending destruction, they select with a stroke of lightning a messenger who dramatizes the ecological threat. And finally, in chapter 16 Lame Deer brings the peace pipe to all humanity, offering its sacred vision to those "on the road to self-destruction."

*Lame Deer*
*Seeker of Visions*

# 1
# Alone on the Hilltop

I was all alone on the hilltop. I sat there in the vision pit, a hole dug into the hill, my arms hugging my knees as I watched old man Chest, the medicine man who had brought me there, disappear far down in the valley. He was just a moving black dot among the pines, and soon he was gone altogether.

Now I was all by myself, left on the hilltop for four days and nights without food or water until he came back for me. You know, we Indians are not like some white folks—a man and a wife, two children, and one baby sitter who watches the TV set while the parents are out visiting somewhere.

Indian children are never alone. They are always surrounded by grandparents, uncles, cousins, relatives of all kinds, who fondle the kids, sing to them, tell them stories. If the parents go someplace, the kids go along.

But here I was, crouched in my vision pit, left alone by myself for the first time in my life. I was sixteen then, still had my boy's name and, let me tell you, I was scared. I was shivering and not only from the cold. The nearest human being was many miles away, and four days and nights is a long, long time. Of course, when it was all over, I would no longer be a boy, but a man. I would have had my vision. I would be given a man's name.

Sioux men are not afraid to endure hunger, thirst and loneliness, and I was only ninety-six hours away from being a man. The thought was comforting. Comforting, too, was the warmth of the star blanket which old man Chest had wrapped around me to cover my nakedness. My grandmother had made it

1

especially for this, my first *hanblechia,* my first vision-seeking. It was a beautifully designed quilt, white with a large morning star made of many pieces of brightly colored cloth. That star was so big it covered most of the blanket. If Wakan Tanka, the Great Spirit, would give me the vision and the power, I would become a medicine man and perform many ceremonies wrapped in that quilt. I am an old man now and many times a grandfather, but I still have that star blanket my grandmother made for me. I treasure it; some day I shall be buried in it.

The medicine man had also left a peace pipe with me, together with a bag of *kinnickinnick*—our kind of tobacco made of red willow bark. This pipe was even more of a friend to me than my star blanket. To us the pipe is like an open Bible. White people need a church house, a preacher and a pipe organ to get into a praying mood. There are so many things to distract you: who else is in the church, whether the other people notice that you have come, the pictures on the wall, the sermon, how much money you should give and did you bring it with you. We think you can't have a vision that way.

For us Indians there is just the pipe, the earth we sit on and the open sky. The spirit is everywhere. Sometimes it shows itself through an animal, a bird or some trees and hills. Sometimes it speaks from the Badlands, a stone, or even from the water. That smoke from the peace pipe, it goes straight up to the spirit world. But this is a two-way thing. Power flows down to us through that smoke, through the pipe stem. You feel that power as you hold your pipe; it moves from the pipe right into your body. It makes your hair stand up. That pipe is not just a thing; it is alive. Smoking this pipe would make me feel good and help me to get rid of my fears.

As I ran my fingers along its bowl of smooth red pipestone, red like the blood of my people, I no longer felt scared. That pipe had belonged to my father and to his father before him. It would someday pass to my son and, through him, to my grandchildren. As long as we had the pipe there would be a Sioux nation. As I fingered the pipe, touched it, felt its smoothness that came from long use, I sensed that my forefathers who had once smoked this pipe were with me on the hill, right in the vision pit. I was no longer alone.

Besides the pipe the medicine man had also given me a gourd. In it were forty small squares of flesh which my grandmother had cut from her arm with a razor blade. I had seen her do it. Blood had been streaming down from her shoulder to her elbow as she carefully put down each piece of skin on a handkerchief, anxious not to lose a single one. It would have made those anthropologists mad. Imagine, performing such an ancient ceremony with a razor blade instead of a flint knife! To me it did not matter. Someone dear to me had undergone pain, given me something of herself, part of her body, to help me pray and make me stronghearted. How could I be afraid with so many people—living and dead—helping me?

One thing still worried me. I wanted to become a medicine man, a *yuwipi,* a healer carrying on the ancient ways of the Sioux nation. But you cannot learn to be a medicine man like a white man going to medical school. An old holy man can teach you about herbs and the right ways to perform a ceremony where everything must be in its proper place, where every move, every word has its own, special meaning. These things you can learn—like spelling, like training a horse. But by themselves these things mean nothing. Without the vision and the power this learning will do no good. It would not make me a medicine man.

What if I failed, if I had no vision? Or if I dreamed of the Thunder Beings, or lightning struck the hill? That would make me at once into a *heyoka,* a contrarywise, an upside-down man, a clown. "You'll know it, if you get the power," my Uncle Chest had told me. "If you are not given it, you won't lie about it, you won't pretend. That would kill you, or kill somebody close to you, somebody you love."

Night was coming on. I was still lightheaded and dizzy from my first sweat bath in which I had purified myself before going up the hill. I had never been in a sweat lodge before. I had sat in the little beehive-shaped hut made of bent willow branches and covered with blankets to keep the heat in. Old Chest and three other medicine men had been in the lodge with me. I had my back against the wall, edging as far away as I could from the red-hot stones glowing in the center. As Chest poured water over the rocks, hissing white steam enveloped me and filled my lungs. I thought the heat would kill me, burn the eyelids off my face! But right in the middle of all this swirling steam I heard Chest singing. So it couldn't be all that bad. I did not cry out "All my relatives!"—which would have made him open the flap of the sweat lodge to let in some cool air—and I was proud of this. I heard him praying for me: "Oh, holy rocks, we receive your white breath, the steam. It is the breath of life. Let this young boy inhale it. Make him strong."

The sweat bath had prepared me for my vision-seeking. Even now, an hour later, my skin still tingled. But it seemed to have made my brains empty. Maybe that was good, plenty of room for new insights.

Darkness had fallen upon the hill. I knew that *hanhepiwi* had risen, the night sun, which is what we call the moon. Huddled in my narrow cave, I did not see it. Blackness was wrapped around me like a velvet cloth. It seemed to cut me off from the outside world, even from my own body. It made me listen to the voices within me. I thought of my forefathers who had crouched on this hill before me, because the medicine men in my family had chosen this spot for a place of meditation and vision-seeking ever since the day they had crossed the Missouri to hunt for buffalo in the White River country some two hundred years ago. I thought that I could sense their presence right through the earth I was leaning against. I could feel them entering my body, feel them stirring in my mind and heart.

Sounds came to me through the darkness: the cries of the wind, the whisper of the trees, the voices of nature, animal sounds, the hooting of an owl. Suddenly I felt an overwhelming presence. Down there with me in my cramped hole was a big bird. The pit was only as wide as myself, and I was a skinny boy, but that huge bird was flying around me as if he had the whole sky to himself. I could hear his cries, sometimes near and sometimes far, far away. I felt feathers or a wing touching my back and head. This feeling was so overwhelming that it was just too much for me. I trembled and my bones turned to ice. I grasped the rattle with the forty pieces of my grandmother's flesh. It also had many little stones in it, tiny fossils picked up from an ant heap. Ants collect them. Nobody knows why. These little stones are supposed to have a power in them. I shook the rattle and it made a soothing sound, like rain falling on rock. It was talking to me, but it did not calm my fears. I took the sacred pipe in my other hand and began to sing and pray: "Tunkashila, grandfather spirit, help me." But this did not help. I don't know what got into me, but I was no longer myself. I started to cry. Crying, even my voice was different. I sounded like an older man, I couldn't even recognize this strange voice. I used long-ago words in my prayer, words no longer used nowadays. I tried to wipe away my tears, but they wouldn't stop. In the end I just pulled that quilt over me, rolled myself up in it. Still I felt the bird wings touching me.

Slowly I perceived that a voice was trying to tell me something. It was a bird cry, but I tell you, I began to understand some of it. That happens sometimes. I know a lady who had a butterfly sitting on her shoulder. That butterfly told her things. This made her become a great medicine woman.

I heard a human voice too, strange and high-pitched, a voice which could not come from an ordinary, living being. All at once I was way up there with the birds. The hill with the vision pit was way above everything. I could look down even on the stars, and the moon was close to my left side. It seemed as though the earth and the stars were moving below me. A voice said, "You are sacrificing yourself here to be a medicine man. In time you will be one. You will teach other medicine men. We are the fowl people, the winged ones, the eagles and the owls. We are a nation and you shall be our brother. You will never kill or harm any one of us. You are going to understand us whenever you come to seek a vision here on this hill. You will learn about herbs and roots, and you will heal people. You will ask them for nothing in return. A man's life is short. Make yours a worthy one."

I felt that these voices were good, and slowly my fear left me. I had lost all sense of time. I did not know whether it was day or night. I was asleep, yet wide awake. Then I saw a shape before me. It rose from the darkness and the swirling fog which penetrated my earth hole. I saw that this was my great-grandfather, Tahca Ushte, Lame Deer, old man chief of the Minneconjou. I could see the blood dripping from my great-grandfather's chest where a white soldier had shot him. I understood that my great-grandfather wished me to take his name. This made me glad beyond words.

We Sioux believe that there is something within us that controls us, something like a second person almost. We call it *nagi*, what other people might call soul, spirit or essence. One can't see it, feel it or taste it, but that time on the hill—and only that once—I knew it was there inside of me. Then I felt the power surge through me like a flood. I cannot describe it, but it filled all of me. Now I knew for sure that I would become a *wicasa wakan*, a medicine man. Again I wept, this time with happiness.

I didn't know how long I had been up there on that hill—one minute or a lifetime. I felt a hand on my shoulder gently shaking me. It was old man Chest, who had come for me. He told me that I had been in the vision pit four days and four nights and that it was time to come down. He would give me something to eat and water to drink and then I was to tell him everything that had happened to me during my *hanblechia*. He would interpret my visions for me. He told me that the vision pit had changed me in a way that I would not be able to understand at that time. He told me also that I was no longer a boy, that I was a man now. I was Lame Deer.

# 2

# That Gun in the New York Museum Belongs to Me

In the Museum of the American Indian in New York are two glass cases. A sign over them reads: "Famous Guns of Famous Indian Chiefs." They have five or six guns there, Sitting Bull's among them. A note next to one of these old breechloaders says that it belonged to the famous Chief Lame Deer, killed in a battle with General Miles, who generously donated this gun to the New York museum. I don't know what right old Bear Coat Miles had to be that free with other people's property. That gun didn't belong to him. It belongs to me. I am the only Lame Deer left.

I am a medicine man and I want to talk about visions, spirits and sacred things. But you must know something about the man Lame Deer before you can understand the medicine man Lame Deer. So I will start with the man, the boy, and we'll get to the medicine part later.

Tahca Ushte—the first Lame Deer—was my great-grandfather on my father's side. He was killed by mistake. You could say he was murdered. A year before this so-called battle with General Miles, Lame Deer had made his final peace with the white man. He had made an agreement with the U.S. Government. By this treaty they measured off four squares miles west of what is now Rapid City, South Dakota. This was to be a reservation for the chief and his people, and it was to be called Lame Deer after him. This land was to be ours forever—"as long as the sun shines and the grass grows." These days smog is hiding the sun and there's little grass left in Rapid City now. Maybe the white people had a gift of foreseeing this when they took our land before the ink on that treaty was dry.

Lame Deer said that he would sign this treaty if he and his people could go out on one last hunt and live for just one more summer in the good old way—going after the buffalo. After that they would all settle down on their new reservation and "walk the white man's road." The Government people said that this was all right and gave him permission for his last hunt. They shook hands on it.

The U.S. Government is a strange monster with many heads. One head doesn't know what the others are up to. The Army had given Lame Deer its word that he could hunt in peace. At the same time it told old Bear Coat Miles that any Indians found hunting off the reservations were to be attacked as "hostiles." Lame Deer had gone north in the spring of 1877 to his favorite buffalo range between the Rosebud and Bighorn rivers. He had camped in the Wolf Mountains along Fat Horse Creek.

The old people have told me that the prairie had never been more beautiful than it was that spring. The grass was high and green. The slopes were covered with flowers, and the air was full of good smells and the song of birds. If the Indians had only one more hunt left, this was how they wished it to be. Lame Deer knew that there were soldiers around, but this did not worry him. He had a right to be where he was. Besides, any fool could see that he was not about to make war on anybody. He had all the women and children with him. His fifty lodges were full of meat and hides. His people had come as to a feast. They were dressed in their finery and beaded goods. They were enjoying their last vacation from the white man.

General Miles was stupid not to grasp this, but I think that he acted in good faith. Nobody had told him about the treaty. He had six companies of walking soldiers and several troops of cavalry, more men

9

than all the Indians together, including the women and children. The blue coats came tearing into the camp, shooting and yelling, stampeding the horses and riding down the people. At the same time one of them carried a white flag of truce.

Seeing the peaceful camp from up close, Bear Coat Miles, I believe, changed his mind and regretted what was happening. He began waving his arms, trying to stop the killing, shouting over and over again, *"Kola, kola*—friend, friend." His Indian scouts took up the cry. They too started shouting, "We are friends!" It sure was a strange way for friends to drop in, but my great-grandfather pretended to believe them. He didn't want his people to be killed. He dropped his gun as a sign of peace.

General Miles rushed up to him, grabbed his hand and started shaking it. He kept shouting, *"Kola, kola."* But peace was not what his soldiers wanted. They wanted Indian scalps and souvenirs. Probably they also wanted to get at the women and girls. One trooper came riding up and fired his carbine at Lame Deer. Miles hung onto my great-grandfather's arm with both hands, but the chief tore himself loose and picked up his gun, shooting the man who had fired on him. Then all the soldiers opened up with everything they had, killing Lame Deer, his second chief, Iron Star, and about a dozen more of the warriors. Then they plundered the tipis, taking what they wanted and destroying the rest. Even General Miles was not too proud to take a few things for himself, and that is why my ancestor's gun is in a New York museum instead of hanging on my wall.

About those four square miles along the Rapid River: When the treaty was signed Lame Deer said, "If I ever die, or the school closes, this land shall go to my first son and, if he dies, to his son, and so on down the line." I tried to sue the Government for this land, and they said, "No personal Indian claims allowed." Maybe it was a good thing that they would not let us

Indians keep that land. Think of what would have been missed: the motels with their neon signs, the pawn shops, the Rock Hunter's Paradise, the Horned Trophies Taxidermist Studio, the giftie shoppies, the Genuine Indian Crafts Center with its beadwork from Taiwan and Hong Kong, the Sitting Bull Cave—electrically lighted for your convenience—the Shrine of Democracy Souvenir Shop, the Fun House—the talk of your trip for years to come—the Bucket of Blood Saloon, the life-size dinosaur made of green concrete, the go-go gals and cat houses, the Reptile Gardens, where they don't feed the snakes because that would be too much trouble. When they die you get yourself some new rattlers for free. Just think: If that land belonged to us there would be nothing here, only trees, grass and some animals running free. All that *real estate* would be going to waste!

My great-grandfather Lame Deer was a chief of the Mni Owoju—the Planters by the Water—one of the seven western tribes of the Sioux nation. He had three wives. His first wife had three sons: Did Not Butcher, Flying By and my own grandfather, Cante Witko, which means Crazy Heart. The second wife had one daughter. The third wife had no children. My other grandfather was named Good Fox.

Both Crazy Heart and Good Fox were famous warriors and had been in the Custer fight. Good Fox was also a survivor of the Wounded Knee massacre. Crazy Heart was a shirt-wearer, which was a great honor. He wore a yellow-and-blue shirt fringed with locks of human hair. He was listened to in our councils and the people sought his advice on all matters of importance. Good Fox, too, was respected for his wisdom. Right up to the time of his death in 1928 he was always given the job of supervising our ceremonies and smoothening up the sacred dancing ground.

I never knew Crazy Heart, but my grandpa Good Fox played a big part in my life, and I looked up to him. He had a great reputation as a warrior, but he was not a killing man. Most of his war honors came from "counting coup," riding up to the enemy, zigzagging among them, touching them with his crooked cup stick wrapped in otter fur. He was a coup-man. That was his way of showing his bravery. Compared to my grandfathers, we reservation people of today are just plain chicken. They say, "Custer died for your sins." I say Custer is alive. We still have too many Custers and Mileses among the white people, but where is our Crazy Horse? One medicine man around here told me he had a vision that Crazy Horse would come back as a black man. That would be something.

I often asked my grandpa Good Fox to tell me about the Custer battle. "I'm not a good witness," he said, "because I was too busy fighting to pay much attention to what was going on. I raced my horse right into the middle of a big cloud of dust where the hottest action was, shouting, 'It's a good day to die and a good day to fight,' but this was a day for the blue coats to die, though one of them hit me in the arm with a bullet from his carbine. It didn't even go all the way through my arm. I was told that after the battle two Cheyenne women came across Custer's body. They knew him, because he attacked their peaceful village on the Washita. These women said, 'You smoked the peace pipe with us. Our chiefs told you that you would be killed if you ever made war on us again. But you would not listen. This will make you hear better.' The women each took an awl from their beaded cases and stuck them deep into Custer's ears. Somebody who saw this told me about it. Grandson, I tell you, hundreds of books have been written about this battle by people who weren't there. I was there, but all I remember is one big cloud of dust."

About the Wounded Knee massacre grandfather Good Fox told me, "There may be some good men among the whites, but to trust them is a quick way to get oneself killed. Every time I hear a lady or child screaming I think of that terrible day of killing. The preachers and missionaries tell you to turn the other cheek and to love your neighbor like yourself. Grandson, I don't know how the white people treat each other, but I don't think they love us more than they love themselves. Some don't love us at all." My grandpa died in 1928. He was almost blind at the end.

My father came from Standing Rock. His name was Wawi-Yohi-Ya, which means Let-Them-Have-Enough. Silas was his first name, which the missionaries gave him. He was a very generous man. He always invited people to a feast or to a give-away ceremony. At such a time he always used to worry about everybody having enough to eat and enough presents. That's why he was known as Let-Them-Have-Enough among the Indian people.

Among the whites he was known as Silas Fire. They had a census and everybody had to go to Rosebud to be put in a big book. The superintendent told my father, "Sign here." My dad couldn't write his name. He told that white man what his name was in Indian. The superintendent said it was too long and complicated. Dad told him, "O.K., give me a short name." A lot of people had come for their rations and put up tents. Just at that moment one of them caught fire. It caused a big uproar. People were running about calling, "Fire, fire!" The superintendent heard it and said, "That's it. You are Silas Fire, short and sweet."

If that tent hadn't caught fire my name would have been Let-Them-Have-Enough. Now it's John Fire on some white man's document, but my Indian name is Lame Deer, after my great-grandfather, and that's as it should be. My father was loved by everybody. He was a kind, smiling man. He had great patience and it was very hard to get him angry. He was the silent type, kept his mouth shut and did very little talking. Some men have their mouths open all the time, but they own only one horse or no horse at all. My dad had over two hundred. He used to tease me, pat me on the head, showing that he loved me in a hundred different ways, but for weeks he did not say one goddam word to me.

My dad never went to school, couldn't read or write, but one could learn a lot from him just by watching. Dad taught me how to rope a horse or how to gentle it down for riding. First I'd watch him do it, then he made a motion with his hand. That meant: "Now you try it!" I caught on easy and I was faster than he was. Once I was thrown from a horse. I came down real hard. My father told me, "Don't kill yourself, son." It was one of the few things he ever said to me. That's why I remember it.

My mother's name was Sally Red Blanket. She was good to look at, a beautiful woman with long, curly hair. She was very skilled with her hands, doing fine beadwork. She used the tiniest beads, the ones you can't get anymore. Much later, when I was half grown, I noticed that whenever a trader looked at her work with a magnifying glass or fingered it too long, the price went up. My mother died when I was seventeen years old.

I was born a full-blood Indian in a twelve-by-twelve log cabin between Pine Ridge and Rosebud. *Maka tanhan wicasa wan*—I am a man of the earth, as we say. Our people don't call themselves Sioux or Dakota. That's white man talk. We call ourselves Ikce Wicasa—the natural humans, the free, wild, common people. I am pleased to be called that.

As with most Indian children, much of my upbringing was done by my grandparents—Good Fox and his wife, Pte-Sa-Ota-Win, Plenty White Buffalo. Among our people the relationship to one's grandparents is as strong as to one's own father and mother. We lived in that little hut way out on the prairie, in the back country, and for the first few years of my life I had no contact with the outside world. Of course we had a few white man's things—coffee, iron pots, a shotgun, an old buckboard. But I never thought much of where these things came from or who had made them.

When I was about five years old my grandma took me to visit some neighbors. As always, my little black pup came along. We were walking on the dirt road when I saw a rider come up. He looked so strange to me that I hid myself behind Grandma and my pup hid behind me. I already knew enough about riding to see that he didn't know how to handle a horse. His feet were hanging down to the ground. He had some tiny, windmill-like things coming out of his heels, making a tinkling sound. As he came closer I started to size him up. I had never seen so much hair on a man. It covered all of his face and grew way down to his chest, maybe lower, but he didn't have hair where it counted, on top of his head. The hair was of a light-brown color and it made him look like a mattress come to life. He had eyes like a dead owl, of a washed-out blue-green hue. He was chewing on something that looked like a smoking Baby Ruth candy bar. Later I found out that this was a cigar. This man sure went in for double enjoyment, because he was also chomping on a wad of chewing tobacco, and now and then he took the smoking candy bar from his mouth to spit out a long stream of brown juice. I wondered why he kept eating something which tasted so bad that he couldn't keep it down.

This strange human being also wore a funny headgear—a cross between a skillet and a stovepipe. He had a big chunk of leather piled on top of his poor horse, hanging down also on both sides. In front of his crotch the leather was shaped like a horn. I thought maybe he kept his man-thing inside to protect it. This was the first saddle I had seen. His pitiful horse also had strings of leather on its head and a piece of iron in its mouth. Every time the horse stuck out its tongue I could hear some kind of roller or gear grinding inside it. This funny human being wore leather pants and had two strange-looking hammers tied to his hips. I later found out these were .45 Colts.

The man started to make weird sounds. He was talking, but we couldn't understand him because it was English. He pointed at my grandmother's pretty beaded moccasins and he took some square green frog hides from his pocket and wanted to trade. I guess those were dollar bills. But Grandma refused to swap, because she had four big gold coins in her moccasins. That man must have smelled them. This was the first white man I met.

When I got home I had a new surprise waiting for me. My grandpa was butchering something that I had never seen before, an animal with hoofs like a horse and the body of a dog. Maybe somebody had mated a dog with a horse and this funny creature was the result. Looking at its pink, hairless body, I was reminded of scary old tales about humans coupling with animals and begetting terrifying monsters. Grandpa was chopping away, taking the white meat and throwing the insides out. My little puppy was sure enjoying this, his first pig. So was I, but the pig smelled terrible. My grandpa said to save the fat for axle grease.

Most of my childhood days weren't very exciting, and that was all right with me. We had a good, simple life. One day passed like another. Only in one way was I different from other Indian kids. I was never hungry, because my dad had so many horses and cattle. Grandma always got up early in the morning before everybody else, taking down the big tin container with the Government-issue coffee. First I would hear her roasting the beans in a frying pan, then I would hear her grind them. She always made a huge pot holding two gallons of water, put in two big handfuls of coffee and boiled it. She would add some sweetener— molasses or maple syrup; we didn't like sugar. We used no milk or cream in our *pejuta sapa*—our black medicine.

Before anything else Grandma poured out a big soup spoon of coffee as an offering to the spirits, and then she kept the pot going all day. If she saw people anywhere near the house she called out to them, regardless of who they were, "Come in, have some coffee!" When the black medicine gave out, she added water and a lot more coffee and boiled the whole again. That stuff got stronger and stronger, thicker and thicker. In the end you could almost stick the spoon in there and it would keep standing upright. "Now the coffee is real good," Grandma would say.

To go with the coffee Grandma got her baking powder each morning and made soda bread and squaw bread. That squaw bread filled the stomach. It seemed to grow bigger and bigger inside. Every spring, as the weather got warmer, the men would fix up Grandma's "squaw-cooler." This was a brush shelter made of four upright tree trunks with horizontal lodge poles tied to the top. The whole was then covered with branches from pine trees. They rigged up an old wood burner for Grandma to cook on, a rough table and some logs to sit on. In the summer, much of our life was spent in the squaw-cooler, where you could always feel a breeze. These squaw-coolers are still very popular on the reservation.

Grandma liked to smoke a little pipe. She loved her *kinnickinnick*—the red willow-bark tobacco. One time she accidentally dropped some glowing embers into an old visitor's lap. This guy still wore a breech cloth. Suddenly we smelled something burning. That breech cloth had caught fire and we had to yank it off and beat the flames out. He almost got his child-maker burned up. He was so old it wouldn't have made a lot of difference, but he still could jump.

One of my uncles used to keep a moon-counting stick, our own kind of calendar and a good one. He had a special staff and every night he cut a notch in it until the moon "died"—that is, disappeared. On the other side of his staff he made a notch for every month. He started a new stick every year in the spring. That way we always knew when it was the right day for one of our ceremonies.

Every so often my grandparents would take me to a little celebration down the creek. Grandpa always rode his old red horse, which was well known in all the tribes. We always brought plenty of food for everybody, squaw bread, beef, the kind of dried meat we called *papa,* and *wasna,* or pemmican, which was meat pounded together with berries and kidney fat. We also brought a kettle of coffee, wild mint tea, soup or stuff like that. Grandfather was always the leader of the *owanka osnato*—the rehearsal ground. He prepared the place carefully. Only the real warriors were allowed to dance there—men like Red Fish or Thin Elk, who had fought in the Custer battle. With the years the dancers grew older and older and fewer and fewer. Grandfather danced too. Everybody could see the scars all over his arm where he had been wounded by the white soldiers.

Some women had scars, too. Grandpa's brother, White Crane Walking, had three wives. They were not jealous of one another. They were like sisters. They loved one another and they loved their husband. This old man was really taking it easy; the women did all the work. He just lay around the whole day long, doing nothing. Once in a while some men called him lazy, but he just laughed and told them, "Why don't you get a second wife?" He knew their wives were jealous and didn't want them to get a second one. When this old man finally passed away, the two wives who survived him buried him in the side of a hill. They took their skinning knives and made many deep gashes in their arms and legs to show their grief. They might have cut off their little fingers too, but somebody told them that this was no longer allowed, that the Government would punish them for this. So they cut off their hair instead. They keened and cried for four days and nights; they loved their husband that much.

I was the *takoja*—the pampered grandson—and like all Indian children I was spoiled. I was never scolded, never heard a harsh word. *"Ajustan*—leave it alone"—that was the worst. I was never beaten; we don't treat children that way. Indian kids are so used to being handled gently, to get away with things, that they often don't pay much attention to what the grownups tell them. I'm a grandfather now myself and sometimes I feel like yelling at one of those brash kids, "Hey, you little son of a bitch, listen to me!" That would make him listen all right, but I can't do it.

When I didn't want to go to sleep my grandma would try to scare me with the *ciciye*—a kind of bogeyman. *"Takoja, istima ye*—Go to sleep, sonny," she would say, "or the *ciciye* will come after you." Nobody knew what the *ciciye* was like, but he must have been something terrible. When the *ciciye* wouldn't work anymore, I was threatened with the *siyoko*—another kind of monster. Nobody knew what the *siyoko* was like, either, but he was ten times more terrible than the *ciciye*. Grandma did not have much luck. Neither the *ciciye* nor the *siyoko* scared me for long. But when I was real bad, Grandma would say, *"Wasicun anigni kte*—the white man will come and take you to his home," and that scared me all right. *Wasicun* were for real.

It was said that I didn't take after my grandpa Good Fox, whom I loved, but after my other grandfather, Crazy Heart, whom I never knew. They said I picked up where he left off, because I was so daring and full of the devil. I was told that Crazy Heart had been like that. He did not care what happened to other people, or to himself, once he was on his way. He was hot-tempered, always feuding and on the warpath. At the same time he saved lots of people, gave wise counsel, urged the people to do right. He was a good speech-maker. Everybody who listened to him said that he was a very encouraging man. He always advised patience, except when it came to himself. Then his temper got in the way.

I was like that. Things I was told not to do—I did them. I liked to play rough. We played shinny ball, a kind of hockey game. We made the ball and sticks ourselves. We played the hoop game, shot with a bow and arrow. We had foot races, horse races and water races. We liked to play *mato kiciyapi,* the bear game, throwing sharp, stiff grass stems at each other. These could really hurt you and draw blood if they hit the bare skin. And we were always at the *isto kicicastakapi,* the pit-slinging game. You chewed the fruit from the rosebush or wild cherries, spit a fistful of pits into your hand and flung them into the other fellow's face. And of course I liked the Grab-Them-by-the-Hair-and-Kick-Them game, which we played with two teams.

I liked to ride horseback behind my older sister, holding onto her. As I got a little bigger she would hold onto me. By the time I was nine years old I had my own horse to ride. It was a beautiful gray pony my father had given me together with a fine saddle and a very colorful Mexican saddle blanket. That gray was my favorite companion and I was proud to ride him. But he was not mine for long. I lost him through my own fault.

*Nonge Pahloka*—the Piercing of Her Ears—is a big event in a little girl's life. By this ceremony her parents, and especially her grandmother, want to show how much they love and honor her. They ask a man who is respected for his bravery or wisdom to pierce the ears of their daughter. The grandmother puts on a big feed. The little girl is placed on a blanket surrounded by the many gifts her family will give away in her name. The man who does the piercing is much admired and gets the most valuable gift. Afterward they get down to the really important part—the eating.

Well, one day I watched somebody pierce a girl's ears. I saw the fuss they made over it, the presents he got and all that. I thought I should do this to my little sister. She was about four years old at the time and I was nine. I don't know anymore what made me want to do this. Maybe I wanted to feel big and important like the man whom I had watched perform the ceremony. Maybe I wanted to get a big present. Maybe I wanted to make my sister cry. I don't remember what was in my little boy's mind then. I found some wire and made a pair of "ear rings" out of it. Then I asked my sister, "Would you like me to put these on you?" She smiled. *"Ohan*—yes." I didn't have the sharp bone one uses for the ear-piercing, and I didn't know the prayer that goes with it. I just had an old awl but thought it would do fine. Oh, how my sister yelled. I had to hold her down, but I got that awl through her earlobes and managed to put the "ear rings" in. I was proud of the neat job I had done.

When my mother came home and saw those wire loops in my sister's ears she gasped. But she recovered soon enough to go and tell my father. That was one of the few occasions he talked to me. He said, "I should punish you and whip you, but I won't. That's not my way. You'll get your punishment later." Well, some time passed and I forgot all about it. One morning my father announced that we were going to a powwow. He had hitched up the wagon and it was heaped high with boxes and bundles. At that powwow my father let it be known that he was doing a big *otuhan*—a give-away. He put my sister on a rug, a pretty Navajo blanket, and laid out things to give away—quilts, food, blankets, a fine shotgun, his own new pair of cowboy boots, a sheepskin coat, enough to fit out a whole family. Dad was telling the people, "I want to honor my daughter for her ear-piercing. This should have been done openly, but my son did it at home. I guess he's too small. He didn't know any better." This was a long speech for Dad. He motioned me to come closer. I was sitting on my pretty gray horse. I thought we were both cutting a very fine figure. Well, before I knew it, Dad had given my horse away, together with its beautiful saddle and blanket. I had to ride home in the wagon and I cried all the way. The old man said, "You have your punishment now, but you will feel better later on. All her life your sister will tell about how you pierced her ears. She'll brag about you. I bet you are the only small boy who ever did this big ceremony."

That was no consolation to me. My beautiful gray was gone. I was heart-broken for three days. On the fourth morning I looked out the door and there stood a little white stallion with a new saddle and a silver-plated bit. "It's yours," my father told me. "Get on it." I was happy again.

After I was six years old it was very hard to make me behave. The only way one could get me to sit still was to tell me a story. I loved to listen to my grandparents' old tales, and they were good at relating the ancient legends of my people. They told me of the great gods Wi and Hanwi, the sun and the moon, who were married to each other. They told me about the old man god Waziya, whom the priests have made into Santa Claus. Waziya had a wife who was a big witch. These two had a daughter called Ite—the face—the most beautiful woman in the universe. Ite was married to Tate, the wind.

The trouble with this pairing was that Ite got it into her mind that the sun, Wi, was more handsome than her own husband, the wind. Wi, on his part, thought that Ite was much more beautiful than his own wife, the moon. Wi was having a love affair with Ite, and whenever the moon saw them misbehaving she hid her face in shame. "That's why on some nights we don't see the moon," Grandma told me.

The Great Spirit did not like these goings-on, and he punished Ite. She still remained the most beautiful creature in the world, but only if one looked at her

22

from one side. The other half of her face had become so hideous and ugly that there were no words to describe it. From that time on she was known as Anunk-Ite, or Double-Face. When it comes to love the women always have the worst of it.

Many of these legends were about animals. Grandma told me about the bat who hid himself on top of the eagle's back, screaming, "I can fly higher than any other bird." That was true enough; even the eagle couldn't fly higher than somebody who was sitting on top of him. As a punishment the other birds grounded the bat and put him in a mouse hole. There he fell in love with a lady mouse. That's why bats now are half mouse and half bird.

Grandpa Good Fox told me about the young hunters who killed a buffalo with a big rattle for a tail. After eating of its meat these young men were changed into giant rattlesnakes with human heads and human voices. They lived in a cave beneath the earth and ruled the underworld.

The stories I liked best had to do with Iktome, the evil spiderman, a smart-ass who played tricks on everybody. One day this spider was walking by a lake where he saw many ducks swimming around. This sight gave him a sudden appetite for roast duck. He stuffed his rawhide bag full of grass and then he showed himself. When the ducks saw him they started to holler, "Where are you going, Iktome?"

"I am going to a big powwow."

"What have you got in your bag, Iktome?"

"It's full of songs which I am taking to the powwow, good songs to dance to."

"How about singing some songs for us?" begged the ducks.

The tricky spider made a big show of not wanting to do it. He told the ducks he had no time for them, but in the end he pretended to give in, because they were such nice birds. "I'll sing for you," he told the ducks, "but you must help me."

"We'll do what you want. Tell us the rules."

"Well, you must form three rows. In the front row, all you fat ones, get in there. In the second row go all those who are neither fat nor thin—the in-betweens. The poor scrawny ones go in the third row, way down there. And you have to act out the song, do what the words tell you. Now the words to my first song are 'Close your eyes and dance!'"

The ducks all lined up with their eyes shut, flapping their wings, the fat ones up front. Iktome took a big club from underneath his coat. "Sing along as loud as you can," he ordered, "and keep your eyes shut. Whoever peeks will get blind." He told them to sing so that their voices would drown out the "thump, thump" of his club when he hit them over the head. He knocked them down one by one and was already half done when one of those low-down, skinny ducks in the back row opened its eyes and saw what Iktome was up to.

"Hey, wake up!" it hollered. "That Iktome is killing us all!"

The ducks that were left opened their eyes and took off. Iktome didn't mind. He already had more fat ducks than he could eat.

Iktome is like some of those bull-shipping politicians who make us close our eyes and sing and dance for them while they knock us on the head. Democratic ducks, Republican ducks, it makes no different. The fat, stupid ones are the first in the pot. It's always the skinny, no-account, low-class duck in the back that doesn't hold still. That's a good Indian who keeps his eyes open. Iktome is an evil schemer, Grandpa told me, but luckily he's so greedy that most of the time he outsmarts himself.

It's hard to make our grandchildren listen to these stories nowadays. Some don't understand our language anymore. At the same time there is the TV going full blast—and the radio and the phonograph. These are the things our children listen to. They don't care to hear an old-fashioned Indian story.

I was happy living with my grandparents in a world of our own, but it was a happiness that could not last. "Shh, *wasicun anigni kte*—be quiet or the white man will take you away." How often had I heard these words when I had been up to some mischief, but I never thought that this threat could become true, just as I never believed that the monsters *ciciye* and *siyoko* would come and get me.

But one day the monster came—a white man from the Bureau of Indian Affairs. I guess he had my name on a list. He told my family, "This kid has to go to school. If your kids don't come by themselves the Indian police will pick them up and give them a rough ride." I hid behind Grandma. My father was like a big god to me and Grandpa had been a warrior at the Custer fight, but they could not protect me now.

In those days the Indian schools were like jails and run along military lines, with roll calls four times a day. We had to stand at attention, or march in step. The B.I.A. thought that the best way to teach us was to stop us from being Indians. We were forbidden to talk our language or to sing our songs. If we disobeyed we had to stand in the corner or flat against the wall, our noses and knees touching the plaster. Some teachers hit us on the hands with a ruler. A few of these rulers were covered with brass studs. They didn't have much luck redoing me, though. They could make me dress up like a white man, but they couldn't change what was inside the shirt and pants.

My first teacher was a man and he was facing a lot of fearful kids. I noticed that all the children had the same expression on their faces—no expression at all. They looked frozen, deadpan, wooden. I knew that I, too, looked that way. I didn't know a word of the white man's language and very little about his ways. I thought that everybody had money free. The teacher didn't speak a word of Lakota. He motioned me to my seat. I was scared stiff.

The teacher said, "Stand," "Sit down!" He said it again and again until we caught on. "Sit, stand, sit, stand. Go and stop. Yes and no." All without spelling, just by sound.

We also had a lady teacher. She used the same method. She'd hold up one stick and say, "One." Then she'd hold up two sticks and say, "Two," over and over again. For many weeks she showed us pictures of animals and said "dog" or "cat." It took me three years to learn to say, "I want this."

My first day in school was also the first time I had beans, and with them came some white stuff, I guessed it was pork fat. That night, when I came home, my grandparents had to open the windows. They said my air was no good. Up to then I had eaten nothing but dry meat, *wasna, papa,* dry corn mixed with berries. I didn't know cheese and eggs, butter or cream. Only seldom had I tasted sugar or candy. So I had little appetite at school. For days on end they fed us cheese sandwiches, which made Grandma sniff at me, saying, "Grandson, have you been near some goats?"

After a while I lost some of my fear and recovered my daring. I called the white man teacher all the bad names in my language, smiling at him at the same time. He beamed and patted me on the head, because he thought I was complimenting him. Once I found a big picture of a monkey in the classroom, a strange animal with stiff, white side whiskers. I thought this must be the Great White Father, I really did.

I went to the day school on the Rosebud Reservation, twelve miles south of Norris, South Dakota. The Government teachers were all third-grade teachers. They taught up to this grade and that was the highest. I stayed in that goddam third grade for six years. There wasn't any other. The Indian people of my generation will tell you that it was the same at the other schools all over the reservations. Year after year the same grade over again. If we ran away the police would bring us back. It didn't matter anyway. In all those years at the day school they never taught me to speak English or to write and read. I learned these things only many years later, in saloons, in the Army or in jail.

When I was fourteen years old I was told that I had to go to boarding school. It is hard for a non-Indian to understand how some of our kids feel about boarding schools. In their own homes Indian children are surrounded with relatives as with a warm blanket. Parents, grandparents, uncles, aunts, older brothers and cousins are always fussing over them, playing with them or listening to what they have to say. Indian kids call their aunt "Mother," not just as a polite figure of speech but because that aunt acts like a mother. Indian children are never alone. If the grown-ups go someplace, the little ones are taken along. Children have their rights just as the adults. They are rarely forced to do something they don't like, even if it is good for them. The parents will say, "He hates it so much, we don't have the heart to make him do it."

To the Indian kid the white boarding school comes as a terrific shock. He is taken from his warm womb to a strange, cold place. It is like being pushed out of a cozy kitchen into a howling blizzard. The schools are better now than they were in my time. They look good from the outside—modern and expensive. The teachers understand the kids a little better, use more psychology and less stick. But in these fine new buildings Indian children still commit suicide, because they are lonely among all that noise and activity. I know of a ten-year-old who hanged herself. These schools are just boxes filled with homesick children. The schools leave a scar. We enter them confused and bewildered and we leave them the same way. When we enter the school we at least know that we are Indians. We come out half red and half white, not knowing what we are.

27

When I was a kid those schools were really bad. Ask the old-timers. I envied my father, who never had to go through this. I felt so lonesome I cried, but I wouldn't cooperate in the remaking of myself. I played the dumb Indian. They couldn't make me into an apple—red outside and white inside. From their point of view I was a complete failure. I took the rap for all the troubles in the school. If anything happened the first question always was "Did you see John do it?" They used the strap on us, but more on me than on anybody else.

My teacher was a mean old lady. I once threw a live chicken at her like a snowball. In return she hit my palms with a ruler. I fixed an inkpot in such a way that it went up in her face. The black ink was all over her. I was the first to smile and she knew who had done it right away. They used a harness thong on my back that time and locked me up in the basement. We full-bloods spent much time down there. I picked up some good fox songs in that basement.

I was a good athlete. I busted a kitchen window once playing stickball. After that I never hit so good again. They tried to make me play a slide trombone. I tore it apart and twisted it into a pretzel. That mean old teacher had a mouth like a pike and eyes to match. We counted many coups upon each other and I still don't know who won. Once, when they were after me again for something I didn't do, I ran off. I got home and on my horse. I knew the Indian police would come after me. I made it to Nebraska, where I sold my horse and saddle and bought a ticket to Rapid City. I still had twelve dollars in my pocket. I could live two days on one dollar, but the police caught me and brought me back. I think in the end I got the better of that school. I was more of an Indian when I left than when I went in. My back had been tougher than the many straps they had worn out on it.

Some doctors say that Indians must be healthier than white people because they have less heart disease. Others say that this comes from our being hungrier, having less to eat, which makes our bodies lean and healthy. But this is wrong. The reason Indians suffer less from heart disease is that we don't live long enough to have heart trouble. That's an old folks' sickness. The way we have to live now, we are lucky if we make it to age forty. The fullbloods are dying fast. One day I talk to one, the next day he is dead. In a way the Government is still "vanishing" the Indian, doing Custer's work. The strange-looking pills and capsules they give us to live on at the Public Health Service hospitals don't do us much good. At my school the dentist came once a year in his horse and buggy with a big pair of pliers to yank our teeth, while the strongest, biggest man they could find kept our arms pinned to our sides. That was the anesthesia.

There were twelve of us, but they are all dead now, except one sister. Most of them didn't even grow up. My big brother, Tom, and his wife were killed by the flu in 1917. I lost my own little boy thirty-five years ago. I was a hundred miles away, caught in a blizzard. A doctor couldn't be found for him soon enough. I was told it was the measles. Last year I lost another baby boy, a foster child. This time they told me it was due to some intestinal trouble. So in a lifetime we haven't made much progress. We medicine men try to doctor our sick, but we suffer from many new white man's diseases, which come from the white man's food and white man's living, and we have no herbs for that.

My big sister was the oldest of us all. When she died in 1914 my folks took it so hard that our life was changed. In honor of her memory they gave away most of their possessions, even beds and mattresses, even the things without which the family would find it hard to go on. My mother died of tuberculosis in 1920, when I was seventeen years old, and that was our family's "last stand." On her last day I felt that her body was already gone; only her soul was still there. I was holding her hand and she was looking at me. Her eyes were big and sad, as if she knew that I was in for a hard time. She said, *"Onsika, onsika*—pitiful, pitiful." These were her last words. She wasn't sorry for herself; she was sorry for me. I went up on a hill by myself and cried.

When grandfather Crazy Heart died they killed his two ponies, heads toward the east and tails to the west. They had told each horse, "Grandson, your owner loved you. He has need of you where he's going now." Grandfather knew for sure where he was going, and so did the people who buried him according to our old custom, up on a scaffold where the wind and the air, the sun, the rain and the snow could take good care of him. I think that eventually they took the box with his body down from the scaffold and buried it in a cemetery, but that happened years later and by then he and his ponies had long gone to wherever they wanted to be.

But in 1920 they wouldn't even allow us to be dead in our own way. We had to be buried in the Christian fashion. It was as if they wanted to take my mother to a white boarding school way up there. For four days I felt my mother's *nagi,* her presence, her soul, near me. I felt that some of her goodness was staying with me. The priest talked about eternity. I told him we Indians did not believe in a forever and forever. We say that only the rocks and the mountains last, but even they will disappear. There's a new day coming, but no forever, I told him. "When my time comes, I want to go where my ancestors have gone." The priest said, "That may be hell." I told him that I'd rather be frying with a Sioux grandmother or uncle than sit on a cloud playing harp with a pale-faced stranger. I told him, "That Christian name, John, don't call me that when I'm gone. Call me Tahca Ushte—Lame Deer."

With the death of my mother one world crumbled for me. It coincided with a new rule the Government made about grazing pay and allotments. Barbed-wire fences closed in on us. My dad said, "We might just as well give up." He went back to Standing Rock, where he was from. He left my sister about sixty horses, forty scrub cows and one bull. I had about sixty head of broken saddle horses and fifty cows. My dad turned me loose. "Hey, I give you these horses; do as you please. If you want to live like a white man, go and buy a car till you are broke and walk on foot." I guess Dad knew what was in my mind.

I started trading my stock for a Model-T Ford and bought things that were in style for the rodeo—fancy boots, silver spurs, gaudy horse-trappings, a big hat. I followed the rodeo circuit, but I wasn't too interested in competing as a rider. It was just an excuse to travel to different reservations. My life was changed and I myself was changing. I hardly recognized myself anymore. I was a wanderer, a hippie Indian. I knew nothing then. Right or wrong were just words. My life was a find-out. If somebody said, "That's bad," I still wanted to experience it. Maybe it would turn out to be good. I wasn't drinking then but soon would be. My horses and cows were gone. Instead I was the owner of a half-dozen wrecked jalopies. Yet I felt the spirits. Always at night they came down to me. I could hear them, something like the whistling from the hearing aid that I am wearing now. I could feel their touch like a feather on a sore spot. I always burned a little sweetgrass for them. Though I lived like a hobo, I was visiting many old medicine men, trying to learn their ways.

I didn't need a house then or a pasture. Somewhere there would be a cave, a crack in the rocks, where I could hole up during a rain. I wanted the plants and the stones to tell me their secrets. I talked to them. I roamed. I was like a part of the earth. Everything had been taken from me except myself. Now and then, in some place or other, I looked at my face in a mirror to remind myself who I was. Poverty, hardship, laughter, shame, adventure—I wanted to experience them all. At times I felt like one of those modern declawed cats, like a lone coyote with traps, poisoned meat, and a ranger's gun waiting for him, but this did not worry me. I was neither sad nor happy. I just was.

I knew an old Indian at this time who was being forced to leave his tent and to go live in a new house. They told him that he would be more comfortable there and that they had to burn up his old tent because it was verminous and unsanitary. He looked thin and feeble, but he put up a terrific fight. They had a hard time dragging him. He was cursing them all the time: "I don't want no son-of-a-bitch house. I don't want to live in a box. Throw out the goddam refrigerator, drink him up! Throw out the chair, saw off the damn legs, sit on the ground. Throw out that thing to piss in. I won't use it. Dump the son-of-a-bitch goldfish in there. Kill the damn cow, eat him up. Tomorrow is another day. There's no tomorrow in this goddam box!"

I felt proud of this old man. He expressed what I felt. He gave me courage. I was cut loose, drifting like a leaf the wind tore from a tree. I listened to many white preachers of all denominations simply because I was curious to hear what they had to say. But I had no need of their churches. I carried my own church within me. I went to peyote meetings and had visions. I wanted to feel, smell, hear and see, but not see with my eyes and my mind only. I wanted to see with *cante ista*—the eye of the heart. This eye had its own way of looking at things. I was going through a change. I didn't resist it. I gave myself up to it wholly. Always I tried to find out. I met a medicine man, one of my uncles. "Tell me about the Great Spirit," I asked him. "He is not like a human being, like the white god. He is a power. That power could be in a cup of coffee. The Great Spirit is no old man with a beard." This answer made me happy, but I would ask the same question again from somebody else.

I had a thirst for women. I wanted to know them. I loved many girls, more than a hundred. Their soft moaning had something to teach me. It could also get me killed. At a dance on one reservation—I won't mention the name of the place, because they could come and want to shoot me again—I met a girl and took her out, brought her to my hideout nearby. Then I noticed that I had left my coat at the powwow and went to get it. When I got there I ran into her husband, pawing the ground, looking mean. Of all things he turned out to be one hell of a big policeman and he had seen me sneaking off with his wife. He had his gun out in a flash and started banging away at me, calling me some very bad names at the same time. I didn't stop to listen but jumped on the nearest horse and away I went. He fired all six shots after me. He didn't hit me, but one of the bullets hit the horse in the rump. Poor horse, he hadn't done a thing.

In 1930 I got what I deserved. I was married by force. The girl's father was a big cheese, a Christian with plenty of pull. They put the pressure on me. I didn't have any choice. I was like the coyote caught with his leg in a trap. At some time I would bite the leg off.

These people were Catholics and I went to their church with them. It didn't work well. People paid more attention to me than to the preacher. Some white people didn't want to sit next to me. It was the boarding school all over again. After three years my wife divorced me. She said I was good during the day but bad in the nighttime.

I was out of the trap. I hadn't been ready to settle down anyway. There were still many things I had to be—an outlaw and a lawman, a prisoner and a roamer, a sheepherder and a bootlegger, a rodeo rider and a medicine man. I still wanted to lead many lives, finding out who I was. The fever was still strong in me. Like my great-grandfather Lame Deer, I wanted to go on one more big hunt, though I didn't know then what I was hunting for or how long the hunt would last, and whether it would kill me, as it had killed my ancestor. Maybe I was looking for his gun. I still say it is mine.

# 3
# The Green Frog Skin

The green frog skin—that's what I call a dollar bill. In our attitude toward it lies the biggest difference between Indians and whites. My grandparents grew up in an Indian world without money. Just before the Custer battle the white soldiers had received their pay. Their pockets were full of green paper and they had no place to spend it. What were their last thoughts as an Indian bullet or arrow hit them? I guess they were thinking of all that money going to waste, of not having had a chance to enjoy it, of a bunch of dumb savages getting their paws on that hard-earned pay. That must have hurt them more than the arrow between their ribs.

The close hand-to-hand fighting, with a thousand horses gally-hooting all over the place, had covered the battlefield with an enormous cloud of dust, and in it the green frog skins of the soldiers were whirling around like snowflakes in a blizzard. Now, what did the Indians do with all that money? They gave it to their children to play with, to fold those strange bits of colored paper into all kinds of shapes, making them into toy buffalo and horses. Somebody was enjoying that money after all. The books tell of one soldier who survived. He got away, but he went crazy and some women watched him from a distance as he killed himself. The writers always say he must have been afraid of being captured and tortured, but that's all wrong.

Can't you see it? There he is, bellied down in a gully, watching what is going on. He sees the kids playing with the money, tearing it up, the women

35

using it to fire up some dried buffalo chips to cook on, the men lighting their pipes with green frog skins, but mostly all those beautiful dollar bills floating away with the dust and the wind. It's this sight that drove that poor soldier crazy. He's clutching his head, hollering, "Goddam, Jesus Christ Almighty, look at them dumb, stupid, red sons of bitches wasting all that dough!" He watches till he can't stand it any longer, and then he blows his brains out with a six-shooter. It would make a great scene in a movie, but it would take an Indian mind to get the point.

The green frog skin—that was what the fight was all about. The gold of the Black Hills, the gold in every clump of grass. Each day you can see ranch hands riding over this land. They have a bagful of grain hanging from their saddle horns, and whenever they see a prairie-dog hole they toss a handful of oats in it, like a kind little old lady feeding the pigeons in one of your city parks. Only the oats for the prairie dogs are poisoned with strychnine. What happens to the prairie dog after he has eaten this grain is not a pleasant thing to watch. The prairie dogs are poisoned, because they eat grass. A thousand of them eat up as much grass in a year as a cow. So if the rancher can kill that many prairie dogs he can run one more head of cattle, make a little more money. When he looks at a prairie dog he sees only a green frog skin getting away from him.

For the white man each blade of grass or spring of water has a price tag on it. And that is the trouble, because look at what happens. The bobcats and coyotes which used to feed on prairie dogs now have to go after a stray lamb or a crippled calf. The rancher calls the pest-control officer to kill these animals. This man shoots some rabbits and puts them out as bait with a piece of wood stuck in them. That stick has an explosive charge which shoots some cyanide into the mouth of the coyote who tugs at it. The officer has been trained to be careful. He puts a printed warning

36

on each stick reading, "Danger, Explosive, Poison!" The trouble is that our dogs can't read, and some of our children can't either.

And the prairie becomes a thing without life—no more prairie dogs, no more badgers, foxes, coyotes. The big birds of prey used to feed on prairie dogs, too. So you hardly see an eagle these days. The bald eagle is your symbol. You see him on your money, but your money is killing him. When a people start killing off their own symbols they are in a bad way.

The Sioux have a name for white men. They call them *wasicun*—fat-takers. It is a good name, because you have taken the fat of the land. But it does not seem to have agreed with you. Right now you don't look so healthy—overweight, yes, but not healthy. Americans are bred like stuffed geese—to be consumers, not human beings. The moment they stop consuming and buying, the frog-skin world has no more use for them. They have become frogs themselves. Some cruel child has stuffed a cigar into their mouths and they have to keep puffing and puffing until they explode. Fat-taking is a bad thing, even for the taker. It is especially bad for Indians who are forced to live in this frog-skin world which they did not make and for which they have no use.

You, Richard, are an artist. That's one reason we get along well. Artists are the Indians of the white world. They are called dreamers who live in the clouds, improvident people who can't hold onto their money, people who don't want to face "reality." They say the same things about Indians. How the hell do these frog-skin people know what reality is? The world in which you paint a picture in your mind, a picture which shows things different from what your eyes see, that is the world from which I get my visions. I tell you this is the real world, not the Green Frog Skin World. That's only a bad dream, a streamlined, smog-filled nightmare.

Because we refuse to step out of our reality into this

frog-skin illusion, we are called dumb, lazy, improvident, immature, other-worldly. It makes me happy to be called "other-worldly," and it should make you so. It's a good thing our reality is different from theirs. I remember one white man looking at my grandfather's vest. It was made of black velvet and had ten-dollar gold coins for buttons. The white man had a fit, saying over and over again, "Only a crazy Indian would think of that, using good money for buttons, a man who hasn't got a pot to piss in!" But Grandpa wasn't a bit crazy and he had learned to know the value of money as well as anybody. But money exists to give a man pleasure. Well, it pleasured Grandpa to put a few golden Indian heads on his vest. That made sense.

I knew a well-educated Indian who had come back to his reservation after working for many years in a big city. With his life savings he opened a cafeteria and gas station. All day long the cars lined up. "Hey, Uncle, fill her up. I can't pay, but you are rich; you let me have it free." And the same thing over at the cafeteria: "Say, Uncle, let me have one of them barbecued-beef sandwiches. Don't bother to write up a bill for a relation of yours."

The owner had done very well living and working in the white man's way among white people. But now he was an Indian again, back among Indians. He couldn't say "no" to a poor relative, and the whole reservation was just one big mass of poor relatives, people who called him Uncle and Cousin regardless of the degree of their relationship. He couldn't refuse them and his education couldn't help him in this situation. We aren't divided up into separate, neat little families— Pa, Ma, kids, and to hell with everybody else. The whole damn tribe is one big family; that's our kind of reality.

It wasn't long before this Indian businessman was broke and in debt. But this man was smart, white-educated. So he found a way out. He hired a white waitress and a white gas-station attendant and spread the word that he had been forced to sell the business to white owners. From then on he did well. Everybody paid, because they knew white men don't give anything away for free.

I once heard of an Indian who lost a leg in an industrial accident. He got about fifteen thousand dollars in insurance money. In no time his place was overrun with more than a hundred hungry relatives. They came in old jalopies, in buckboards, on horseback or on foot. From morning to night a pick-up truck was making round trips between his place and the nearest store, hauling beef and bread and crates of beer to keep all of those lean bellies full. In the end they bought a few scrub steers and did their own butchering. The fun lasted a few weeks, then the money was gone. A day after that the relatives were gone, too. That man had no regrets. He said he wished he'd lose his other leg so that he could start all over again. This man had become quite a hero, even to other tribes, and he was welcome everywhere.

I made up a new proverb: "Indians chase the vision, white men chase the dollar." We are lousy raw material from which to form a capitalist. We could do it easily, but then we would stop being Indians. We would just be ordinary citizens with a slightly darker skin. That's a high price to pay, my friend, too high. We make lousy farmers, too, because deep down within us lingers a feeling that land, water, air, the earth and what lies beneath its surface cannot be owned as someone's private property. That belongs to everybody, and if man wants to survive, he had better come around to this Indian point of view, the sooner the better, because there isn't much time left to think it over.

I always remember listening to my first radio. That was in the little town of Interior, way back in the twenties. There was a sign over a door: "Listen to wireless music from Sioux Falls—300 miles away! $1.50 per person." You had to plunk that much down to be allowed inside this café to give your ears a treat. We saw a guy fooling around with a needle on a crystal and heard a tinny, crackling voice saying something about winter feed, corn and the price of prime hogs. At that moment an old Indian spoke up. "They took the land and the water, now they own the air, too." So we have the green frog-skin world in which all things have a price tag.

Indians don't like to haggle. A long argument about money is painful. But we can drive a shrewd bargain. My uncle, Poor Thunder, bred a special brand of Appaloosas. At that time you could get a saddle-broken horse for twenty bucks, not one of Poor Thunder's Appaloosas. If a white man came and asked for a price my uncle would tell him it was seventy-five dollars per head. The buyer used to scratch his head and say the price was too high. They always came back in a day or two, because these horses were really something. But when they returned with cash in their hands my uncle would tell them, "That was yesterday's price. Now it will cost you a hundred dollars." If they were foolish enough to do some more head-scratching the price would go up to 125 dollars. But the cheerful buyer who didn't haggle, who made up his mind at once, got ten bucks off. Uncle loved his ponies. He once told me, "An Indian can love one horse so much, he'll die for it." He had a great head for business—he was one hell of a horse trader—but he gave most of what he got away to his poor relations. The trader in him couldn't get the better of the Indian.

Old Uncle would sometimes leave a heifer or steer in front of a poor cousin's house. He used to tell me, "There's more to food than just passing through your body. There are spirits in the food, watching over it. If you are stingy, that spirit will go away thinking 'that bastard is so tight, I'll leave.' But if you share your food with others, this good spirit will always stay around." I was brought up to regard food as something sacred. I can foresee a day when all you have to give us are capsules with some chemicals and vitamins instead of food, with the missionaries telling us to fold our hands over a few tablets on our plates, saying, "Heavenly Father, bless our daily pill." I'm glad I won't be around to see it.

I'd rather have a glass of *mini-sha,* red water, with one of my neighbors. He is an old wino but very generous. He'll share his last bottle with a friend. He told me, "The whisky can't get away from me. The more I give away, the more it comes. I've got to be careful, or I'll drown in it."

The anthropologists are always saying that there is still too much of the old buffalo hunter in us. Share your food, share your goods, or the tribe will perish. That was good for yesterday. Today it's saying "No, no, no" to a poor cousin. That's the practical thing to do. Trying always to remake people in one's own image is a white man's disease. I can't cure that. I tell those anthros, "You have green frog skins on your brains. If we Indians were such filthy savages as you tell us, we should have eaten you up when you first came to this turtle continent. Then I could have some peace and quiet now." That shuts them up for a while.

They are also wagging their fingers at us when we have a give-away feast. What they are trying to tell us is that poor people can't afford to be generous. But we hold onto our *otuhan,* our give-aways, because they help us to remain Indians. All the big events in our lives—birth and death, joy and sadness—can be occasions for a give-away. We don't believe in a family getting wealthy through inheritance. Better give away a dead person's belongings. That way he, or she, will be remembered.

If a man loses his wife, his friends come and help him cry. He cries for four days, but no longer, because life must go on, and if he cries too much the spirits will give him something extra to cry about. Not so long ago I saw an old lady who still cut her hair short to mourn for a dead grandson. After four days she and her husband emptied the whole house. They gave away the grand piano, the TV, even their bed. They were sitting on the bare floor calling out to the people coming to pay their respects, "Say, brother, sister, do you need this thing? If it is useful to you, take it." Only the empty walls were left at the end of the day. Friends gave them a new bed. A *wopila*—a thanksgiving for something good that happened to a person—is also a time for giving away things. But your white man's day of thanksgiving—that's a day of mourning for the Indians, nothing to be thankful for.

You put "In God We Trust" on your money. I'm glad you left the Great Spirit out of it. What you want to use your God for is your own business. I tried to show you that the green frog skin is something that keeps whites and Indians apart. But even a medicine man like myself has to have some money, because you force me to live in your make-believe world where I can't get along without it. Which means that I have to be two persons living in two different worlds. I don't like it, but I can't help it. I will try to tell you how I managed this. Whether I have been successful at it you may judge for yourself.

As long as I still had some of the horses and cattle left which my father had given me, I had no thought about earning money. I roamed. I didn't let myself get swallowed up by the frog-skin world, but I was curious enough to explore it. I liked to go to town on horseback. I used to pick up my pals on the way, like Ben Rifle, who later became a congressman. We played around the little reservation towns called Wososo, or Upper Cut Meat. I was like an elk dreamer with a power to charm the girls. I had a good voice and liked to sing Indian. My grandparents had taught me all the old songs. I had no education, but always I was thinking, finding out, trying to fit what I saw and heard into my kind of reality.

Then the day came when I swapped or sold the last of my livestock. I was almost happy. Now I no longer had any property to take care of, to tie me down. Now I could be what I wanted—a real Sioux, an *ikce wicasa,* a common, wild, natural human being. How such a creature could survive in frog-skin land was something I would have to find out. I thought I'd do some hunting to keep meat on my table. I found out that I needed a hunting license if I wanted to go after deer or antelope. The idea of an Indian having to pay for a fancy piece of paper in order to be allowed to hunt on his own land to feed his own, genuine, red man's belly seemed like a bad joke to me. It made me laugh, but it also made me angry. The same people who had killed off the buffalo, who were chopping up the last wild horses into dog food, now were telling me that I was a danger to wildlife preservation if I wanted some red meat on my table, that I had to be regulated. Why couldn't I be satisfied with the starches they were handing out to us? They told me I should be flattered, that having to buy a license put me up there on the same level with the white gentleman hunter. I answered, through an interpreter, that I was no goddam sportsman, just a hungry, common, natural Indian who did not like fancy stamped papers and knew of only one way he could use them.

I was not the only one to feel this way. Most Indians would have been ashamed to hunt with a license. So we did without. The only catch was that there was really not much game left. A few hungry Indians, when they came across some white man's scrub steer, pretended that he had antlers and there was a little bit of "night-butchering" on the reservation, and some people were eating "slow elk." There was some satisfaction in this, like stealing horses from the Crow Indians in the good old days.

No matter how much I hated it I had to face up to the fact that I would have to earn some money. I was like many other fullbloods. I didn't want a steady job in an office or factory. I thought myself too good for that, not because I was stuck up but simply because any human being is too good for that kind of no-life, even white people. I trained myself to need and want as little as could be so that I wouldn't have to work except when I felt like it. That way I got along fine with plenty of spare time to think, to ask, to learn, to listen, to count coup on the girls.

I hit the rodeo circuit. The riding suited me fine and put some cash in my pocket. I still had my fancy saddle and clothes, so I dressed myself up like a sore toe and hit the trail. I was good at this kind of life. I had been raised among horses, was almost part horse myself. I had learned about horses through the seat of my pants. In those days, when I started out, the rodeos were still fun. Most of the spectators could ride as well as the guys in the arena. They understood what you were doing and there was no faking.

Nowadays rodeos are frog-skin business, and the riders are just people working at a job. They could as well be TV repairmen, the way I look at it. There are no wild bucking horses anymore. Horses are trained to buck just as elephants are trained to walk around in the circus. The same horses show up again and again. The riders take movies of them so that, when they draw that horse to ride, they already know how he's going to buck. That's not riding; you might just as well drive a milk truck. It's all a scramble for money, points and championships now. The excitement is gone.

In the old days you got a wild horse or cow that had never been ridden or roped before, and you had a lot to do. After you were through with that horse, or he with you, you most likely never set eyes on him again. And there were no specialists. I did every goddam, mad-dog thing you can think of—bulldogging, bronc-busting, buffalo riding. Those were real wild horses we rode, real cloud-hunters and sun-fishers. You could be the first man to sit on one of them. You had to blindfold them to get them in a chute. Then it was hold onto their ears and away you go. You volunteered to ride the bad ones—"Bring on that man-killer"—just for that one girl watching you.

You had the wild cattle from the unfenced range for your steer-roping and bulldogging. In my days you went after that "renegade," roped it by the horns and rode your horse in such a way that it flipped the steer up high and over like a flapjack. It usually knocked him out long enough for you to have a chance to hog-tie him before he came to. Some riders grabbed the steer's nose between their teeth and spread their arms to show the onlookers who was boss. The flipping was called "throwing the hoolihan," and it could break a steer's neck or yours. It's now forbidden, which is a good thing for man and beast.

The most exciting thing that I did was buffalo riding. Those buffalo looked big and clumsy, but they went as fast as a dollar bill. I don't know where these creatures came from, probably Custer State Park. Once I rode seven of them in one day. Those buffalo gave me a workout. I stayed with the first one for just one jump. He was a real fart-knocker. On the second one I hung on long enough for two jumps. On the fourth buffalo I lasted for six full jumps. He went so fast the cowboys couldn't pick me off. Number seven came out of the chute so quick I missed him altogether. I spilled hard, but the sand was soft and good to me.

I guess the spirits were watching over me, because I never broke an arm or leg except once, in Martin, South Dakota. I had my right shoulder put out of joint riding bareback. They had no doctors in attendance in those days. They just put a pillow under my arm and yanked away. I still have a bum shoulder after all these years.

I used to go to the White River Frontier Days, which was rated as a big shindig around here. I traveled to Gilette, Wyoming, to Oregon, and all the way down to the border. Sometimes we didn't have a proper fairground. Those old jalopies, Model T's and horse buggies just formed a big circle at some place, and that was the arena. The spectators stayed in their cars and wagons, and if you did something they admired they honked their horns good and loud. The prize money was small then, but the excitement was big. Today it's just like a picture show.

I figured it was time to quit bronc-busting while I was still in one piece. Besides, I got bored whenever I was too long at one job. But I still kept traveling to the fairs as a rodeo clown. It was a little less dangerous than bulldogging, but only a little. Our name for clown is *heyoka*. For us Indians a clown is somebody strange, who always does the opposite of what's expected of him. A clown's work is sacred; it's a medicine man's job. I'll have more to say about this when we get to the *heyoka* part of my story, when we'll be talking about dreams of the thunderbeings, visions, medicine and boiled dog.

It was my job as a clown to divert the bulls from the riders who had been thrown, so that they wouldn't be gored. We had to do this in a funny way to amuse the crowd, waving blankets and having barrels around us like in a cartoon showing a fellow when the income-tax man is through with him. If the bull attacked me I withdrew into my barrel like a snail into its shell, pulling in my horns, letting the bull bang me around from one end of the ring to the other.

I had a special act. I was dressed up as a lady with a big yellow wig and two pillows stuffed in my chest for a make-believe "babies' bar," as the cowboys called a girl's bumpers. My stage name was Alice Jitterbug. I always made my entry riding on a cow, a very hot cow with the love wink in her eye. Once we were chased by a bull that took a real shine to her. The spectators thought it was very funny, but it wasn't funny to me. I waved my red underskirts at the Brahma bulls to take their minds off the fallen riders. Sometimes I had to dive head first into my barrel, letting the folks admire my lace underpants. Often I teamed up with another Indian clown, Jake Herman, who was famous for his funny stories and fairy tales. He's been dead now for a number of years, "gone south," as we say.

I had a lot of fun doing my act and made a little money off it, too. The old-timers in the little cow towns for a hundred miles around still remember me. They don't remember me as a rider, because there were so many good ones in those days, but there was only one Alice Jitterbug.

Riding or clowning, it wasn't a bad life. There was always somebody to treat you to some bumblebee whisky—the drink with a sting—people to get friendly with, Indian boys from other tribes I could talk to. I slept under the grandstand, if there was one, or in my bedroll out in the sagebrush. And I seldom slept alone. It was a rare night when a girl didn't keep me company. My elk power must have been strong.

When it came to women I looked upon them as a part of mother earth which no man should treat as just a chunk of fenced-in property. If my bedroll looked soft and inviting to some girl, if she felt like taking a short rest and asked me could I spare a drink of sneaky Pete or dago red, who was I to say no, or to make her swear on a stack of Bibles that she was single and had no brand on her. I figured that was none of my business.

Some men didn't see eye to eye with me on this. I got into some good fights. I wasn't one to back down then. I told those jealous men: "Guarding an unwilling girl is like watching a sockful of fleas—hopeless."

It was a sociable life, but also lonely, happy and sad at the same time. That was what I wanted. I heard a young Indian rider sing:

I ain't got no father
I ain't got no father
To pay for the boots I wear.

I ain't got no ma
I ain't got no ma
To mend my socks.

I ain't got no gal
I ain't got no gal
To kiss my ugly puss.

I'm just a *pteole Lakota hoksila*
A poor Sioux cowboy
A long ways from home.

That's how I felt, except that once in a while some girl kissed my ugly puss. I joined that boy singing, *"Tokiya blahe?*—where am I riding to, where am I going?" I didn't know and I didn't care.

It was rodeo in the summer and square dancing in the winter. We liked that white man's dancing, because it gave a boy a chance to touch a girl, get a feel of her body. In an Indian powwow, the girls dance separately from the boys, moving in a circle, the girls going one way and the boys circling in the opposite direction. So one Indian got things started, a quadrille, Western style. He got a fiddler, a mouth harp and a good harmonica player. He did the calling himself. We caught on fast. I tried to be a caller, too, because I always stuck my neck out. Sometimes this guy had a sore throat, so he told me to go ahead and give her a whirl. I was excited and shy at the same time and made a lot of mistakes.

It added up to one big confusion—dancers bumping into one another, running around like chickens when the fox gets into the henhouse. I was never a good English talker, and at that time I could hardly pronounce the words, even when I understood their meaning, which mostly I didn't. I just tried to remember the sound. The man who ran the dance told me, "Just so long as you make a big racket, it will be all right." I damn near busted my throat. After a while I got the hang of this square-dance calling. I got no frog skins out of it, just free meals. Here is how it went:

> Now rope that heifer, swing her high,
> Don't get lost, and away you go,
> Swap your partners, do-see-do!
> Hug your honey and pat her on the head,
> Turn her out to grass,
> Don't fall on your . . . do-see-do.
> I swing mine, and you swing yours,
> I swing yours, and you swing mine,
> Aahaa, get going, hit her hard
> All the way round and promenade,
> Up the middle, march home.

A good dance started at sundown and didn't stop until after sunup. Everybody went home red-eyed and sleepy but with a lot of good memories. We slept all day on Sundays. Some of the old fiddlers always ended up with a slow, slow waltz, so slow you could watch the snails whizz by. I held onto my girl of the moment, closing my eyes, having some good vision of her that meant more to me than the music. These visions weren't always pure, but they sure were nice. We kept this square dancing up for seven years, but it's dead now. The last old-style fiddler in our little town passed away not long ago and the dancers are long married and white-haired, if they are still alive.

Well, this is what we did indoors in the wintertime. Summers I wanted to be out in the open. That was powwow time, time for Indian-style dancing. But the powwows too have become a green frog-skin business. When I was young there was never an admission charge to a dance, and you didn't come to watch; you came to take part. Now they dance for the contest money. It discourages those who don't compete, who have come for the fun of it. At first the judges gave the prize money to a poor man who needed it; now they give it to their relatives. Once this money business starts, everything turns sour.

At the last sun dance in Pine Ridge the organizing committee charged a buck and a half admission. They threw two poor old Indians out of the dance ground because they couldn't pay. Imagine, charging an Indian to go to his sun dance! The people didn't like this, and in the evening, when they called for the Indian dancers to come in, well, there were all the dancers on the high ground, bunched up in little groups, decked out in their feathers, bustles and ankle bells, leaning against their cars and pick-ups, making a fine show but not moving. They wouldn't dance in a place where two old full-bloods couldn't come without paying. It made us happy to see this. We won that round, but later we heard that two of the men who handled the organization of this dance were being accused of having embezzled some funds from the sacred sun dance. The green frog-skin world is closing in, even on our most sacred ceremony.

During my time of wandering, my *oyumni,* or roaming, period, I got into card games, got drunk or spent money on some girl. One way or another I had to sell my fine saddle and take my fancy boots and doodads to the hock shop. So I didn't care to make the rodeo circuit anymore. Somebody tried to give me a steady job as a ranch hand. I told him, "I want to raise cain, not cattle." I wasn't through roaming yet. Something was driving me on, keeping me from settling down. I was still young, a born world-shaker, or just plain foolish. A fellow told me that spud pickers were needed in Nebraska, five cents a bushel. I used my last ten frog skins as a down payment on a broken-down jalopy, an early Ford, a real museum piece even then. I jacked her up, cranked her up and chug-chugged to Pine Ridge. There I picked up three other guys and we started out as a crew. They told us, "The farther south you go, the less competition you'll have, and the more you'll get paid." South we went, past Gordon, Agate, Haysprings. In the morning we rolled into the town of Alliance. A truck with a farmer came along. "Want a job, fellows, five cents a bushel?"

That farmer had maybe one hundred acres of spuds, so and so many plowed lines. We measured how many bushels there were to a line. It came to about thirty or forty bushels. The farmer fixed us up with a lot of sacks and a team of horses. You have a belt with a long dragging sack between your legs. You go up and down the line from sunup to sundown. That first day I picked seventy-five bushels and they almost broke my back. Three dollars and two bits for twelve hours of hard work. That farmer didn't feed us; we had to eat raw potatoes and sleep in the hayloft. I became a champion spud picker. My record was 150 bushels, or seven and a half bucks a day. That was the most I ever made.

Later we switched to another farmer. He was nicer. He paid us the same as the first one, but he had a heart and fed us—bread and butter, sowbelly and coffee. The old barn he gave us to sleep in, though, had a lot of extra wildlife we weren't keen on—pants rats and seam squirrels. I didn't make 150 bushels there because I had to stop and scratch. We four Indians pooled our frog skins and shared the gas. We got paid every day. Once a month we bought canned goods, a big slab of bacon, a sack of sugar, and drank up what money was left over.

When the season was finished we had a big drunk in town. That day the moonshine was good. You drank it, filled yourself up, and the next day you felt nothing —no hangover. That was about the best **mo**onshine I ever had. One of our crew had been without a woman for too long. He made up a song:

> I count coup on the girls
> The moment I am on top of them.
> I'm on top of the world.
> I am the top man.

Nobody could top this song, I guess. Two of our little crew got involved with girls and left us, breaking up our gang. I had learned something about farmers and potatoes; time to try something else.

I went up north to Standing Rock. I felt a great need to be by myself, think about what I had experienced so far. One day I was wandering aimlessly through the streets of Belle Fourche when a white woman came up to me and asked could I do some sheepherding. Her husband had been out in the hills for a long time now, taking care of the woollies, and she was growing kind of hot for him to come back. I could see she had a soft, warm, moist spot there waiting for that man of hers.

She took me out to where her husband was, a long way off in the unfenced country where they had a big flock of sheep. That husband sure was glad to see me, a jolly man with a barefoot head that was shining in the sun whenever he took off his hat to wipe it. They were in a hurry to leave me and be off by themselves. I had a notion these two wouldn't drive straight home but rest a few times under some cottonwoods. They hadn't seen each other for some time. That's sheepherding for you.

There was a big sheep wagon there with a stovepipe sticking out, loaded with everything I needed, food and stuff to last me for six months at least. This was to be my home. I had all the grub I wanted and the pay was good. Barefoot Head had left me a .30–.30 rifle, a handful of shells and two sheep dogs. These dogs did all the work, whipping the strays into line. I was just a lonesome decoration.

The place where the sheep sleep is called the bed ground, and that's where I slept, too; the spot I put the wagon. Every morning at five o'clock I took the sheep out for lunch, or rather the dogs did, with me following on horseback. Each time we picked a different place where the grass was plentiful. The sheep always spent the first five hours of the day eating, the next hour drinking, and then about three hours doing nothing in particular. That's when I gave the dogs time off to chase rabbits and did my own thinking. After this rest period the sheep would eat some more, and finally came the grand parade home to the bed ground.

Every few weeks, as soon as the sheep had eaten off all the grass around the wagon for as far as could be reached in a day's walk to and from the feeding grounds, it was time to move and find some more grass. Usually I picked a place with a nice view from my wagon. And then the whole routine would start all over again.

Herding seems very boring until you try it for yourself. The fact is that the woollies can keep a man pretty busy. The reason is that they are man-bred, unnatural cousins of the wild mountain sheep, critters so dumb that they can't take care of themselves. They are always rolling over on their backs, and once they get themselves into that position they can't get up again. Did you know that? I didn't. I would have never believed this, even from a white-man-bred animal. But there they were with their four legs sticking up in the air, looking helpless and stupid. For some reason, once a sheep is lying on its back, it gets bloated like a balloon, and it will die soon, unless somebody comes along and put it on its feet again. Sometimes you have to stick an awl into them and they go pfftt . . . like a pricked balloon. They don't seem to mind. They simply deflate and start munching grass again within a few minutes as if nothing had happened.

Well, some days I was busy turning those damn

woollies over like flapjacks. Once I overlooked one and it died on me within an hour.

Some sheep are so dumb they won't recognize, or feed, their own lambs. These orphans are called bums and you have to hand raise them, unless you can trick, or cajole, another lady sheep into adopting one, which can be done if you know how. In spite of having no brains to speak of, sheep can think up a lot of ways to keep a herder busy.

At night I ran the sheep up to the wagon and put out two kerosene lamps with reflectors so that I could keep an eye on the woollies and watch out for coyotes, bobcats or maybe a stray mountain lion. When the dogs started barking I knew the coyotes had arrived. I could see their eyes like so many points of light in a wide circle around me. I didn't have to shoot. The moment I threw another log on the fire and got my .30–.30 out, they took off and I could go back to sleep. Coyotes are smart, smarter than some people I know.

So here I was, a Sioux Indian, running woollies, a flock-master. In the morning I went to the creek for water, which was so cold it hurt my teeth. I filled my cowboy hat with it and let the dogs drink from it, because I was told that's what a proper sheepherder does. I was happy to be alone, closing my eyes, thinking, figuring, listening to the voices, letting the spirits come to me. But after about a month I began to get restless. I got tired of hearing nothing but the bleating of sheep. I began wishing for that man, or his wife, to come back for me, to send someone to spell me. I got so damn lonely out there I prayed for a squaw to keep me company, even an ugly one. But day after day went by without my seeing another human being or hearing a human voice.

There was no radio, but Barefoot Head did leave me a stack of colored magazines, *Saturday Evening Post*s and such. I practiced my reading, tracing the printed lines with my finger. The stories and pictures in those magazines were all foreign country to me, something from another world. I also found a Bible in the wagon, and I studied that, too. So my English and my reading improved with time. "And Shem begat Uz, and Uz begat Lud, and Lud begat Mash, and Mash begat Nush." Begat, begat, begat! Those ancient Hebrews, I gathered, were all sheepherders like me. With all that begetting, who in hell was watching their woollies? They had no .30–.30s, but plenty of lions. All this begetting made me think of women, and that didn't help. I began to mumble to myself.

I used to go out and holler just to hear my own voice. Those yellow-eyed sheep watched me. They thought I had gone crazy. Once in a while one of them died through some accident, and I went on a diet of sheep, ram, lamb and mutton, as they say. I lost all track of time, didn't know which day of the week it was. Hell, I wasn't even sure of the month.

One day I saw a cloud of dust. Barefoot Head and his old woman were coming up in their rattling wagon to see if I was still alive. When they stopped I was all packed up and ready to go. They asked if anything was wrong. Was it the food or the pay? I told them that they had treated me real nice but that I wasn't cut out to be a sheep man. I'd better quit before I forgot how to talk, before I got married to a lady sheep.

I had been alone out there for over three months, and I got home with a big wad of frog skins. Not long ago I ran into a modern sheepherder who had a tape recorder in his wagon. I asked him what it was for. He told me he used it to talk to himself. He had only one tape. When he got tired of arguing with himself on one subject, he erased it and started a dispute about something else. I think all old sheepherders are *witko*—crazy—from being too much by themselves. I felt very sociable for a while after this, and my money was soon gone.

Always, after working at a white man's job or a time of hell-raising, I would go back to the old men of my tribe and spend many days learning about medicine and the ancient ways. Visions, a world beyond the frog-skin world, have always been very important to us. You could almost say that a man with no vision can't be a real Indian. Out in the plains we get our visions the hard way, by fasting and by staying in the vision pit for four days and nights, crying for a dream. Other tribes have the same quest for visions but search for them in a different way. Eighty years ago the ghost-dance religion came to us from the south, from a Paiute holy man. People danced themselves into a trance until they saw their dead relatives. The ghost dancers were massacred at Wounded Knee and their dream wiped out with Gatling guns. Dreams are dangerous to the frog-skin world, which tries to keep them away with cannons.

I was about twenty-one years old when some men told me, "There's a new, powerful medicine. It's going to whirl you around. It will make you see God." As with the ghost dance, the men who brought us this new medicine were not from our own tribe. One was an Arapaho and the other a Black Foot, a man called Lone Bear.

I wanted to experience this and I went to their first meeting in a lonely shack. Six men were sitting on the floor of an empty room. They had a half-gallon can full of cut-up peyote. The Arapaho and the Black Foot were talking in their language. I couldn't make it out, but I understood what they were trying to say: "Eat this and you will see a new light!" I felt strange taking this new medicine and took only a few tablespoons at first. The peyote was powerful. The drum got into me. The gourd got into me. There were voices coming to me out of that rattle. I was closing my eyes, looking inward, into myself, hunkered down on my haunches, my back against the wall, feeling my bones through my skin. I like the pejuta because it whirled me around. By midnight I was having visions. First I saw a square turning into a circle, into a half moon, into a beaded belt—green and blue—which was spinning around me. I could see myself as if looking down from a high mountain, sitting with the other six men, seeing myself crouching in the corner of that log house.

Suddenly I was back within myself. My eyes were on the logs, which seemed very close by, like looking through a magnifying glass. I saw something crawling out between the chinks. It was a big ant, maybe ten feet high, the biggest ant there ever was, all horns, shiny like a lobster. As the ant grew bigger, the room expanded with it. I saw insects starting to eat me. I got scared and tried to get away but couldn't move. The leader, the road man, could tell that I was seeing something. He knew how I felt. He whirled his gourd around, shook his fan of feathers at me. I came back to life, back from someplace outside the log house, it seemed to me.

I was confused. I tried to think about somebody I loved, my grandmother, my uncle—but it didn't work. My thoughts were getting away from me like a stampeding herd. I tried to think about white men, about the frog-skin world—and that didn't work. I tried to think about animals but was unable to concentrate. The men had told me, "Eat this and you will see God." I did not see God. I couldn't think in complete words, only in syllables, one syllable at a time.

I made a prayer to the Great Spirit to help me, show me. A sweet smell came up not in my nostrils but in my mind. It wasn't a perfume or a scent from nature. Only I could smell it. I saw a book turn into a rock, the rock turn into a cave. I didn't know what to make of it, but there was something *wakan,* something sacred there. I knew it was good, but it scared me at the same time.

The leader handed me the staff and the gourd. It was my turn to sing, but I didn't know how and they had to pass me by. When the sun finally came up I was exhausted and lightheaded. I was shook up. Something had happened that I could not explain. It would take a long time to think about it.

I became a peyoter for a number of years and went regularly to their meetings, but I did not give myself up wholly to it. I also got myself deeper into our old Sioux beliefs, the spirit world; listened to preachers, herb men and the *yuwipi*. I was slowly forming an idea of where I wanted to go. I could dimly see my place, but I could also see a number of different roads leading up to it and I did not yet know which one to take. So I tried them all, coming to many dead ends.

The police tried to stamp out this new peyote cult, as they had stamped out the ghost dance, not because peyote was a drug—drugs weren't on our mind then —but because it was Indian, a competition to the missionaries. The police didn't like me very much anyhow, aside from the peyote. I had a place in Pine Ridge and another one in Rosebud. At Pine Ridge I kept a girl. We weren't married according to the white man's view. The missionaries called it a common-law arrangement. They didn't allow this at that time and threw you in jail for it. They said, "You can't stay together with a girl unless you are properly married— our way."

I had gone to a peyote meeting and the police came and raided it. They came at twilight. I guess they must have smelled it or somebody had tipped them off. They broke the door open looking for the peyote but couldn't find any. It was kept two miles away from the house and hadn't been brought in yet for the meeting. As they turned the kerosene lamp up, they saw me. At once they forgot about the peyote and took after me. I was a badman in their eyes, a bad example to all the little sheep on the reservation.

The cabin was only a thousand feet away from the border line between the reservations. The Pine Ridge *and* the Rosebud police were in on the raid, but each had to stay on his own side of the line. They were not supposed to cross it. I ran along the boundary, the Rosebud patrol car on one side, the Pine Ridge wagon on the other. They were taking pot shots at me to make me stop, but I knew they weren't trying to hit me; they didn't dare. If the Rosebud police came too close, I jumped across into Pine Ridge territory and the other way round, hopping back and forth across that line like some oversized grasshopper. Just when I was all tuckered out, my heart pounding like mad, I got into the pine hills where their cars couldn't follow me. They got out with their guns drawn, trying to keep up with me, but I lost them in the dark. They arrested my girl friend, but when I completely disappeared they turned her loose. They watched her, put her out as bait. But I wasn't that easy to catch. I lit out for Standing Rock for a while to let things cool down. I had a beautiful nest out there on the prairie for my girl.

I was a peyoter for six years. After that I quit it. I found out that it was not my way. It was a dead end, a box canyon, and I had to find my way out of it. I don't want to talk down this peyote cult. In many Indian tribes they have people believing in this medicine. Grandfather Peyote brings many people together, not only as members of this religion but as Indians, and that is good. Some tribes have had peyote for so long that it has become their main and only religion. Many people have forgotten their old beliefs, which the missionaries stamped out, and only the peyote is left; it is the only Indian belief they know. But for us Sioux it is something fairly new, different from our belief in the Great Spirit and the sacred pipe. Slowly I came to realize that I should not mix up these two beliefs, confuse them with each other. I felt that the time had come for me to choose—the pipe or the peyote. I chose the pipe.

At the time I quit peyote I had found out what a real Sioux vision was like. If you dream, that's no vision. Anybody can dream. And if you take an herb—well, even the butcher boy at his meat counter will have a vision after eating peyote. The real vision has to come out of your own juices. It is not a dream; it is very real. It hits you sharp and clear like an electric shock. You are wide awake and, suddenly, there is a person standing next to you who you know can't be there at all. Or somebody is sitting close by, and all at once you see him also up on a hill half a mile away. Yet you are not dreaming; your eyes are open. You have to work for this, empty your mind for it.

Peyote is for the poor people. It helps to get them out of their despair, gives them something to grab hold of, but I couldn't stop there, I had to go further. Once you have experienced the real thing you will never be satisfied with anything else. It will be all or nothing for you then.

The find-out, it has lasted my whole life. In a way I was always hopping back and forth across the boundary line of the mind. For three years I was a bootlegger. I ran a little café and pool hall in Parmelee, with a dice table and a nickelodeon. I had the best red-eye anywhere. I played with the police. I had a certain kind of bottle of an unusual shape in which I kept the real hot, hard stuff, the genuine rattlesnake piss. When the stoolie came in I let him have a big swig of that gut-warmer—guaranteed to maim and kill. In no time he was back with the police, and there was the evidence still standing on the table. They marched us off to the judge, me and the bottle.

The judge said, "What have we got here, a quart of bust-head?" He poured himself a drink, in his official capacity only, as he explained, and then he made a big face. "Brr, that stuff is cold tea—awful!" I had two of those funny bottles and had switched them. They had to let me go. I played so many tricks on them, the police left me alone for a while.

Being a kind of two-face, I then wanted to find out how it looked from the other side. When there was an opening for a tribal policeman in the Black Pipe district, I went for it. I was surprised when they gave it to me, because I was a hell-raiser, but I was popular with the people. They handed me a badge and a gun, but I put the shooting iron away in a drawer. I never carried it. I carried only a loaded sap for emergencies, but the emergency never came. Right on my first day as a lawman I found out how it felt to have a drunk cuss the shit out of you. I was known as the relationship cop; everybody was my relative. Now when your cousin gets drunk you don't arrest him; you take him home. I followed that policy. When I saw a drunk I told him, "Cousin, I am a real mean man. Instead of taking you to jail, I take you to your old woman, let her use the rolling pin on you. That's how mean I am."

When I saw a young squaw tying one on, hanging around with the wrong buck, I took her aside. "Say, my girl, let me take you home to your ma. That man is no good. He has a half-dozen girls already. He only wants to get you in the family way." "How do you know?" "Because I do that myself. One son of a bitch with the squaw fever can recognize another." "Well, I guess you can take me home then. I guess you know what you are talking about."

I kept it up for a while, being a night cop, until the novelty wore off—for me, for the drunks and for the council. Some tribal cops are mean half-bloods. They can't beat the white man, so they beat the Indian, the bottom guy. It makes them feel like somebody. I had made a big change. After I turned in my badge I think the drunks began to miss me, but I wouldn't stay put in one place.

The years passed. I was getting older and had tried almost everything. I was like a big jigsaw puzzle. Year by year new pieces were added to form the complete picture. A few pieces are still missing. In 1941 I was working for a farmer in Nebraska. He was a nice guy, very sociable, with a wonderful wife and kids. There was a love there between myself and that white family. He lived close to the earth, in a very natural way, not many machines or gadgets, in a self-built house made of the stones and trees that were around him, a part of the land. You could tell that this man was all right by the many trees that surrounded his place. In Nebraska and Dakota a lot of those hog and corn farmers are so stingy they won't have more than four trees standing on their property, two at the front porch to give a little shade and two in back. All the rest of the trees go under to make room for whatever they are growing. They don't waste a square foot, because they could maybe lose a nickel or a dime that way. And those stingy frog-skinners with their shriveled souls raise only one cash crop and live out of tins.

My farmer wasn't like this. He had himself a little forest of trees, and now and then when he passed one of them, he would pat its trunk absent-mindedly as if it were some kind of pet. And he raised his own food. I could get along fine with a man like him. He let me have a piece of his land to use for myself, and I planted my own corn and potatoes there. He was a cripple and I had to do most of his job for him, the hard labor, running his tractor, but he treated me like one of his family. His wife made wonderful pies and I put some meat on my bones at their place.

Then one day I got this notice from the Government, from the Great White Father himself: "Greetings!" They wanted me to kill some white people. Suddenly that's all right. What do you know! That farmer gave me my pay, a lot more than he owed me, and put on a big send-off for me and my relations, one big, two-day, son-of-a-bitching drunk. They put me on a train to Fort Leavenworth, Kansas. I was as drunk as a boiled owl. There were a lot of other Indian boys on that train, all going to the same place.

The Army doctors who examined me first put me in 4F. I guess they thought I was too old by that time. But I wanted to stay with my buddies, go where they were going. So I joined a few Sioux in another line, and this time I passed. I was with a lot of different outfits, wearing a helmet and a gun. At home, when I was a kid, a bow and arrow was a "concealed weapon." The soldiering business was a big disappointment to me. They were wasting our time with a lot of foolish orders, drill, red tape, saluting; 90 percent of all my time in the Army was just standing around, waiting for orders. Counting coup Indian-style in the old way made a lot more sense.

One day, after basic training, we had to pass in review before some big-shot general. Some of the white boys had their relations coming down to see them, but they didn't ship in our folks from the reservation. Well, we were standing stiff like nine-pins, and that big chief was making a speech: "Men, you are soldiers now, not civilians. Is there anybody here who doesn't like the Army, any complaints?" He didn't expect an answer, but I stepped forward. "Shit, I don't like this white man's army. Teach us to shoot, but forget about the rest. You are wasting our time." They tried to hold me back, make me shut up, but I got to that general. "They treat us like slaves. I don't mind fighting, but you can't make a windup toy out of me."

The general looked at me and saw that I was an Indian. He made another speech: "You soldier boys, we all know that nobody likes this man's army. But nobody admits it. Only this guy here is telling the truth." He gave me an extra stripe then and there and I marched the platoon home. Next pay day—the day the eagle shits, as they called it—I got good and drunk and they took my stripes off.

I finally got shipped out. I was the oldest man in the outfit, the others were kids compared to me. When things got hairy they cried real tears and I was their baby sitter. I was a very rough baby sitter, I guess. I thought I'd scalp me a German, lift that blond hair, here's one in the eye for Custer and all that. But I changed my mind. I guess it was the cheap wine that made me think of it in the first place.

A lot of nonsense is talked and written about war: fight for your country, for America, for democracy, for your loved ones. Hell, a soldier fights only to protect himself. Somebody shoots at him, so he shoots back before the other guy can kill him. He runs like a deer. He comes back and brags: "I fought for my flag." That's a lot of *ta-chesli,* a lot of bull. When he's shot at, nobody thinks of a piece of cloth.

The Government takes our Indian boys, our uncles, cousins, brothers, sons, all of us, to fight their wars. World War I, World War II, Korea, Vietnam. As long as the shooting keeps on, we are the heroes, like Ira Hayes, who won the Congressional Medal of Honor at Iwo Jima. When we come back we are once again incompetent wards of the Government and wind up in a ditch, also like Ira Hayes. It wasn't white men who killed Sitting Bull, but Indians, Hunkpapa Sioux like himself, paid off in green frog skins. A white soldier stabbed Crazy Horse with his bayonet, but it was Indian police who kept his arms pinned to his sides so that the white trooper could use him for bayonet practice. You always find some hungry Indians to do your fighting.

The anthropologists say we came over from Asia over this land bridge to Alaska, but maybe we have been all the time, right from the beginning, and traffic moved the other way, from this continent to over there. Maybe those Vietnamese are all former Indians and we are all Crow and Rhee scouts riding point for a new Custer. I have seen pictures of Song My, My Lai, and I have seen pictures of Wounded Knee—the dead mothers with their babies. And I remember my grandfather, Good Fox, telling me about the dead mother with a baby nursing at her cold breast, drinking that cold milk. My Lai was hot, and Wounded Knee was icy cold, and that's the only difference.

They are playing around with the sacred fire of the sun, making it into atom bombs. They'll only succeed in blowing their own heads off in the end. How not to do this they could learn this from us, but maybe they think we are too uneducated, not worth listening to. I have saved one copy of our tribal newspaper. It is a couple of years old. I kept it because it has a poem in it written by one of our Sioux boys in Vietnam, Spotted War Bonnet, who was stationed in the DMZ when he wrote it. I wished I could have written this poem, because it expresses what I feel, what most of us feel.

THE LAMENT OF THE SIOUX RESERVATION INDIAN

They took the whole Sioux Nation
And put it on this reservation
They took away our way of life
The tomahawk, the bow and knife
They put our papoose in a crib
And took the buckskin from our rib
They took away our native tongue
And talk their English to our young
The old teepee we all love so
They're using now for just a show
And all our beads we made by hand
And nowadays are made in Japan
Altho they've changed our ways of old
They'll never change our hearts and souls
Though I wear a man's shirt and tie
I'm still a red man deep inside.
*Hi ya yoh, hi ya yoh ho*

—from the Rosebud *Sioux Herald*

Within a month after Normandy somebody discovered that I was over thirty-nine years old and I was released from the Army. That was also my release from the green frog-skin world. My roaming was at an end and I settled down to my only full-time job—being an Indian.

# 4
# Getting Drunk, Going to Jail

Those clever white men always try to teach us poor, dumb Indians something new. I sure wish they'd teach us how to drink. When you buy a camera or a tape recorder, it always comes with a little booklet which tells you how to use it, but when they brought us the white man's whisky, they forgot the instruction book. This has caused us no end of trouble.

Look at that pitiful old wino over there at the curb. He's picking up empty Coke bottles. As soon as he has collected twenty of them, he'll cash them in at the grocery store. It will buy him a pint of cheap booze, Muscatel—Mustn't Tell. He'll be drunk before noon.

That wino has one thing going for him, though: He is white. This is the white part of town, and that means lots of empties. Over there is Indian Town, with its tar-paper shacks, rusty house trailers, disintegrating log cabins and toppling privies. You settle down in one of those ancient two-seaters and you never know whether the next gust of wind will blow you down. Some people live in old auto bodies. That's the only home for them.

There are few empty Coke bottles in Indian Town. We don't have money to buy that much pop, and the kids get to the empties first. It is hard for the Indian wino to find enough of the bottles to get his pint of bug juice. But that's the least of his troubles. When a white man gets drunk around here, the police are real nice to him, putting him in the patrol car and taking him home to his old lady. He can be as drunk as a boiled owl; it doesn't matter. I've seen them stagger out of that saloon, their pants soaked in urine and their shirts covered with "happy returns"—that's wino for vomit. I've seen a drunk white man piss in the street in front of the big store in broad daylight, and the police zipped him up and got some black coffee into him to make him sober enough to find his way home.

It's very different when an Indian gets drunk. The police love to play games with us, the way a cat plays with a mouse or a young bird. Not only here in Winner but in all those little white cow towns around the reservation. Any day you can watch an Indian couple coming out of a store with their sack of groceries and the cop in his wagon eyeballing them, trying to figure out whether the Indians have any liquor or beer in their bag. The cop will follow them at a distance, but outside the city limits, on the reservation border, he will pounce on them and confiscate the stuff. That's one way for the police to get free booze. You can buy liquor in town, but you can't drink it on the reservation. We don't have equal justice around here. It's always open season on Indians.

I stay most of the time on the good side; that is to say *sober*. But once in a long while I start taking some whisky to find things out, and then I really get my feet wet. Sometimes I'd be on a drunk for a whole week, and it takes me two days to sober up. Once, a long time ago, I didn't come home from a New Year's powwow. They found me in a snowbank with just my feet sticking out. They filled up an old bathtub with snow and put me in. At the same time they made me swallow a big jar of moonshine to warm me up. That snow felt hot and I got real red all over. After a while I got cold again and I could feel my ears and toes freezing up. They took me to my uncle's place and put me to bed. I was so weak that for about ten days I could do nothing but look at the ceiling. My lungs were out of gear and I had a big pain in my side. My uncle, who was a medicine man, got me on my feet again with all kinds of herbs. Up to this day I can't remember how I got into that snowbank. I must have been drunk, I guess.

In the old days, when Indians couldn't buy liquor, we used to drink anything with a kick in it—wood alcohol, lemon extract, varnish. We used to hide behind the houses, anywhere we wouldn't be seen. We didn't even have time to enjoy our drinking. We had to guzzle down whatever we had right away and were in trouble real soon, inside half an hour. Now we are free to drink. In the towns you see Indian boys and girls zigzagging from bar to bar, begging for a handout to get one more drink. It's a big problem. Many of us die in car accidents, because these two white man's inventions—whisky and cars—don't get along. And the men fight. They don't fight the white people; they fight each other—for nothing.

The white police around here like to work Mister Indian over just because he is a little drunk, cusses a little bit. So they pound him, and because he is drunk he feels nothing. They mash him up, hurt him bad. Sometimes the Indian dies; sometimes he comes out of it with a fractured skull or a cut mouth. He is drunk and can't fight back. We have some undersized policemen, skinny little good-for-nothing lightweights, who use their guns, irons, clubs and saps to hit the "big, tough Indian." It makes them feel like men.

One night, some years back, I had a few too many. I wasn't really drunk, just a bit unsteady, friendly like, and in a mood for fun. But they arrested me all the same, pushing and manhandling me. I tried to make a joke of the whole thing, but one of the officers didn't have a sense of humor. He snarled at me like a dog, "Get in there, you red son of a bitch," and slugged me with his sap. I turned around and knocked him down; then the other two jumped me, working me over with their blackjacks. I hit them a few good ones, but in the end the three of them pinned me down, with the meanest cop, the one who had slugged me first, sitting on my chest.

He had a heavy ring on his finger and he smashed it again and again into my face while his two buddies held me down. I can still see that big hunk of carved silver coming at me. I suppose he wore it for just such occasions. Well, he smashed the bone under my eye, really splintered and crumbled it. Finally his arm got tired and I passed out.

I came to with a doctor fussing over me. I guess they worried about word leaking out over what they had done to me. "You are all right," said the doctor, "except for a little bruise. You must have fallen down when you was drunk." I didn't say anything. They fined me ten dollars and let me go. My wife, Ida, is a hot girl with a temper. "Who did this to you?" she cried. "Which one hit you? I'll take a gun to him." She went for that old broken-down .38 I kept around, but I brought her back to reality. This wasn't the Little Big Horn. "Don't be a hero," I said, more to myself than to her.

A week later I went to Rosebud, where the Government doctor examined me. He told me I had a bad fracture. That was no news to me. My face was all caved in where that policeman had hammered at it with his ring. I still don't have any feeling there after all these years. Maybe I should get even, but my inner voice says no. Those Indian-haters are destroying themselves, going to hell in a super-jet. Why bother with that one?

Every time I see that guy with his big silver ring my cheek begins to hurt, but I'm thinking of my family, what would happen to them if I'd take justice into my own hands. But I don't forget. I wait, I watch. One voice tells me: "Don't play the hero; that's not in your line. You are a healer, not a hurter." But another voice tells me: "Be a man!" Maybe one of these days, when that old cheek is acting up again, I'll get mad. Soon I'll be too old to take a good swing at somebody, but when I'm mad I feel thirty years younger.

Before our white brothers came to civilize us we had no jails. Therefore we had no criminals. You can't have criminals without a jail. We had no locks or keys, and so we had no thieves. If a man was so poor that he had no horse, tipi or blanket, someone gave him these things. We were too uncivilized to set much value on personal belongings. We wanted to have things only in order to give them away. We had no money, and therefore a man's worth couldn't be measured by it. We had no written law, no attorneys or politicians, therefore we couldn't cheat. We really were in a bad way before the white man came, and I don't know how we managed to get along without the basic things which, we are told, are absolutely necessary to make a civilized society.

But now visible progress is everywhere—jails all over the place, and we know these jails are for us Indians. What a pity that so many of us don't appreciate them! They are good-humor jails with big "Welcome" signs painted on their walls. Some have "Heartbreak Hotel" written over their doors. Tourists like to photograph them, but they never take a picture of the drunk tanks inside.

If the police find a drunk Indian woman, they often amuse themselves by driving her way out into the sagebrush, turning her loose miles away from the nearest house. Indian girls are even worse off than the men. In some places the police take advantage of them in jail and rape them. Many of the drunk charges on which they are booked are phony. A girl doesn't have to be drunk to wind up in a cell, just pretty. The police know that the girls will be too embarrassed to tell, but even if they do complain, who'll believe a "drunken Injun"?

The white bar owners have a sense of humor, too. Not so long ago they had those signs in their windows, "No Indians or Dogs Allowed." You don't see them anymore nowadays, except way off in the back country. I could still show you one or two, but officially the state and people of South Dakota don't discriminate against us nowadays; they just have a sense of humor. So they put these "Red Power" signs in the bars on top of the beer cans and between the liquor bottles. Here is a paragraph from one of our Indian newspapers.

## WANBLEE INDIANS ON THE WARPATH!

Ever since the white man first occupied our land, we have been the objects of derision and prejudice. This prejudice has assumed many forms, ranging from outright violence to much more subtle forms such as racist jokes and poorly concealed disdain. We, the people of Wanblee, are against all forms of prejudice, since we are the ones who have suffered, and continue to suffer, its effects.

A blatant example of racial prejudice is the "Indian Power" sign which appears on the wine cabinet at the Kadoka Municipal Bar. This sign has, no doubt, been found quite humorous by many patrons of the bar. We assert that, far from being humorous, it is insulting and prejudicial. It is indeed regretful that there are still large numbers of people who indulge in classifying whole races of people simply on the basis of their own limited personal experience. What is even more troubling is the fact that fellow citizens would fail to aid those of limited scope and understanding in realizing that there is very little humor to be found in a joke of this nature.

There is a mood sweeping this nation, in which minority groups are demanding that they be perceived as people. We concur in this mood and we trust that it will not be long before the residents of Kadoka shall have advanced to a stage where they, too, can begin to treat their neighbors as people.

Community of Wanblee, South Dakota.

Wanblee—you can hardly find it on the map. Just a few huts and shanties. White people would say that it is just one more rural slum of a handful of poor, illiterate Indians. Well, they don't write badly, those illiterates. They can even spell. They have made up their mind to "be perceived as people." A few years ago no Indian would have raised his voice about this matter. He would have just shrugged his shoulders with that "what can you do about it?" look on his face. But times are changing. I am glad of being alive to see this.

Alcoholism is a problem for us, and as long as all this liquor is lying about here, it won't get better. I have often thought about the special effect liquor has on us Indians. In two hundred years we still haven't learned how to handle it. It is just like the measles and other diseases the white man brought us. The illness was the same for them as for us, but we died from it, while for them it was usually just a few days of discomfort.

I figured out a few reasons for our drinking. They might not be the right ones; I'm just speculating. We call liquor *mni wakan*—holy water. I guess visions were so important and sacred to us that having our minds altered and befuddled by whisky impressed us in the beginning like a religious experience, a dream, a vision. It didn't take much to make us drunk; it still doesn't. Those old French traders out of St. Louis were thrifty people. They wouldn't think of wasting good stuff on the Indians. The whisky they sold us in return for our beaver pelts was mostly Missouri water mixed with a few rattlesnake heads, gunpowder and a lot of black pepper to give a kick, with just a little jigger of real booze in every bottle. It sure was powerful even without much alcohol.

But you can't blame our drinking nowadays on a desire to have visions, or say that we guzzle the stuff because it is holy—though I want to tell you that even glassy-eyed winos often hold up their bottles and spill a little of the precious stuff on the ground for spirits of the departed, saying, "Here, my friend who left us, here's something for you," or "Here, my old girl friend who died, share this drink with me."

So here is the question: Why do Indians drink? They drink to forget, I think, to forget the great days when this land was ours and when it was beautiful, without highways, billboards, fences and factories. They try to forget the pitiful shacks and rusting trailers which are their "homes." They try to forget that they are treated like children, not like grown-up people. In those new O.E.O. houses—instant slums I call them, because they fall apart even before they are finished—you can't have a visitor after ten o'clock, or have a relative staying overnight. We are even told what color we must paint them and what kind of curtains we must put up. Nor are we allowed to have our own money to spend as we see fit. So we drink because we are minors, not men. We try to forget that even our fenced-in reservations no longer belong to us. We have to lease them to white ranchers who fatten their cattle, and themselves, on our land. At Pine Ridge less than one percent of the land is worked by Indians.

We drink to forget that we are beggars, living on handouts, eight different kinds of handouts: ex-servicemen, the disabled, widows, gold-star mothers, old-age support, foster-parent contracts, Social Security, ADC—aid to dependent children. That ADC! The mothers get more money by kicking their husbands out. "I don't want him," they say. "If he stays with his family, the money stops. We'd rather have the money than him." In my town close to forty girls live that way.

We drink to forget that there is nothing worthwhile for a man to do, nothing that would bring honor or make him feel good inside. There are only a handful of jobs for a few thousand people. These are all Government jobs, tribal or federal. You have to be a good house Indian, an Uncle Tomahawk, a real apple

—red outside, white inside—to get a job like this. You have to behave yourself, and never talk back, to keep it. If you have such a job, you drink to forget what kind of person it has made of you. If you don't have it, you drink because there's nothing to look forward to but a few weeks of spud-picking, if you are lucky. You drink because you don't live; you just exist. That may be enough for some people; it's not enough for us.

When an Indian is arrested for drunkenness, he gets thirty days in jail. As soon as the weather gets cold, you can always find thirty-five to forty Indians in the tank. They get themselves arrested to get warm, to have something to eat and to have a place to sleep. That's one way to solve the "Indian Problem."

The wino might be warm in his cell, but what about his family? That's the sad part of the whole business —what it does to the children. No matter how down a man is, he has to go on caring for his helpless ones, the women, the kids. We Indians always say that kids are our most important possessions, not cars, houses, TV sets. These count for nothing. But half of our kids never make it, never live long enough to grow up.

We have a bird out here, about the size and shape of a pigeon. It has a circle on each side of its head. It doesn't chirp. Whenever it opens its beak it makes a sound like a fart. The white man calls it a night hawk. We call it *pishko*. This bird doesn't build a nest. It doesn't take care of its chicks. The *pishko* drops its eggs any place, in a ditch or on the highway. Some winos are like that, forgetting that they have kids to take care of, letting them hatch themselves out. They talk big in public and have a big mouth but very little wisdom. But who is to blame? Who will let them be anything else but what they are?

I am no wino or *pishko*, but I am no saint either. A medicine man shouldn't be a saint. He should experience and feel all the ups and downs, the despair and joy, the magic and the reality, the courage and the fear, of his people. He should be able to sink as low as a bug, or soar as high as an eagle. Unless he can experience both, he is no good as a medicine man.

Sickness, jail, poverty, getting drunk—I had to experience all that myself. Sinning makes the world go round. You can't be so stuck up, so inhuman that you want to be pure, your soul wrapped up in a plastic bag, all the time. You have to be God and the devil, both of them. Being a good medicine man means being right in the midst of the turmoil, not shielding yourself from it. It means experiencing life in all its phases. It means not being afraid of cutting up and playing the fool now and then. That's sacred too.

Nature, the Great Spirit—they are not perfect. The world couldn't stand that perfection. The spirit has a good side and a bad side. Sometimes the bad side gives me more knowledge than the good side.

When I was a young man I roamed the country on foot like a hippie, sleeping in haystacks or under the stars on the open prairie. I joined five or six different churches, worked at many jobs. It was almost as if I were several different people—a preacher, a spud-picker, a cowhand, a clown, a sign painter, a healer, a bootlegger, a president of the Indian YMCA. I managed to be both a Christian and a heathen, a fugitive and a pursuer, a lawman and an outlaw. I was uneducated but soaked up knowledge like a sponge. All that knowledge, as yet undigested, made a big racket in my brain. This period of roaming and cutting up lasted from 1926 to 1935. I was a hobo and a hippie then for much of the time, but also I spent many quiet months as a budding healer and medicine man.

I had many loves then. One day, one girl; the next day, another one. Sometimes even one girl in the evening, and then another one later in the night. They are all grandmothers now. When I run into one of them these days, at the store or on the road, I say to myself: Here comes that old scarecrow, that girl I used to make love to. Now she calls me an old buzzard and uses me to scare her grandchildren. They are white-haired and some have faces all wrinkled like walnuts, faces landscaped like the Badlands. But I imagine I still see that twinkle in their eyes. That never dies.

I have to tell you about one time I got drunk and went on a big tear, my biggest one. I was with a buddy of mine. We had gotten hold of a bottle of moonshine. Remember, this was in 1930, in the days of Prohibition. The stuff was so powerful I wondered how they kept it corked. When we had finished it we were *itomni*—very happy, scouting for some excitement. We were thinking of how we could get some more moonshine. I had heard that some bootlegger down in Nebraska was trading moonshine for anything. I also knew of a white man who had a lot of baling wire lying around someplace on his ranch.

When I told my buddy he said, "Hey, here's a car with no driver. Let's go get that baling wire. *Hiyupo, hopo, hoka-hay!*" This car was a 1929 Model T with a very careless owner who had left the key in the ignition. It was snowing, a real Dakota blizzard; you could hardly see the road. We didn't mind. Things worked out real good. We had loaded up fifteen bales of wire when a dog started to bark. My buddy got scared and ran off, but I finished the job and drove off to swap my load for moonshine. Well, on the road I met another friend of mine. When we came to Upper Cut Meat this guy said, "It's a long way to Cody to get rid of that wire. Let's stop here for a while and get something to drink. I know a guy here who has real strong stuff."

He took me to someone he knew, an old white man, who took us down into his cellar. "Gentlemen, what's your pleasure?" What he served us was good—pure grizzly milk and rattlesnake piss. It snowed so hard we couldn't leave right away but had to stay awhile, passing the bottle and playing cards. That bootlegger was just a frying-size oldster, so drunk he couldn't find his nose with both hands. Every now and then he would pass out. Still, he won all of my friend's money, which wasn't very much. When the snow let up we got rolling again. We made Cody, Nebraska, at daybreak and traded that wire for thirty gallons of moonshine.

All that day we were enjoying ourselves. There was a café in town with a sign: "Ladies Invited—No Indians or Minors!" We went in all the same, and that started a big fight. We scraped the enamel off some white pool players who objected to our presence and counted plenty of coups. The police broke up the powwow and arrested us on a "drunk and disorderly" charge, but they couldn't hold onto us. We somehow got loose in that weather and they couldn't trail us. We made it back to the Model T. By that time we began feeling sorry for the owner and thought he might appreciate our returning it to him. But we met more people high on moonshine, some good-looking young squaws among them, and resolved to give them all a ride home. We dropped them off all over the map, one by one, in Upper Cut Meat, Bad Nation, Potato Creek, Porcupine, Wososo, all those little places. Then I headed south again into Nebraska. At Kilgore we stalled in the snow and stayed overnight with a man who helped us drink up some of that red-eye. A day later the road was open again. We went through Valentine and sold some moonshine in Crookston. I think I must have been drunk, because I whirled that car around and got stuck. Trying to get out of the ditch, I busted the rear end. Well, we walked away from the Ford then. We waded into Crookston through waist-high snow drifts. The white stuff piled up in some places as the wind blew it about, covering some spots, baring others. It was all fluffy; one could still drive—at least I could. On the main street I came across a 1928 Chevy, left with the motor running on account of the cold, right in front of the pool hall. It was too much of a temptation.

I told my buddy to get all the moonshine that was left in that abandoned Model T and wait at the highway, where I'd pick him up in my new Chevrolet. I was still full of ginger. On the way to Gordon we met another Indian. He was marooned in the drifts and half frozen to death. He was sure glad to see us. We revived him, but this took all that was left of the hard stuff. I decided to replenish our supply in Pine Ridge, where we were told that the police were all over looking for me. When he heard this my buddy said, "I'm going to rest awhile," and he never came back. Chickened out on me. But that man who had wanted to go to Gordon, the guy we thawed out, said he had too much fun to quit. He was a jolly fellow, but he passed out on me. No use waiting for that one. He'd be out cold for days.

I was looking for a new companion but ran into the tribal police instead. "Hey, John, you stole a Model T in Norris, South Dakota. You're under arrest." I just laughed at them. "See for yourself. My car is a Chevy with a Nebraska license. Can't you guys tell the difference? Some police we got here!" They looked sheepish. They couldn't figure it out. "Don't look so sad," I told them. "Here, have a swallow of bug juice." They had to let me go.

I was on my own then. Going east was a little bit rough. The snow was four feet high and the road a mere wagon track. I made it to a gas station at Wounded Knee and told the man to put chains on all four wheels, fill up the tank. When he had done this I told him to go back in his place and bring me some extra oil. While he was in there getting it I took off with all the speed I had, but the snow slowed me down. Looking back, after I had gone about two hundred yards, I could see that man had his rifle out and was shooting at me. He must have been a good shooter, because he missed me real close. One bullet whistled by my sheepskin collar and the other went straight through my hat. That one burned up a little of my hair. There was a .30–.30 rifle in the back seat of my Chevy. I stopped and started firing back. After a few bang-bangs we both cooled off. This wasn't surprising, considering that the temperature had dropped to 20° below.

I was still heading east, still had a pint of *mni-wakan* to keep me warm inside. When I got near Martin, I left the Chevy among some cottonwoods outside town. I figured nobody would be looking for me on foot. Night had fallen and I was huddling in a doorway. I was in a kind of haze but still sharp enough to keep an eye on the main chance. I watched the police fooling with cars, checking the door handles for fingerprints, checking the eating places and speakeasies. I had a hunch who they were looking for. A young thing walked close to the place where I was hiding. *"Wincincala,* pretty girl," I whispered, "come here." She wasn't afraid of me or the dark. "Where are you?" she asked. She had her skinning knife out. No wonder she wasn't afraid. I told her to make friends with the police, find out what was going on. She was back in no time. "Say, John, word's out that you stole all them cars. They are sure anxious to get their hands on you. Wow, you are some warrior, some desperado. Six cars!"

Six cars! I was dumfounded. I didn't know then that some other man was loose on exactly the same kind of spree, borrowing cars right and left. It sure confused the law. They had reports by wire and phone of my committing depredations as far north as Holabird, Tennis, Grassrope, Grindstone and Eagle Butte in South Dakota, while at the same time they had me going berserk in Hire, Cherry, Valentine and Nonpareil, Nebraska. The funny thing is that I never met up with that other joy-rider though our paths must have crossed sometimes. He was sure covering a lot of ground. The police must have thought I had some powerful medicine to pop up in all these different places at one and the same time.

Meanwhile, here I was huddling in a doorway at Martin, getting real friendly with that pretty girl. "It's too cold here, John," she said. "Let me take you someplace and warm you up." I didn't need much warming up. The red-eye had lit a nice cozy fire in my stomach. The *wincincala* took me to a half-blood bootlegger. He was bare to the waist on account of the red-hot stove in his place. He had two big tattoos over each nipple; one said "beer" and the other "wine." I had heard about this man and his old woman, who was rumored to have tattoos over her nipples, too, only hers read "sweet" and "sour." She was nowhere in sight. This man was supposed to be very sharp with a dollar when sober. That's when his white man's nature took over. But when he got drunk, he was all Indian with a sharing heart. He was drunk enough then to open his shirt collar to piss, as they say. He motioned toward the cellar. "Help yourselves. It's on me." Then he lay down on the floor and started to snore. It was that kind of a night. Well, we didn't need him to help us. Boy, was his moonshine good! Our clothes were steaming like the hot pools in Yellowstone Park. We stayed in that place until morning, when I experienced a powerful urge to get moving again. I picked up a gallon of bug juice, so I wouldn't dry up, and found myself another car, a brand-new Chevy with only twenty-five miles on it. The pretty girl hugged me goodbye and wished me luck.

I headed for Rosebud. The snow was so deep that shiny new car was about to give up. When I got back into Todd County a rider on a black horse was blocking my path. Through the whirling snow I could make him out as a tribal policeman. Before he had a chance to get his gun I got the .30–.30 pointed right at his chest. I ordered him to drop his Government .38 special. He didn't argue but threw his pistol down. I told him, "Hang on, Uncle," and fired a shot close by his horse's ears, and it took off like a greased fart on a lightning rod. I walked back about twenty yards and picked up the .38.

Driving on, I met some Indian folks who were stuck in the snow. They told me, "Be real careful, because two states and all the Government police are on the lookout for you. The radio says you are dangerous and will resist arrest." I made it back to Parmelee, where I had lots of friends, but none of them wanted to come near me. So I made tracks toward Kadoka. The snow reached up to the windows in the dips, soft and fluffy like soap suds. I looked for cigarettes in the glove compartment but found a .44 instead. Things got pretty confused. Somewhere, somehow, I lost about twelve hours that I don't remember. By the time I hit Norris, where my big spree had started, I was sobering up—a hell of a thing! I gave a man the new spare tire in exchange for five gallons of grizzly milk. I ran into the owner of the Model T, the car I had started out with. He seemed in a hurry to talk to me, but when he saw all the artillery I carried, he changed his mind fast.

After that things are kind of blurred again. Between Norris and Belvidere, two miles south from where I then lived, I abandoned the car in a gully. I stuffed two revolvers into my pockets and somehow made it to my cabin. I was good and tired. After all, I had been hard at work for three days—or was it four?

I woke up when I heard the dogs bark. I knew the law had come for me. Luckily, the first to arrive were the Indian police, Sioux men with an understanding heart. They stopped fifteen yards short of my cabin and called out, "Nephew, we take you peacefully. Look, we throw down our thirty-thirties." They threw their guns right down in the snow before me. It made me feel good to see this. I rummaged for my guns and threw them on the ground, too.

"Uncles, don't handcuff me," I begged. "We have to

do it, Nephew," they said. "The white police is coming behind us. They'll shoot you if they find you with your arms free. But we'll protect you." Well, I thanked them. They took me back to the road, and there, sure enough, were about a dozen white deputies waiting for me with shotguns, rifles and pistols sticking out of their cars. More and more patrol wagons arrived from everywhere, from as far away as Rapid City, Pierre, Chamberlain, Yankton, Wall and Hot Springs. The newspapermen were all over me, snapping pictures, telling me to turn this way and that way, smile. It turned into a regular funeral procession. They had me in irons, two fellows at my back and two more holding my arms. They sure treated me like somebody, all of a sudden. I tried to make them understand that I was not all that dangerous, but they told me that I was a desperate character and had to be handled carefully.

I wound up in the reservation *kaśka,* our own heartbreak hotel in Rosebud. It was decided pretty quickly that my crimes were too enormous to be handled by the tribal court. They took me out of the bullpen and transported me up to Deadwood City in the Black Hills. There, in a big hall, I was booked and had to make a statement. They had four or five stenographers to take it all down; they even had footprints of me made out of plaster. What for I don't know. They arraigned me under the Dire Act, taking stolen cars across a state line, which was a federal offense. They had eleven charges on me, but they needed time to sort out the facts. This I could believe. I stayed two months in Deadwood. By then my friends and relatives had collected money to put up my bond, and I was on the loose again.

I felt the need for fasting and going up on the hill for a *hanblechia,* a vision quest. I stayed up there alone in a hole dug for me, working out my problems, letting the dreams come to me. My uncle, who was himself a well-known medicine man, interpreted my visions for me after I came down. He told me then: "Nephew, you are going in, but you'll be out in less than a year. It will be hard on you, but don't be afraid. There's a lesson for you in all this. You'll come out of it as a complete human being, so be of good heart."

It was June when my case finally came up. I was two days late for my own trial and they made a fuss about it. "What do you want?" I asked. "I'm here. I operate on Indian time. You people are always in such a damn hurry." For the duration of the trial I was paid three dollars a day, one dollar for the hotel and two dollars for food. I spent these two dollars every day in the cat house to complete my education. Deadwood was a wide-open mining town then and probably still is. It had sporting houses and plenty of fancy women. Nowadays it is also a tourist center, you know, Wild Bill Hickock, Calamity Jane and all that jazz. They are buried there up on boot hill, and during the tourist season they have nightly pageants like "The Shooting of Wild Bill" in the historic old saloon where it really happened. Deadwood was just the right setting for my trial. It had style.

The trial was one big confusion. I had been drunk when I borrowed those cars. My buddies and everybody I had come in contact with had been drunk. All the witnesses had been drunk. Some of the police had been hitting the bottle, and even the owners of the cars we took, the reason those guys were not behind their wheels was probably that they had all holed up somewhere putting the hard stuff away. There must have been something in the air at the time of my joyride, maybe the Cayuse wind blowing all that soft snow our way, making every man in South Dakota, white or red, suddenly get up and say, "Let's get drunk!"

The witnesses contradicted one another and themselves. The police did the same. On top of that they always confused me with Running Horse, that other fellow. There had even been a few minor actors out on some little, half-sized sprees, nothing worth mentioning, but they kept cropping up all the same so that nobody knew anymore who had done what.

The judge threw up his hands. He was ripe for a nervous breakdown. "Please, Chief," he begged me, "please plead guilty to the first charge, and I'll throw out the other ten. Just listening to all this has given me one big hangover. Make it easy on me, Chief, and I'll make it easy on you." That seemed fair enough. I had a lawyer, a friend of my father, I let him work it all out. He and the judge put their heads together and my lawyer came back telling me, "Plead guilty on that first charge, John. They are willing to send you to the reformatory only, not to the pen. It's like school— half learning, half work. They'll give you a year and a day. That's nine months with time off for good behavior."

So I stood up very solemnly and said, "I did it, what it says in the first charge." The judge was so glad to be rid of me, he shook my hand over and over again. The U.S. marshal took me to the reformatory at Chillicothe, Ohio. For the first thirty days I was kept at hard labor. After that it was easier—school in the morning and job training in the afternoon. They told me to pick a trade and I chose sign painting. It had something to do with art, which had always appealed to me. The boss was a fellow convict named Nolan who was in for five years. He was a good sign painter and taught me well. They started me painting the hardest way, putting lettering at the top of a huge silo, a grain elevator. Suspended on a little board dangling from two ropes, the wind tossing me about up there like a dry leaf, I splattered paint all over the countryside. Ohio looked mighty small from where I was dangling. I still am a sign painter on and off. The local Chamber of Commerce billboard on the highway, the front of

the supermarket, the pictures on the delivery wagon
—that's all my work. But I think I will have to give it
up. Those new colors I have to use nowadays are full
of chemicals and poisons. You can't help inhaling the
fumes and it makes you feel sick. You cough and your
eyes hurt. That's still another form of pollution. I
don't think I can stand it any longer.

But I learned more than just a trade at Chillicothe.
When I went to jail I was almost illiterate. I spoke
almost no English. The reason was that, as I mentioned earlier, when I was a child we had only the
third grade. I, and all the other kids of my age, had to
go to the third grade for eight years, doing the same
thing over and over again. On top of that, we didn't
understand the teachers and they couldn't understand
us.

In jail I went to school every day except Sunday. I
found out that I was good at math, which seemed
strange to me. I learned even more from my fellow
prisoners than I learned from school. There was lots of
time to talk, to listen, to tell stories. One thing I
learned was cussing and all the dirty four-letters
words. That was a big accomplishment, because we
Indians didn't know how to curse. If a white man
called me a dirty name, all I could do was to make the
bear sound—hrrrhn, hrrrhn—to show my anger. But
this wasn't very satisfactory, because he didn't understand it. Also, making the bear sound, you were
supposed to follow it up, fight, and go for your knife.
It wasn't always worth it. Now I could simply say,
"You lousy son of a bitch!" and let it go at that. It
surely made social intercourse with whites a lot easier
and less complicated.

When I came out of the reformatory I felt that I had
grown up. I had been nine months in there. That's the
time it takes to have a baby. I felt reborn. I sometimes
wonder what made me do it, going on my big tear. The
nearest I can come to an answer is this: In the old days

a man could win respect by his generosity, by his giving, but we had nothing left to give. One could win respect by being a medicine man. I was a medicine man, but my religion was being repressed and driven underground. It was treated as something shameful —a savage superstition. I had to practice secretly, if at all. At this time you were more often than not ashamed of being a medicine man and wouldn't admit it to strangers.

Once a man had been honored for being a good hunter and provider, but there was nothing left for us to hunt anymore. Bringing home the scanty Government rations, food that we didn't like, that was not natural for us, that we never got used to, didn't bring us honor. We had been warriors once, admired for our bravery. Now we were nothing. In the past a man might have been born a cripple, unable to do the things which brought honor and admiration, but if he was clear-minded and thoughtful he would still be respected for his wisdom alone. But now our wisdom was measured against the white man's cleverness and we were told, over and over again, that we were stupid, uneducated, good for nothing.

We didn't want to be nothing. We wanted to be somebody. I felt that I was only half a man, that all the old, honored, accepted ways for a young man to do something worthy were barred to me. Just as there was a fence around the reservation, so they had put a fence around our pride. Well, I had to invent a new way of making a name for myself, of breaking through that fence. I couldn't live on the glory of my great-grandfather, who had died fighting General Miles. Going on that joy ride was for me like going on the warpath, like counting coup.

I was young and maybe this was a childish way of saying, "Look, I'm a man. I exist. Take notice of my existence!" I'm an old wood-tick now, as they say, supposedly very wise and respectable, but I still can't help smiling when I think of the big commotion I caused. It had made me feel like a man who was letting the world know of his manhood. It had made me feel that my living was a matter of some importance, that it had a purpose. This was worth going to jail for.

# 5

# Sitting on Top of Teddy
# Roosevelt's Head

Here we are, sitting on Teddy Roosevelt's head, giving
him a headache, maybe. If we get tired of the view
from here, we could move over and sit for a while on
Washington or Lincoln or Jefferson, but Teddy is by
far the best. There is moss growing near the back of
his skull, lots of trees, firewood, boulders to lean your
back against, a little hollow surrounded by pines,
which makes a nice campground—especially with
that cliff rising behind it on which that big "Red
Power—Indian Land" sign is painted. It looks nice,
doesn't it? Actually, we're not sitting exactly on
Teddy's head, which is bald and smooth, but in back
of it, halfway toward Lincoln. We are really higher
than any of these heads. One good thing about being
on top of Mount Rushmore, it's the only place around
here where you don't have to look at those big faces,
these giant tourist curios, ashtrays, paperweights. I
know a Santee Indian who some years ago climbed up
here one night with a few friends just to pee down on
the nose of one of those faces. He called it a "symbolic
gesture." The way he told it to me it was quite a feat.
They had to form a human chain to make it possible
for him to do it.

Don't get me wrong—we hold no grudge against
Lincoln, Jefferson or Washington. They signed a few
good treaties with us and it wasn't their fault that they
weren't kept. What we object to is the white man's
arrogance and self-love, his disregard for nature which
makes him desecrate one of our holy mountains with
these oversized pale faces. It's symbolic, too, that this

"Shrine of Democracy," these four faces, are up to their chins in one tremendous pile of rubble, a million tons of jagged, blasted, dynamited stone reaching all the way down to the visitors' center. If you look up the mountain, the way most tourists do, you see these four heads rising out of something like a gigantic, abandoned mine dump. But nobody seems to notice that.

It's funny that we all got the sudden urge to be up here—you, a white artist with your wife, I, an old Sioux medicine man, a handful of Indian ladies with their children and grandchildren, and a bunch of young, angry "Red Power" kids. We are all different and have come here for different reasons, each of us bringing his own private anger with him. Well, a good anger is a good thing too. It could turn into love in the end. Anger is something we can share, like food.

Listen, my white friend Richard here told me some reasons why he doesn't like Mount Rushmore. We Indians have many reasons why we don't like it, but he has thought up a few we never hit on. He calls these faces one big white ego trip. He says good art can't be made with a jackhammer, and I think, being an artist, he knows what he is talking about. He says that anything which is in such disharmony with nature is bad art. Even if Michelangelo had made this monument it would still be ugly, because it fits into these mountains, our sacred Black Hills, like a red-hot iron poker into somebody's eye. Did I get you right so far?

Richard also called it a disease of our society—I guess you meant white society, not us—to confuse bigness with greatness. I got this right away, because that's what we think, too, but you also told me something I had not known before. It was this: that the only other mountains carved up like Rushmore are some huge cliffs in Asia. They always show some Babylonian big cheese, or Egyptian pharaoh, trampling some people underfoot, and the inscriptions always go like this: "I, the great king, the king of kings, the living god, I smote fifty towns over there and buried the inhabitants alive, and I smashed fifty cities down here and had everybody impaled, and I conquered another fifty places on this side and had everybody in them burned up, and to show you what a big guy I am I had a thousand slaves carve up this mountain."

That really got me thinking. What does this Mount Rushmore mean to us Indians? It means that these big white faces are telling us, "First we gave you Indians a treaty that you could keep these Black Hills forever, as long as the sun would shine, in exchange for all the Dakotas, Wyoming and Montana. Then we found the gold and took this last piece of land, because we were stronger, and there were more of us than there were of you, and because we had cannons and Gatling guns, while you hadn't even progressed far enough to make a steel knife. And when you didn't want to leave, we wiped you out, and those of you who survived we put on reservations. And then we took the gold out, a billion bucks, and we aren't through yet. And because we like the tourist dollars, too, we have made your sacred Black Hills into one vast Disneyland. And after we did all this we carved up this mountain, the dwelling place of your spirits, and put our four gleaming white faces here. We are the conquerors."

And a million or more tourists every year look up at those faces and feel good, real good, because they make them feel big and powerful, because their own kind of people made these faces and the tourists are thinking: "We are white, and we made this, what we want we get, and nothing can stop us." Maybe they won't admit it to themselves, but that's what many of them are thinking deep down inside. And this is what conquering means. They could just as well have carved this mountain into a huge cavalry boot standing on a dead Indian.

One man's shrine is another man's cemetery, except that now a few white folks are also getting tired of having to look at this big paperweight curio. We can't get away from it. You could make a lovely mountain into a great paperweight, but can you make it into a wild, natural mountain again? I don't think you have the know-how for that.

A reporter from the Rapid City *Journal* asked me why I come up here. I told him that the Presidents' faces on Mount Rushmore had become dirty and that I wanted to plant a staff up there, like an altar, on the very top, making this a sacred mountain again. That guy really looked puzzled. For a while he said nothing. Finally he asked, "What is the true significance of this staff?" I told him, "The lower part of the staff is painted black. That stands for night. It stands for black face paint in war. It also represents people praying, either with their eyes closed or in the dark. It also means that I am putting a blanket, or shroud, over the mountain by planting this staff, and the Presidents' faces shall remain dirty until the treaties concerning the Black Hills are fulfilled. The upper part of the staff is red, which represents the day and the sun, the red face paint of gladness. It means that when the Government's promises to the Indians will be fulfilled, the Black Hills will be covered with brightness again, but this could take some time. In the meantime we Indians renamed Mount Rushmore 'Crazy Horse Mountain.'"

"Well," said the reporter, "I hope I've gotten all this right." I told him I hoped so, too.

Now, Richard here had another good idea. He said there should be a law that all statues over a hundred feet high should be put in abandoned mine shafts. This way nobody would be forced to look at them. Those interested would pay a quarter and take an elevator down to see the giant sculptures. That way everybody would be happy. I wished we'd had a law like this before this big thing was started. Maybe it's not too late to put an elevator under this whole shrine of democracy—press a button and the whole monument disappears. And once a week—say, every Sunday from nine to eleven—you press the button again and those four heads come up again with the music going full blast. The guys who got an astronaut on the moon should be able to do this much for us Indians, artists and nature lovers.

In one thing you're wrong, though. You said we could relax now, the worst was over; they had done everything they could to the Black Hills. There was no room left for more. So now I have to tell you about a white fellow artist of yours—a sculptor. I have the name written down somewhere, back in my hip pocket. We Indians are so uneducated we can't even remember a simple name. We should be able to do it, because our own names are so complicated—Red Cloud, Lame Deer, Gall—after this it should be easy to catch on to a simple, civilized white man's name. But I can't memorize it, I have to look it up. Here it is: Mr. Korczak Ziolkowski, pupil of Gutzon Borglum, who built Mount Rushmore. It seems Ziolkowski and Borglum had a falling-out at one time. Ziolkowski felt bad at having to work at such a measly thing as Mount Rushmore.

He went off and started working on Thunderhead Mountain, which is about twice as big as Mount Rushmore. Now Ziolkowski says he is a friend of the Indians. He says he wants to do something for us. If a white man says this, it's time for us Indians to run. What Ziolkowski wants to do for us is put up a giant statue of Crazy Horse which will make those four Presidents look like dwarfs.

This statue of the chief sitting on his pony is supposed to be about 650 feet long and 560 feet high. It will have a forty-foot feather sticking out from its head. Ziolkowski has made a huge model of his monument. Crazy Horse doesn't look very Indian and neither does his pony. Crazy Horse doesn't have braids and the feather coming out of his hair looks like an air valve sticking out of a tire. The chief's arm is pointing ahead like "this way to the men's room." It is said that all the people on our reservation could stand on that arm, or maybe just on his hand. That statue is supposed to be wired for sound. Maybe its jaws will open and war whoops will come out that you will be able to hear all the way to Sioux Falls. The heap of rubble all this will make could be ten times as big as the rock dump at the foot of Mount Rushmore. The advertising says, "An entire mountain is being carved in the likeness of Chief Crazy Horse by sculptor-genius Korczak Ziolkowski." That man thinks big.

This genius, I am told, makes more than 100,000 green frog skins a year tax-free from tourist admissions and by selling plaster models of his statue from three dollars up—tax-free, because he is doing all this for us poor Indians. Somewhere in, or under, that statue is supposed to be a fifty-million-dollar university for Indians, maybe in the big toe or a hoof, I'm not quite sure where, but I'm fairly sure that we Indians never got any money out of this.

There are two things wrong with this statue. Crazy Horse never let a white man take his picture. He didn't want white people to look at him. He died fighting before he would let white soldiers shut him up in a stone guardhouse. He was buried the way he wanted it, with nobody knowing his grave. The whole idea of making a beautiful wild mountain into a statue of him is a pollution of the landscape. It is against the spirit of Crazy Horse.

Mr. Fools Crow, one of our most respected medicine men, says, "This mountain doesn't want the statue to be built. The ghost of Crazy Horse doesn't want it. It will never be finished."

Godfrey Chips, our youngest medicine man, told me, "This man Crazy Horse, in the beginning he was a peaceful man, but when he sees that all his people are massacred down the line, well, he had been given a power, so he starts to fight with it. He used to be gentle, but life made him into a man-killer. The hate was in him. He never liked the white people and he died that way. So his spirit told me he doesn't want them to build a tourist monument of Crazy Horse."

Another Yuwipi man said, "Thunderhead Mountain, that's an old name. It could mean some thunderbirds were up there once. They won't like this. Our dead people don't want it being built. The trees and the animals don't want it. All of us medicine men know this."

The second thing wrong with this statue is that the time has passed when a white man could simply decide for us to build a monument on our behalf according to what he had in mind, in our sacred hills, without asking us. When he started it all over thirty years ago, he could still find Indians who were flattered that a white sculptor-genius wanted to do a statue of an Indian chief. But these days are over.

Ziolkowski sometimes says that the Indians are superstitious and that the main trouble is our lack of vision to understand him. The trouble is that we understand him too well. It's he who doesn't understand. He might have good intentions, but he doesn't see that all that gigantic carving up of our sacred mountains is just another form of racism.

But don't worry. The genius-sculptor is getting long in the tooth, while his statue isn't making much progress. Also he is very busy collecting admission fees from tourists, taking them on guided tours, selling them plaster models of all sizes, letting them look through a pay telescope, letting them touch off dynamite blasts, and what not. Maybe it's the spirit of Crazy Horse which is sending him all these interruptions. My father was a betting man. In a fight between Korczak Ziolkowski and the spirit of Crazy Horse, he wouldn't have put his money on Ziolkowski. I am telling you, this statue will remain faceless.

Why am I wasting my time talking about white men's giant statues? Because they are a form of discrimination. It's discrimination which brought us all up here on top of Teddy Roosevelt's head. And that's what I want to talk about. Some of our young Indians have bumper stickers on their cars—"Custer Died for Your Sins!"—but I'm telling you, Custer is alive! Not one but many Custers are at work at their trade, which is beating down on the Indians. Custer's spirit is in all those tourist traps which desecrate these mountains. It's in the Mother Goose Story Book Island, in the All-Aboard, Narrow Gauge, Scenic 1880 Train, in the Flintstone's Bed-Rock Village, the Doll-House Museum, the Horseless Carriage Museum, the Unforgettable Fun for the Family Gravity House, the Pan Your Own Gold Dust Place, all the phony pageants, the whole crap. There's a little Custer in all those sightseers, souvenir hunters, rock hounds, tourist scalpers, sharps and Deadwood hookers which cover these hills like so many ants.

Well, I came up here to pray, to do a ceremony, plant a stick. So I'll crawl into the boulders back there, do a little singing, listen to the voices. In the meantime, you can ask these ladies here, Muriel Waukazoo and Lizzy Fast Horse, why they are up here.

MURIEL WAUKAZOO and LIZZY FAST HORSE: "This idea of coming up here originated from a woman in Pine Ridge, South Dakota. And first they started a demonstration down on Sheep Mountain, near Scenic. The Government took two hundred thousand acres of Indian land for a bombing range. They promised to give it back after World War Two ended and they haven't given it back yet. So we printed up some handbills about the movement, told them everything that was happening. Then we took those handbills from home to home and gave them out, and we told the Indians who we gave them to not to say anything. So the Indian population of Rapid City knew about occupying Mount Rushmore a month before it happened. But the white people never knew it. We just didn't let it out.

"So we started in on a Monday morning, the

twenty-fourth of August. There were only us three women. We thought other people were coming up, but they didn't. I guess they were scared. And it lightninged all the way up, so we thought about Crazy Horse and we knew he was with us. We were really scared that the rangers would arrest us. For a few days we were handing out handbills to the tourists in the parking lot. Then Lee Brightman came to support us, and then the Indian students came in. We got braver and braver and now we're not afraid of anyone."

LEE BRIGHTMAN: "I'm a Sioux from Cheyenne River. I feel proud of my family. My great-grandfather was killed at Custer's Last Stand. I had some relatives killed at Wounded Knee. I'm forty years old and I'm heading an Indian Studies program at a California university. I brought a group of people here. Well, we started up in the dark and those mounties with flashlights caught us. They were afraid we were going to dump red paint on those faces. They told us to move on, get off the mountain, but we just sat down. We were laughing because they didn't have any weapons. So what could they do to us? At a given signal we just got up and split. Some rangers on top had guns. We had to hide out all night, and next morning we climbed the peak and let out our Sioux Indian Power flag. We decided to stay all summer, and now it's October and we are still here. The Indian people from the community are bringing us food and water.

"These were the reasons we invaded Mount Rushmore. The Federal Government took two hundred thousand acres from us to build a gunnery range. They didn't return it as promised. We've been waiting twenty-six years. And now the Secretary of the Interior has made a statement that he's going to turn it into a national park. That's a violation of the damn agreement they made with us.

"So we dramatize this, and we wanted to dramatize the plight of the Black Hills. Around 1868 they made a treaty with us giving us this land for as long as the sun shines and the grass grows. And, of course, this treaty didn't mean shit. Six years later Custer discovered gold. Immediately they took the land from us, and they haven't paid us for it since. They have been taking billions of dollars out and given us nothing. And they took the timber, too, iron, uranium, and lime. And they also make millions off the tourist trade—'Come to Indian Land'—but we get no cut. And this land is sacred to us, so what do they do? They further desecrate it by putting the faces of four white men on it.

"And this is another gripe we want to dramatize, this discrimination against us. My organization, United Native Americans, did a survey on discrimination in the United States, listing the different states according to their rank as far as racism is concerned. And South Dakota is by far the most racist state for Indians, and Rapid City is the worst city in South Dakota. And this is why we took the mountain.

"These are our demands. We want payment for the Black Hills, for all the minerals mined, for the timber taken out. And we want our sacred mountains back. The Cheyennes probably will want Bear Butte back—that was their most holy place. And here we find they're selling souvenir picture postcards of our dead from Wounded Knee, where the Seventh Cavalry massacred two hundred fifty Indian women and children. And the soldiers were awarded thirty-two Congressional Medals of Honor for that massacre. That's the most horrible thing about it. And we demand that they remove those obscene postcards right away. And we demand that the Indian people be allowed to sell their own arts and crafts here on their own land. Now, white concessionaires are selling 'genuine Indian beadwork' made in Hong Kong—all that crap. And we want more Indian forest rangers employed. And they have this big amphitheater here, which is going to waste, and we want our people to be able to come here and put on a pageant of their own.

"And we have been selling our land to white people for too goddam long, and we're going to wind up with nothing. The soil-conservation people made a survey which said that half of the Indian land was severely or critically eroded and the other half slightly eroded. So we Indians own fifty-six million acres of erosion. If I had anything to say I'd make damn sure no white people got to lease or buy our land. Right now they're getting hundred-year leases on our land. Most of our Indians wind up being serfs on their own land. About ninety percent of the Pine Ridge reservation is leased out to white ranchers and farmers, and those leases are renewable after a hundred years.

"Some of this leasing and selling is done by men who call themselves Indians, because we've got many crooked tribal leaders who allow this stuff. I think you are going to see a new Indian emerge. A young Indian who's mad and frustrated and disgusted. People like myself, who are sick and tired of tribal leaders and white politicians exploiting us. And a lot of older people have joined us. They've been beaten down for a long time. They used to accept their lot because they were accustomed to their misery. But they are finding out that's a lot of bullshit.

"It's hard to speak out on a reservation, because the Bureau of Indian Affairs will cut you down. Maybe you are a young boy and want to speak out, but your father works for the B.I.A. Well, he'll get it in the neck if you open your mouth. The B.I.A. controls Indian people through fear, intimidation and a form of blackmail. If you stand up for your people they make it hard on you and your relatives. If you work for the B.I.A. they'll transfer you to another reservation. The old divide-and-conquer crap.

"And those white boss superintendents. At Bemiji, in the Minnesota area, they found their superintendent was doing a lot of unscrupulous things and after months of griping they finally got rid of this man. So the B.I.A. transferred him from Minnesota to South Dakota and they shoved him off on the Sioux, this incompetent bastard. Then they gave him a raise and a higher position. Now that's how they transfer their incompetents. At this rate, if you're incompetent enough, you can wind up being Commissioner of Indian Affairs.

"I get so mad, I start yelling. But I want to clear this up. I don't hate white people, I only hate what white people have done to us. This mountain climb is going to make many Indian kids and old folks swell with pride seeing us take over this monument from the strongest government in the world, take this mountain and rename it. And this is the significance of it, to gain confidence to run our affairs, to direct our own destiny, to be your own man—that's what we are striving for. And I think there's going to come a time in the very near future when Indians are going to take this right. We are just sick and tired of having other people tell us what to do and how to do it. That's one of the reasons we are up here."

Well, I'm done with my singing and come out of the rocks. Lee Brightman here, he sure scared a lot of our old folks when he used all those strong words in public, "bullshit" and all that. They aren't used to that, except in private among themselves. But I think this is very educational. Once an old Indian lady gets up and says "bullshit" loud and clear to some B.I.A. official, or on a public address system, things will never be the same again. It's working already. Look at Lizzy Fast Horse here, a grandmother climbing up this mountain day after day. That's pretty good. Do you know why this is such a great thing? Only a short while ago Indian women wouldn't have taken part in a thing like this. Some college girls at a big university, maybe, but not our local ladies. And an old wood tick like myself, I wouldn't have taken part either. I would have told myself: "You are a medicine man, stay on the spiritual side, don't mix in politics." But when we heard about Mount Rushmore, you looked at me, and I looked at you, and we both said together: "Let's get up there!"

And a year ago most young people wouldn't have bothered with an old medicine man. What part could he play in their fight? But now everything is changed. Those young, educated Indians come to me and say: "Tell us about the old ways, about the sacred pipe; it will make us more Indian." And when they came to take over this mountain, they asked me to plant a sacred stake there and perform a ceremony. And here we are, old and young, men and women, a big bunch of Indians and you, your wife, and that blond, blue-eyed girl over there who tagged along with us. None of us will be the same when we come down. This mountain will have changed us in some way.

How will it change me? I guess for a start I'm going to sue the city of Winner for discrimination. That will be something new for me. I have been thinking about it, on and off, but now I'll do it. What's going on in our little town of Winner, where I live, is another reason why I'm up here. There are really two towns. On the high ground is white Winner—paved streets, sidewalks, fire hydrants, street lights, plumbing, flush toilets and all the services that go with them.

And down at the bottom is the other Winner, Indian Town, with about eighty Sioux families, what you might call the "native quarters." No paved streets, bright lights, hydrants or flush toilets for us. We are primitive aborigines, as they say. We don't need these things; we prefer outhouses. Everybody knows that. We have a few white families living in Indian Town. They are as poor as us, maybe poorer. And for this crime they are treated like Indians— white Indians.

Even the rain in Winner is racist. It runs down those

beautifully paved white streets, flooding the native quarters, with Mister Indian up to his ass in mud when he takes his exercise walking from his shack to his outdoor privy.

And we don't just have two cities; we also have two kinds of law around here, one for whites and one for Indians. I've lived in Winner close to twenty years, and now and then, like any other bad boy, I got thrown in jail on a drunk-and-disorderly. And at other times I just go there as a visitor. But one way or another I know that jail well. They put Mister Indian in there overnight and next morning he goes to court. There is a little office there with a judge and you go in alone. And the judge reads the complaint and tells Mister Indian: "If you plead guilty you're finished right now, but if you plead not guilty you'll have to get a bondsman, and before you get bailed out, you might be staying here for two weeks. So why don't you make it easy on yourself and plead guilty—fifteen days and a ten-dollar fine." And Mister Indian pleads guilty, because he might stay in jail forever before he can raise the bail.

One time I saw this Indian—he was just on his way home, sober as a judge. The police stop right in front of him. "Get in this car!" He said, "I'm not drunk," but they tell him again, "Get in!" and start pounding him up with their saps and then throw him in the jug. I don't know what they have against him. Probably he had spoken his mind about something bothering him. They treat him this way not only to scare him but to scare us others as well. Nobody talks openly about discrimination in that town, because they know the police will be watching them.

But the worst kind of two-faced justice happens when there is a killing. When White Hawk, an Indian boy, killed a white jeweler he was sentenced to death. This sentence was later commuted to life imprisonment, and yet we all know that White Hawk wasn't in his right mind when he did this. That's the sentence for killing a white man—death.

The sentence for killing a red man is different. When a seventeen-year-old white boy shot an Indian father in his fifties, shooting him seven times with a German Luger, he got away with two years. When a white man from White River killed an Indian boy from Murdo he got thirty days in jail and a hundred-dollar fine for assault and battery. They said they couldn't convict him for murder because he simply married the main witness to the killing, an Indian girl who had seen the crime.

And a rich white rancher shot and killed a young Indian, a very quiet and shy churchgoer. The white man was armed, the Indian was not. There were no witnesses, but the rancher admitted having shot that Indian boy. The white man wasn't even arrested for two weeks. When the trial came up he was acquitted. Justifiable homicide, that's what they called it. These things stay in our memory.

I see the sun coming up and it's red—a real Indian Power sun. It was good spending the night up here, talking to each other, on top of Teddy Roosevelt's head. It's time to plant this sacred staff on the highest spot. Where is it? You want me to go up *there?* Way up that narrow cleft? I think I better take my high-heeled cowboy boots off. My socks are kind of slick, no traction—that's not much better. How are you doing? We need you up there with your camera. I don't think you are doing that well either. After telling me about all those mountains you climbed in Austria. You must have been thinner then. That crack is a little narrow; you are too wide in the beam now. What you call your "fried chicken cemetery" seems to get in the way. But we made it. Let me catch my breath, and you too, brother—I'd like us to be twenty years younger for a crazy stunt like this. Well, I'll say a prayer with my peace pipe. And this is my sacred staff with a feather tied to it, the staff of an old medicine man. I want one of the young men to plant it in that cleft in the rock. Use the ax, drive it in deep. Now this eagle feather is waving once more over the Paha Sapa, the sacred Black Hills. Someday they will be ours again.

## AFTERTHOUGHT

In August 1971, about half a year after we had put this chapter together, John, myself, and our families were camping together in the Black Hills. We decided on the spur of the moment to drop in on Korczak Ziolkowski. The place looked pretty much as we expected—a paved road, a tollgate with an admission charge of two dollars per car, a giant-sized parking lot and, rising behind it, the huge mountain showing as yet no sign of becoming a statue. A flattened area on top and a very big hole tunneled through the granite was all that Ziolkowski had to show for his twenty-four years of battling the mountain.

His studio-home is a rabbit warren of fifty-seven pine-paneled rooms dominated by a vast, timbered hall, the Grand Central Station of the Plains, where tourists sit at the lunch counter munching buffalo-burgers or buying pink and chartreuse replicas of Crazy Horse Monument at the souvenir shop. Loud-speakers were blaring as the sculptor's daughters conducted gaping crowds through various exhibits and points of interest. We were finally led deep into the bowels of the hive into a small, cozy study where the noise of the crowd had faded to a faint hum: Korczak's Inner Sanctum.

It is probably always a mistake to meet a man after you have criticized him. The fact is that both John and I liked Korczak at first sight. Shaggy as a bear, with a big, unkempt beard, he was wearing a sun-bleached Levi jacket with the sleeves ripped off, waving his bare arms in a grizzlylike welcome.

We told him that we had written some bad things

about his monument, and why. He just grinned and put a bottle of very palatable French wine before me and a bottle of good whisky before John. He readily agreed with some of what we had to say. He, too, thought that maybe his mountain would be a better sight if left uncarved. He was sorry for having very little contact with Indians now. He dismissed his tourist mill and its pink Crazy Horse replicas with an obscene gesture.

At the same time, he was in no way apologetic. He was doing his thing and liking it. He was an egomaniac and proud of it. He admitted to getting close to 200,000 dollars a year in admission fees, but pointed out that almost all of this goes back into the project. He told us of having enemies among the local whites who do not want a monument to an Indian Chief. He motioned to a few loaded guns lying around: "I even taught my wife how to shoot."

He admitted that nowadays Indians were cool toward his project, but brought out a letter from a Sioux Chief Henry Standing Bear saying, "Please carve us a mountain so the white man will know that the red man had great heroes, too." This letter, according to Korczak, set the whole project in motion. He spoke of a fifty-million-dollar Indian center with hospital, university and museum, which would come into being as a result of his work. He seemed very sincere about this, though it could have been a superb put-on.

Being sixty-three years old and with nothing but a big hole to show for his labors, we asked him if he thought that he would finish his monument. "Some people say I won't," he answered. "So what! They can go to hell. It didn't cost them a dime." He then startled us with this strange bit of philosophy: "You know, if the Russians, or Chinese, ever conquer this country, they'll blow Mount Rushmore to bits, but they'll leave my Crazy Horse Monument alone; it will dwarf the pyramids of Egypt."

Korczak was a good and entertaining host and we

talked till late into the night, winding up by joining him in his favorite song:

> If I had the balls of a bison,
> And the prick of a bull buffalo
> I'd stand on top of Crazy Horse Mountain,
> And piss on the bastards below.

Driving back to our campsite John and I agreed that we still did not like Korczak's project, but that we liked Korczak, the man.

# 6
# The Circle and the Square

What do you see here, my friend? Just an ordinary old cooking pot, black with soot and full of dents.

It is standing on the fire on top of that old wood stove, and the water bubbles and moves the lid as the white steam rises to the ceiling. Inside the pot is boiling water, chunks of meat with bone and fat, plenty of potatoes.

It doesn't seem to have a message, that old pot, and I guess you don't give it a thought. Except the soup smells good and reminds you that you are hungry. Maybe you are worried that this is dog stew. Well, don't worry. It's just beef—no fat puppy for a special ceremony. It's just an ordinary, everyday meal.

But I'm an Indian. I think about ordinary, common things like this pot. The bubbling water comes from the rain cloud. It represents the sky. The fire comes from the sun which warms us all—men, animals, trees. The meat stands for the four-legged creatures, our animal brothers, who gave of themselves so that we should live. The steam is living breath. It was water; now it goes up to the sky, becomes a cloud again. These things are sacred. Looking at that pot full of good soup, I am thinking how, in this simple manner, Wakan Tanka takes care of me. We Sioux spend a lot of time thinking about everyday things, which in our mind are mixed up with the spiritual. We see in the world around us many symbols that teach us the meaning of life. We have a saying that the white man sees so little, he must see with only one eye. We see a lot that you no longer notice. You could notice if you wanted to, but you are usually too busy. We

Indians live in a world of symbols and images where the spiritual and the commonplace are one. To you symbols are just words, spoken or written in a book. To us they are part of nature, part of ourselves—the earth, the sun, the wind and the rain, stones, trees, animals, even little insects like ants and grasshoppers. We try to understand them not with the head but with the heart, and we need no more than a hint to give us the meaning.

What to you seems commonplace to us appears wondrous through symbolism. This is funny, because we don't even have a word for symbolism, yet we are all wrapped up in it. You have the word, but that is all.

Look at this belt. My grandmother made it. You say it is beautiful and this makes me glad, because I want to give it to you. But it is more than just beautiful; it tells a story. All you see is a geometric pattern of beads—lines, triangles and diamond shapes—but these are a tale of my grandfather's deeds.

This diamond shape represents a feather given to a warrior to wear after doing a brave thing like counting coup.

These rectangles with one line missing represent horses' tracks. They stand for the ponies captured from the enemy.

This shape means a horse killed in battle and its rider rescued by my grandfather.

These two triangles are arrows shot at the enemy.

108

This belt tells of a battle. A woman could make a different kind of belt, expressing her love of nature.

These lines are the trail she walked.

These are leaves she brushed against.

This is a pretty butterfly resting on her shoulder.

These up-and-down steps are a distant mountain.

These are clouds.

And these three shapes are the whirlwind.

This belt tells us about a young woman taking a walk, running into a storm, getting wet hurrying home, where she gets down to making this belt. Of course a girl could make a belt for her lover with all kinds of secret heart-to-heart things put in it. He would understand.

Such abstract designs are always women's work. Men draw figures of humans and animals realistically, the way they see them, but there's a lot of meaning hidden within a man's picture, too. Take this landscape. A friend of mine painted it. All you see are two round hills beneath a sky, the prairie, a dark valley with some bushes, a cleft, a spring. Well, this is no landscape at all. This is a woman's body. The hills are her breasts, the soft, grassy plain is her belly and that valley with the spring—well, that's her *winyan shan,* her female part. My friend didn't paint this to make you smirk. I suppose he saw his woman's body as a beautiful landscape. He couldn't leave out that valley with its cleft. That's a central part of her womanhood; it's her essence, it's holy. It stands for love and child-bearing. I think this is a beautiful picture.

Symbolism helped us to "write" without an alphabet. By way of symbols we can even describe abstract thoughts precisely so that all may understand them.

Two hands like this, open, reaching for each other, is our sign for peace.

A man holding a peace pipe means prayer.

This is a medicine man. His eyes are closed; he is having a vision, an insight. The wavy lines coming down on his head is the spirit power descending to him.

A man surrounded by dots like this means he is afraid; things are closing in on him.

You know, it always makes me laugh when I hear young white kids speak of some people as "squares" or "straights"—old people, hardened in their ways, in their minds, in their hearts. They don't even have to be old. You can be an "old square" at eighteen. Anyway, calling these people "squares"—an Indian could have thought it up. To our way of thinking the Indians' symbol is the circle, the hoop. Nature wants things to be round. The bodies of human beings and animals have no corners. With us the circle stands for the togetherness of people who sit with one another around the campfire, relatives and friends united in peace while the pipe passes from hand to hand. The camp in which every tipi had its place was also a ring. The tipi was a ring in which people sat in a circle and all the families in the village were in turn circles within a larger circle, part of the larger hoop which was the seven campfires of the Sioux, representing one nation. The nation was only a part of the universe, in itself circular and made of the earth, which is round, of the sun, which is round, of the stars, which are round. The moon, the horizon, the rainbow—circles within circles within circles, with no beginning and no end.

To us this is beautiful and fitting, symbol and reality at the same time, expressing the harmony of life and nature. Our circle is timeless, flowing; it is new life emerging from death—life winning out over death.

The white man's symbol is the square. Square is his house, his office buildings with walls that separate people from one another. Square is the door which keeps strangers out, the dollar bill, the jail. Square are the white man's gadgets—boxes, boxes, boxes and more boxes—TV sets, radios, washing machines, computers, cars. These all have corners and sharp edges—points in time, white man's time, with appointments, time clocks and rush hours—that's what the corners mean to me. You become a prisoner inside all these boxes.

More and more young white people want to stop being "straight" and "square" and try to become round, join our circle. That is good.

From birth to death we Indians are enfolded in symbols as in a blanket. An infant's cradle board is covered with designs to ensure a happy, healthy life for the child. The moccasins of the dead have their soles beaded in a certain way to ease the journey to the hereafter. For the same reason most of us have tattoos on our wrists—not like the tattoos of your sailors—daggers, hearts and nude girls—but just a name, a few letters or designs. The Owl Woman who guards the road to the spirit lodges looks at these tattoos and lets us pass. They are like a passport. Many Indians believe that if you don't have these signs on your body, that Ghost Woman won't let you through but will throw you over a cliff. In that case you have to roam the earth endlessly as a *wanagi*—a ghost. All you can do then is frighten people and whistle. Maybe its not so bad being a *wanagi*. It could even be fun. I don't know. But, as you see, I have my arms tattooed.

Every day in my life I see symbols in the shape of certain roots or branches. I read messages in the stones. I pay special attention to them, because I am a Yuwipi man and that is my work. But I am not the only one. Many Indians do this.

*Inyan*—the rocks—are holy. Every man needs a stone to help him. There are two kinds of pebbles that make good medicine. One is white like ice. The other is like ordinary stone, but it makes you pick it up and recognize it by its special shape. You ask stones for aid to find things which are lost or missing. Stones can give warning of an enemy, of approaching misfortune. The winds are symbolized by a raven and a small black stone the size of an egg.

*Inyan-sha*—the red pipestone—is maybe the most sacred of all, its red color representing the very life blood of our people.

In the old days we used to have many boulders which we painted and covered with feathers, or sage, praying to them, using them like an altar. Sometimes a dog was sacrificed to such a boulder. North from here, in Montana near the town of Busby, is an enormous stone called Medicine Deer Rock. It is as tall as a building and you can climb on top of it. It is covered all around with the images of men and animals, or with abstract designs such as whorls, spirals and zigzag lines. Some are painted on, some are scratched into the rock. There are layers upon layers of these images overlapping each other, because generations after generations of Indians have left their pictures on that stone.

Just before the battle of the Little Big Horn the Sioux and Cheyennes held their sun dance at Medicine Deer Rock, and Sitting Bull sacrificed a hundred pieces of his flesh from each arm and had a vision: "Many white soldiers falling backward into camp," which foretold Custer's defeat.

Whenever I'm up in Montana and get a chance I go to pray at that rock. It stands smack in the middle of some cattle rancher's land. He's a nice enough man, that rancher. He opens the gate for us and waves us on through his fence. I guess he wonders what a truckload of crazy Indians is up to busting in on him like that.

A stone fits right into our world of symbols. It is round and endless. Its power is endless too. All round things are kin to each other, like *wagmuha*—the gourd, the holy rattle—which has 405 little stones inside it, pebbles collected from anthills.

Nothing is so small and unimportant but it has a spirit given to it by Waken Tanka. Tunkan is what you might call a stone god, but he is also part of the Great Spirit. The gods are separate beings, but they are all united in Waken Tanka. It is hard to understand— something like the Holy Trinity. You can't explain it except by going back to the "circles within circles" idea, the spirit splitting itself up into stones, trees, tiny insects even, making them all *wakan* by his ever-presence. And in turn all these myriad of things which makes up the universe flowing back to their source, united in the one Grandfather Spirit.

Tunkan—the stone god—is the oldest spirit, we think, because he is the hardest. He stands for creation, you know, like the male part. Hard, upright, piercing—like the lance and arrowheads fashioned from it in the old days.

Inyan Wasicun Waken—the Holy White Stone Man—that's what we call Moses. He appeals to us. He goes up all alone to the top of his mountain like an Indian, to have his vision, be all alone with his God, who talks to him through fire, bushes and rocks. Moses, coming back from the hill carrying stone tablets with things scratched on them—he would have made a good Indian medicine man.

Tunkan, the stone spirit; Wakinyan, the thunder spirit; Takuskanska, the moving spirit; Unktehi, the water spirit—they are all *wakan:* mysterious, wonderful, incomprehensible, holy. They are all part of the Great Mystery. These are our four great supernaturals, which brings us to yet another form of symbolism—the magic of numbers which we share with many other peoples.

*Four* is the number that is most *wakan,* most sacred. Four stands for Tatuye Topa—the four quarters of the earth. One of its chief symbols is Umane, which looks like this:

It represents the unused earth force. By this I mean that the Great Spirit pours a great, unimaginable amount of force into all things—pebbles, ants, leaves, whirlwinds—whatever you will. Still there is so much force left over that's not used up, that is in his gift to bestow, that has to be used wisely and in moderation if we are given some of it.

This force is symbolized by the Umane. In the old days men used to have an Umane altar made of raised earth in their tipis on certain special occasions. It was so *wakan* you couldn't touch it or even hold your hand over it.

Even today we still set up altars—mounds of earth

decorated with tobacco ties and flags—for our Yuwipi ceremonies.

Four, the sacred number, also stands for the four winds, whose symbol is the cross.

The Great Mystery Medicine Bag contained four times four things. Unktehi, the water spirit, created the earth and the human beings in it. Everything has its beginning in the water. Unktehi gave us this Bag of Mysteries. In it the down of the swan stood for all the fowls, a tuft of buffalo hair symbolized the four-legged animals, grass stood for all the herbs, bark and roots for the trees. The bundle contained four kinds of skins from the birds, four kinds of fur from the animals, four kinds of plants, four kinds of rocks and stones.

Four things make the universe: earth, air, water, fire.

We Sioux speak of the four virtues a man should possess: bravery, generosity, endurance, wisdom. For a woman these are bravery, generosity, truthfulness and the bearing of children.

We Sioux do everything by fours: We take four puffs when we smoke the peace pipe. Those of us who believe in the Native American Church take four times four spoons of peyote during a night of prayer. We pour water four times over the hot rocks in the sweat lodge. For four nights we seek a vision during a *hanblechia*. Men abstain for four days and nights from the company of women before an important ceremony. The women in their turn stay away from the men's camp for four days when they are *isnati*— menstruating—or after giving birth. At least they used to.

Seven is a holy number too, representing the seven campfire circles of the Sioux Nation, the seven sacred rites, the seven bands of the Teton Sioux, but four is more *wakan*. We set up four colored flags for all our ceremonies, which reminds me of the symbolism and the power of the colors.

Black represents the west; red, the north; yellow, the east; white, the south. Black is night, darkness, mystery, the sun that has gone down. Red is the earth, the pipestone, the blood of the people. Yellow is the sun as it rises in the east to light the world. White is the snow. White is the glare of the sun in its zenith.

Red, white, black, yellow—these are the true colors. They give us the four directions; you might also say a trail toward our prayers. One reason we are so fascinated with these colors is that they stand for the unity of man—for the black race, the scarlet race, the yellow race, the white race as our brothers and sisters.

Words, too, are symbols and convey great powers, especially names. Not Charles, Dick and George. There's not much power in those. But Red Cloud, Black Elk, Whirlwind, Two Moons, Lame Deer— these names have a relationship to the Great Spirit. Each Indian name has a story behind it, a vision, a quest for dreams. We receive great gifts from the source of a name; it links us to nature, to the animal nations. It gives power. You can lean on a name, get strength from it. It is a special name for you and you alone—not a Dick, George, Charles kind of thing.

Each Indian name tells a story that remains hidden to outsiders unless it is explained to them. Take our famous chief Man-Afraid-of-His-Horse. It sounds funny in English. Man-Afraid once led the warriors in battle against the enemy who fled before him. The medicine men wanted to honor him and so they bestowed this name on him, which really means: He is so brave, so feared, that his enemies run away when merely seeing his horse, even if he is not on it. That is a powerful name. He had to live up to it.

Besides the names by which we were known, we Sioux also used to have a secret, second name, which was never spoken aloud. This was our good-luck, long-life name. Sometimes the grandfather or a medicine man gave a child this secret name, but it was best to go to a *winkte* for it.

116

*Winktes* were men who dressed like women, looked like women and acted like women. They did so by their own choice or in obedience to a dream. They were not like other men, but the Great Spirit made them *winktes* and we accepted them as such. They were supposed to have the gift of prophecy, and the secret name a *winkte* gave to a child was believed to be especially powerful and effective. In former days a father gave to a *winkte* a fine horse in return for such a name.

To a white man symbols are just that: pleasant things to speculate about, to toy with in your mind. To us they are much, much more. Life to us is a symbol to be lived. Here you see me spread some red earth on the floor. I flatten it with my palm and smoothen it with an eagle feather. Now I make a circle in it with my finger, a circle that has no end. The figure of a man is part of this circle. It is me. It is also a spirit. Out of its head come four horns. They stand for the four winds. They are forked at the end, split into a good and a bad part. This bad part of the fork could be used to kill somebody. If you look again at that circle without end you can see that it also forms a half moon. With my thumb I make twenty-four marks around the circle. This represents the twenty-four new medicine men who I was told I would have to ordain. Eighteen I have ordained already. A wise old woman once told me that I would die after I had ordained the

last one. So you can see that I am in no hurry to do this. Study my earth picture well. It is a spiritual design a man has to think about.

The twenty-four marks also represent the four directions of the universe, four dots each for the north, the east, the west, the south, the sky above and the earth below. I point my peace pipe toward all these directions. Now we are one with the universe, with all the living things, a link in the circle which has no end. It means we were here long before the first white man came, we are here now, we will still be here at the end of time—Indian Time. We will live! Now let us smoke. *He-hetchetu.*

# 7

# Talking to the Owls and Butterflies

Let's sit down here, all of us, on the open prairie, where we can't see a highway or a fence. Let's have no blankets to sit on, but feel the ground with our bodies, the earth, the yielding shrubs. Let's have the grass for a mattress, experiencing its sharpness and its softness. Let us become like stones, plants, and trees. Let us be animals, think and feel like animals.

Listen to the air. You can hear it, feel it, smell it, taste it. *Woniya waken*—the holy air—which renews all by its breath. *Woniya, woniya waken*—spirit, life, breath, renewal—it means all that. *Woniya*—we sit together, don't touch, but something is there; we feel it between us, as a presence. A good way to start thinking about nature, talk about it. Rather talk to it, talk to the rivers, to the lakes, to the winds as to our relatives.

You have made it hard for us to experience nature in the good way by being part of it. Even here we are conscious that somewhere out in those hills there are missile silos and radar stations. White men always pick the few unspoiled, beautiful, awesome spots for the sites of these abominations. You have raped and violated these lands, always saying, "Gimme, gimme, gimme," and never giving anything back. You have taken 200,000 acres of our Pine Ridge reservation and made them into a bombing range. This land is so beautiful and strange that now some of you want to make it into a national park. The only use you have made of this land since you took it from us was to blow it up. You have not only despoiled the earth, the rocks, the minerals, all of which you call "dead" but which are very much alive; you have even changed the animals, which are part of us, part of the Great Spirit, changed them in a horrible way, so no one can recognize them. There is power in a buffalo—spiritual, magic power—but there is no power in an Angus, in a Hereford.

There is power in an antelope, but not in a goat or in a sheep, which holds still while you butcher it, which will eat your newspaper if you let it. There was great power in a wolf, even in a coyote. You have made him into a freak—a toy poodle, a Pekingese, a lap dog. You can't do much with a cat, which is like an Indian, unchangeable. So you fix it, alter it, declaw it, even cut its vocal cords so you can experiment on it in a laboratory without being disturbed by its cries.

A partridge, a grouse, a quail, a pheasant, you have made them into chickens, creatures that can't fly, that wear a kind of sunglasses so that they won't peck each other's eyes out, "birds" with a "pecking order." There are some farms where they breed chickens for breast meat. Those birds are kept in low cages, forced to be hunched over all the time, which makes the breast muscles very big. Soothing sounds, Muzak, are piped into these chicken hutches. One loud noise and the chickens go haywire, killing themselves by flying against the mesh of their cages. Having to spend all their lives stooped over makes an unnatural, crazy, no-good bird. It also makes unnatural, no-good human beings.

That's where you fooled yourselves. You have not only altered, declawed and malformed your winged and four-legged cousins; you have done it to yourselves. You have changed men into chairmen of boards, into office workers, into time-clock punchers. You have changed women into housewives, truly fearful creatures. I was once invited into the home of such a one.

"Watch the ashes, don't smoke, you stain the curtains. Watch the goldfish bowl, don't breathe on the parakeet, don't lean your head against the wallpaper; your hair may be greasy. Don't spill liquor on that table: it has a delicate finish. You should have wiped your boots; the floor was just varnished. Don't, don't, don't . . ." That is crazy. We weren't made to endure this. You live in prisons which you have built for yourselves, calling them "homes," offices, factories. We have a new joke on the reservation: "What is cultural deprivation?" Answer: "Being an upper-middle-class white kid living in a split-level suburban home with a color TV."

Sometimes I think that even our pitiful tar-paper shacks are better than your luxury homes. Walking a hundred feet to the outhouse on a clear wintry night, through mud or snow, that's one small link with nature. Or in the summer, in the back country, leaving the door of the privy open, taking your time, listening to the humming of the insects, the sun warming your bones through the thin planks of wood; you don't even have that pleasure anymore.

Americans want to have everything sanitized. No smells! Not even the good, natural man and woman smell. Take away the smell from under the armpits, from your skin. Rub it out, and then spray or dab some nonhuman odor on yourself, stuff you can spend a lot of money on, ten dollars an ounce, so you know this has to smell good. "B.O.," bad breath, "Intimate Female Odor Spray"—I see it all on TV. Soon you'll breed people without body openings.

I think white people are so afraid of the world they created that they don't want to see, feel, smell or hear it. The feeling of rain and snow on your face, being numbed by an icy wind and thawing out before a smoking fire, coming out of a hot sweat bath and plunging into a cold stream, these things make you feel alive, but you don't want them anymore. Living in boxes which shut out the heat of the summer and the chill of winter, living inside a body that no longer has a scent, hearing the noise from the hi-fi instead of listening to the sounds of nature, watching some actor on TV having a make-believe experience when you no longer experience anything for yourself, eating food without taste—that's your way. It's no good.

The food you eat, you treat it like your bodies, take out all the nature part, the taste, the smell, the roughness, then put the artificial color, the artificial flavor in. Raw liver, raw kidney—that's what we old-fashioned full-bloods like to get our teeth into. In the old days we used to eat the guts of the buffalo, making a contest of it, two fellows getting hold of a long piece of intestines from opposite ends, starting chewing toward the middle, seeing who can get there first; that's eating. Those buffalo guts, full of half-fermented, half-digested grass and herbs, you didn't need any pills and vitamins when you swallowed those. Use the bitterness of gall for flavoring, not refined salt or sugar. *Wasna*—meat, kidney fat and berries all pounded together—a lump of that sweet *wasna* kept a man going for a whole day. That was food, that had the power. Not the stuff you give us today: powdered milk, dehydrated eggs, pasteurized butter, chickens that are all drumsticks or all breast; there's no bird left there.

You don't want the bird. You don't have the courage to kill honestly—cut off the chicken's head, pluck it and gut it—no, you don't want this anymore. So it all comes in a neat plastic bag, all cut up, ready to eat, with no taste and no guilt. Your mink and seal coats, you don't want to know about the blood and pain which went into making them. Your idea of war—sit in an airplane, way above the clouds, press a button, drop the bombs, and never look below the clouds—that's the odorless, guiltless, sanitized way.

When we killed a buffalo, we knew what we were

doing. We apologized to his spirit, tried to make him understand why we did it, honoring with a prayer the bones of those who gave their flesh to keep us alive, praying for their return, praying for the life of our brothers, the buffalo nation, as well as for our own people. You wouldn't understand this and that's why we had the Washita Massacre, the Sand Creek Massacre, the dead women and babies at Wounded Knee. That's why we have Song My and My Lai now.

To us life, all life, is sacred. The state of South Dakota has pest-control officers. They go up in a plane and shoot coyotes from the air. They keep track of their kills, put them all down in their little books. The stockmen and sheepowners pay them. Coyotes eat mostly rodents, field mice and such. Only once in a while will they go after a stray lamb. They are our natural garbage men cleaning up the rotten and stinking things. They make good pets if you give them a chance. But their living could lose some man a few cents, and so the coyotes are killed from the air. They were here before the sheep, but they are in the way; you can't make a profit out of them. More and more animals are dying out. The animals which the Great Spirit put here, they must go. The man-made animals are allowed to stay—at least until they are shipped out to be butchered. That terrible arrogance of the white man, making himself something more than God, more than nature, saying, "I will let this animal live, because it makes money"; saying, "This animal must go, it brings no income, the space it occupies can be used in a better way. The only good coyote is a dead coyote." They are treating coyotes almost as badly as they used to treat Indians.

You are spreading death, buying and selling death. With all your deodorants, you smell of it, but you are afraid of its reality; you don't want to face up to it. You have sanitized death, put it under the rug, robbed it of its honor. But we Indians think a lot about death.

I do. Today would be a perfect day to die—not too hot, not too cool. A day to leave something of yourself behind, to let it linger. A day for a lucky man to come to the end of his trail. A happy man with many friends. Other days are not so good. They are for selfish, lonesome men, having a hard time leaving this earth. But for whites every day would be considered a bad one, I guess.

Eighty years ago our people danced the Ghost Dance, singing and dancing until they dropped from exhaustion, swooning, fainting, seeing visions. They danced in this way to bring back their dead, to bring back the buffalo. A prophet had told them that through the power of the Ghost Dance the earth would roll up like a carpet, with all the white man's works—the fences and the mining towns with their whorehouses, the factories and the farms with their stinking, unnatural animals, the railroads and the telegraph poles, the whole works. And underneath this rolled-up white man's world we would find again the flowering prairie, unspoiled, with its herds of buffalo and antelope, its clouds of birds, belonging to everyone, enjoyed by all.

I guess it was not time for this to happen, but it is coming back, I feel it warming my bones. Not the old Ghost Dance, not the rolling-up—but a new-old spirit, not only among Indians but among whites and blacks, too, especially among young people. It is like raindrops making a tiny brook, many brooks making a stream, many streams making one big river bursting all dams. Us making this book, talking like this— these are some of the raindrops.

Listen, I saw this in my mind not long ago: In my vision the electric light will stop sometime. It is used too much for TV and going to the moon. The day is coming when nature will stop the electricity. Police without flashlights, beer getting hot in the refrigerators, planes dropping from the sky, even the President can't call up somebody on the phone. A young man will come, or men, who'll know how to shut off all electricity. It will be painful, like giving birth. Rapings in the dark, winos breaking into the liquor stores, a lot of destruction. People are being too smart, too clever; the machine stops and they are helpless, because they have forgotten how to make do without the machine. There is a Light Man coming, bringing a new light. It will happen before this century is over. The man who has the power will do good things, too—stop all atomic power, stop wars, just by shutting the white electro-power off. I hope to see this, but then I'm also afraid. What will be will be.

I think we are moving in a circle, or maybe a spiral, going a little higher every time, but still returning to the same point. We are moving closer to nature again. I feel it, your two boys here feel it. It won't be bad, doing without many things you are now used to, things taken out of the earth and wasted foolishly. You can't replace them and they won't last forever. Then you'll have to live more according to the Indian way. People won't like that, but their children will. The machine will stop, I hope, before they make electric corncobs for poor Indians' privies.

We'll come out of our boxes and rediscover the weather. In the old days you took your weather as it came, following the cranes, moving south with the herds. Here, in South Dakota, they say, "If you don't like the weather, wait five minutes." It can be 100 degrees in the shade one afternoon and suddenly there comes a storm with hailstones as big as golf balls, the prairie is all white and your teeth chatter. That's good—a reminder that you are just a small particle of nature, not so powerful as you think.

You people try to escape the weather, fly to Miami where it's summer all the time, miss the rains, miss the snow. That's pitiful. Up to 1925 we had some old men who had a sort of a club where they could get together. Somehow they could tell what the weather would be. They needed no forecaster with all those gimmicks, satellites and what have you. They just had their wisdom, something which told them what nature was up to.

Some medicine men have the power to influence the weather. One does not use it lightly, only when it is absolutely necessary. When we hold our sun dance, we always try to have perfect weather. When we had a wedding ceremony in Winner, last spring, you saw me draw a design in the earth, the figure of a turtle. I picked this up from the old people. When I was a little boy I had a party where we played games. It was drizzling and I was mad. We wanted to play and the weather wouldn't let us. My grandma said, "Why don't you make the picture of a turtle?" Before we were through making it, the rain stopped. I could dry the country up, or make a special upside-down turtle and flood everything. You have to know the right prayer with it, the right words. I won't tell what they are. That's too dangerous. You don't fool around with it. I see that white man's look on your face. You don't believe this. Ask my friend Pete Catches here, a brother medicine man.

PETE CATCHES: "John is right. That sun dance he was referring to, when we chopped down the sun-dance pole, we had to catch the tree. It is not supposed to touch the ground. We stood in line and I was close to the trunk of the tree, and when it fell it hit me right above the knee. I went through the sun dance with that suffering in me. And I really liked it. My sun dance was as near close to authentic as I could make it. I pierced my flesh in the morning and broke loose around three o'clock in the afternoon, the longest piercing since we revived this sacred dance. And after I broke loose, there was a big thundercloud forming in the west. A lot of people wanted to get away, to go home before the storm broke. And it was nearing, coming on fast. So, during the course of the dance, they handed me my pipe, the pipe that I always use. I call it my chief pipe. So I took that and asked the Great Spirit to part that thunder, part it in half, so we can finish our ceremony. Before all the people that great storm parted, right before their eyes. The one part went to the north, wrought havoc in the White River country, clear on in, tore off the roofs, destroyed gardens and acted like that. The part of the storm which went south, toward Pine Ridge, covered everything with hail, but on the dance ground the sun kept shining. So, to me, that sun dance in 1964 was the best one I ever did.

"And the power of the turtle design, what John told you about it, we know this to be true. The heart of Keha, the turtle, is about the strongest thing there is. I keeps on beating and beating for two days after you kill the turtle. There is so much strength and endurance in it. To eat such a heart makes you tough. It imparts its power to whoever has eaten of it. My sister ate that turtle heart. They had to cut it in half for her to make it possible to swallow it. This made her into a strong woman, stout-hearted like a warrior. She had a growth on her breast. The doctors said it was cancer. She lit five cigarettes. She told the children to puff on them, to keep those cigarettes glowing. Then she took the lighted cigarettes, one after the other, and burned this evil thing out of her. On and on she went, deep into her breast, and her face remained calm all the while; not one muscle twitched. She is cured now. A turtle heart will do this for you.

But all animals have power, because the Great Spirit dwells in all of them, even a tiny ant, a butterfly, a tree, a flower, a rock. The modern, white man's way keeps that power from us, dilutes it. To come to nature, feel its power, let it help you, one needs time and patience for that. Time to think, to figure it all out. You have so little time for contemplation; it's always rush, rush, rush with you. It lessens a person's life, all that grind, that hurrying and scurrying about. Our old people say that the Indians of long ago didn't have heart trouble. They didn't have that cancer. The illnesses they had they knew how to cure. But between 1890 and 1920 most of the medicines, the animal bundles, the pipes, the ancient, secret things which we had treasured for centuries, were lost and destroyed by the B.I.A., by the Government police. They went about tearing down sweat lodges, went into our homes, broke the pipes, tore up the medicine bags, threw them into the fire, burned them up, completely wiped out the wisdom of generations. But the Indian, you take away everything from him, he still has his mouth to pray, to sing the ancient songs. He can still do his *yuwipi* ceremony in a darkened room, beat his small drum, make the power come back, make the wisdom return. He did, but not all of it. The elk medicines are gone. The bear medicine, too. We had a medicine man here, up the creek, who died about fifteen years ago. He was the last bear medicine man that I knew about. And he was good, too. He was really good.

But it is coming again, the bear power. We make bear sounds, talk bear language when we are in a fighting mood. "Harrnh"—and you are as good as gone. A bear claw, properly treated, you pierce a man for the sun dance with it, he won't feel the pain. Let me tell you about the power of the bear, natural animal power when it comes up against one of those artificial, non-animals.

When I was a boy, a long time ago, I was traveling with my father. We were on our way back to Standing Rock. It happened on the road. My dad stopped for a poker game at a saloon. In the next room a young bear was sitting on the counter, hardly more than a cub. He

128

was chained down, really pitiful. They teased him, made him stand up on two legs.

The card players paid it no mind. They had big stacks of silver dollars before each player. I was sitting under the table. I liked those big, round, shiny silver pieces. I reached up and helped myself to some. Nobody noticed, or maybe they didn't mind. A big white man in a shaggy black coat and a derby walked into the place and sat down at the counter. With him he had a huge bulldog, really huge.

"You have a nice pet here," said the big man, chomping on a big cigar, to the bartender. "But you'd better watch him. If my dog gets loose, your bear will be all chewed up."

"That bulldog is good for nothing. He can't lick my pet!"

"I bet you fifty bucks he can. I give you odds—five to one—my bulldog will tear up this pet. Let's have a big fight!"

They put all this money up, the gamblers tripping over each other to get into the action. They took the bulldog and the bear outside. There was a big brown tent there where they used to hold revival meetings. There were four or five big cowboy hats full of betting money for the dog and for the bear. The news of the fight spread like wildfire, with more and more people coming all the time.

My dad had sold some cattle and had money on him. He told me, "Son, I'm going to bet a hundred dollars on that little pet bear." The big white man with the derby was so sure of his huge brute that he put up fistfuls of money against my dad—those big old twenty-dollar bills, gold and silver coins. They drew a circle inside the tent. Nobody was supposed to step in there. Those who had bet money could sit up front. They knelt or sat down so that the others could see what was going on. There were no bleachers. They put up some blankets, like a fence, to keep the two animals in the circle. The dog owner and the saloon keeper sat inside the circle together with the man who held the bank. I never again saw such a big heap of money all in one place. They were all puffing on their big cheroots, filling the tent with smoke. At last the big man with the dog said, "Five minutes more, after that no more bets!"

That caused a big commotion. Everybody tried to get into the act then. People got so heated up arguing about who was going to win, they started fist fights all over the place, the money rolling on the ground. Those were the old gambling days!

"Quit fussing and bet!" said the big man. Then he pulled out his watch. "Time's up. No more." He turned to his dog and pulled his ears a little. "Okay, get that bear, kill the little bastard. Tear him apart!"

That poor thing of a bear was sitting up like a baby, as if the whole show was no concern of his. "One round, that's all," said the bartender, "one round to the finish." Still a few ranchers and cowhands came running, money in their hands. They were out of luck, or maybe lucky, depending on what they had in mind, because the dog owner pulled a gun and fired it as a starter.

The poor little bear was still sitting up there when they sicked the dog on him. Boy, that bear came on slow. Under the old gas lamps his eyes looked blue. The dog was growling, snarling, his nose more wrinkled than my face is now. The bear just moved a foot closer and sat down again. He looked at that growling thing, all full of white teeth. The little bear just rubbed his paw on the earth, put some dirt on his head. That bulldog, maybe he was smarter than his owner. Maybe he knew something. He snarled, growled, made a big racket, but kept his distance. The big man in the derby got annoyed. "Come on, get on with it," he said and kicked the dog in the backside. The dog gathered himself up for the charge and finally here he comes.

The bear just reached out with his paw, the claws shooting out like so many knives, and made one swipe at the dog, just one swipe, and that old bulldog is out and cold, throat ripped out, dead and gone. And the little bear made the killing sound, "harrrnh," like a Sioux Indian.

My dad won over 700 dollars on that little bear. Most of the whites had bet on the bulldog; all the Indians had put their money on that puny bear. They knew he had the power.

It is the same with the buffalo. They have the power and the wisdom. We Sioux have a close relationship to the buffalo. He is our brother. We have many legends of buffalo changing themselves into men. And the Indians are built like buffalo, too—big shoulders, narrow hips. According to our belief, the Buffalo Woman who brought us the peace pipe, which is at the center of our religion, was a beautiful maiden, and after she had taught our tribes how to worship with the pipe, she changed herself into a white buffalo calf. So the buffalo is very sacred to us. You can't understand about nature, about the feeling we have toward it, unless you understand how close we were to the buffalo. That animal was almost like a part of ourselves, part of our souls.

The buffalo gave us everything we needed. Without it we were nothing. Our tipis were made of his skin. His hide was our bed, our blanket, our winter coat. It was our drum, throbbing through the night, alive, holy. Out of his skin we made our water bags. His flesh strengthened us, became flesh of our flesh. Not the smallest part of it was wasted. His stomach, a red-hot stone dropped into it, became our soup kettle. His horns were our spoons, the bones our knives, our women's awls and needles. Out of his sinews we made our bowstrings and thread. His ribs were fashioned into sleds for our children, his hoofs became rattles. His mightly skull, with the pipe leaning against it, was

131

our sacred altar. The name of the greatest of all Sioux was Tatanka Iyotake—Sitting Bull. When you killed off the buffalo, you also killed the Indian—the real, natural, "wild" Indian.

The buffalo has wisdom, but man-bred cattle—that's just a factory-made thing. They have no sense. Those Mexican fighting bulls get fooled by the cape every time. They are brave, yes, but not very smart. Imagine those bullfighters taking on a buffalo. They'd all get killed. The man-bred bull, he keeps looking at the cape. But a buffalo wouldn't be horn-swoggled by a red piece of cloth. He'd be looking for the man behind the cape, and his horns would find him. Buffalo are smart. They also have a sense of humor. Remember when we were together last in the Black Hills? When it suddenly snowed after a very hot day? Those six big black bulls we saw near Blue Bell, just like six large pick-up trucks. They were so happy over that snow. Gamboling, racing around, playing like kittens. And afterward we came across the tame cattle, hunched over, miserable, pitiful. "Moo, moo, moo—I'm cold." The real, natural animals don't mind the cold; they are happy with the kind of fur coat and galoshes the Great Spirit gave them. White hunters used to call the buffalo stupid because they were easy to shoot, weren't afraid of a gun. But the buffalo was not designed to cope with modern weapons. He was designed to deal with an Indian's arrows.

I told you about the little bear and the bulldog. Let me tell you about the buffalo and the bull. Word got around that some ranchers were staging a fight between a buffalo and a bull at the Philips ranch. We Sioux are all natural gamblers. We used to have many betting games long before the white man came. Betting was something you didn't have to teach us. We could have taught you. My dad knew how to judge things. This happened in 1919 or 1920. We had one of those funny old Fords. It took three dollars to get from

Fort Pierre to the Philips ranch. On three bucks you could go, maybe, a hundred miles. I was about sixteen years old. Dad was still taking care of me. Well, we got to that ranch. The corral was loaded, black with people. They had two roosters fighting each other first, to warm up the crowd, get the money moving. My dad wouldn't bet on a chicken. Two poor chickens, scratching and pecking at each other, who could get excited about such a thing?

At last they drove the buffalo into the trap. The bull was already waiting in a chute. It was owned by a man from Wyoming. It had a short name, but I don't remember it. You hear me, the buffalo is a "he" always, unless we are talking about a cow. But a man-bred bull, that's an "it." It was big all right, a real Bull Durham bull, the meanest bull in the country. Its balls dangled so low it almost tripped over them. They opened the chute. Boy, I've seen lots of bulls in my days, but wow—those horns! They were huge, light with black tips.

The old buffler was blowing dirt this way and that, pawing the ground, looking at the crowd. Some men were sitting on top of the corral, some ladies too, I noticed. They had long skirts in those days, but I saw some nice legs. That was some crowd! They were hollering like at Billy Graham's. All that commotion stirred up the buffalo, made him excited.

My dad picked up many two-to-one and three-to-one bets. He bet the buffalo to win, but this I don't have to tell you. I thought there would be a hundred-miles-an hour collision. The bull was about ready to charge. Its tail was sticking up in the air. I was scared it might break through the corral. My dad said, "Stay behind that big post just in case. Something could go wrong." My dad talked only when it was necessary. For a moment I was afraid that the buffalo would chicken out, because he ignored the bull. They had only about twenty yards to make their charge. The whole corral was maybe a little over a hundred feet across. At last here they came. They missed each other, horns straight up, like two passing trains coming from opposite directions. There was a big, disappointed "oh" from the crowd. But then we saw that the buffalo had ripped the side of the bull open as if with a razor blade. The ribs of the bull were cut. Two cowboys were yelling, "That bull is dead!" It still kicked a few times, but it was deader than hell. Those tame animals don't have the power.

A *hoka*—a badger—now there's a real animal. One day my uncle was on his gray horse, the one he uses to round up his other ponies with. He was riding bareback, just with a rope, a hitch around the gray's nozzle. Then he saw the badger. Once a badger is in his hole, not three or four men can drag him out. My uncle roped that *hoka,* but he couldn't pull it out. The badger was going into his hole; the rope was going in, too. Pretty soon there was the horse coming on. My uncle tried to unhitch it around the nose, but the horse's head was already too close to the hole. My uncle had to shoot the rope in two. Once a badger dips in, there isn't much you can do about it.

With the body of a dead badger, you can foretell how long you are going to live. There's a gift of prophecy in it. I knew a man called Night Chaser. He cut a dead badger open and let the blood stand there. You are supposed to see a vision in it. It's like a red looking glass, like seeing yourself in a mirror. Only you see yourself in that badger's blood as you will look when you are about to die. Three or four men were looking inside that *hoka.* I was there, too. We were all young. The first man to look said, "Boy, I'm an old man, wrinkled and white-haired, stooped, no teeth left." He was happy about it. He knew he'd live to be an old granddaddy. The second one was not so happy. "I think I'm about through," he said. "I'm looking as you see me now. I die before one of my hairs gets gray!" Then it was my turn, but I didn't see anything, just the dark blood. But the two others were right. The one who had seen himself as an old man is still around. The other one died long ago, only a few months after he had looked inside that badger, just as he said, before his hair turned gray.

We use a badger's bone pizzle, his penis, for sewing, or as an awl. You polish it, make it shiny. It lasts forever. This is a good tool, so valuable that you get a good horse in exchange for it.

There are some animals, a kind of gopher, very fast, with a black line down their faces. They got a lot of power; they can hypnotize you, even kill you. The power is in their eyes. They live with the prairie dogs. They are real subway users, traveling underground. They are so fast, your eyes can hardly follow them. Your eye is still here, he's already over there. They tell a funny story about a man who wanted to get one of these creatures. He was told to be fast. Shoot it and then run like hell, grab it before it disappears into its hole. The man made up his mind to be real quick about it. He shot and ran like the dickens. Something hit him in the seat of his pants—his own bullet! The earth from a gopher hole is also very powerful. It can protect you in war, make you bulletproof. I use it for curing certain illnesses.

An animal doesn't have to be big to be powerful. There's an ant power. Some ants have no eyes, but they can feel their way. They go out and bring back those rocks, called *yuwipi,* to put on their anthills. Tiny rocks, the size of seed beads, shiny, agate-like, little stones as clear as snow. Sometimes instead of these they bring tiny fossils. It takes two ants to get one of those rocks. One might be stepped upon and die. The ants take no chances.

We medicine men go out to look for anthills and get these tiny rocks. They are sacred. We put 405 of them into our gourds and rattles which we use in our ceremonies. They represent the 405 trees which grow in our land. *Tašuška šaša*—the red ants—we mash them up and put them in our medicine. If somebody gets shot we give this to him to drink. This ant medicine makes the wound heal faster. As to what you people call fossils, these too are used by us. Deep in the Badlands we find the bones of *unktegila,* the giant, the water monster, which lived long before human beings appeared. On a hill there lies the backbone of one of them, right along the spine of that mound. I have been up there, riding the ridge like a horse; that's the only way you can move on it. It's spooky, like riding the monster. At night there are spirit lights flitting about on that hill. I find things here which I use in my doctoring.

*Iktomé*—the spider—has a power, too, but it is evil. His body is short, and everything is in one place, in the center, with its legs spread out. It's sitting in its web, waiting for a fly. Iktomé is really a man. He's a foolish guy, a smart-ass; he wants to trick everybody, wants to tantalize people, make them miserable. But he is easy to outwit.

You have to listen to all these creatures, listen with your mind. They have secrets to tell. Even a kind of cricket, called *ptewoyake,* a wingless hopper, is used to tell us where to find buffalo. It has nothing to tell us now.

Butterflies talk to the women. A spirit will get into a beautiful butterfly, fly over to a young squaw, sit on her shoulder. The spirit will talk through that butterfly to the young squaw and tell her to become a medicine woman. We still have a couple of these ladies. I helped one, taught her what she must know, and she is doing a good job on the reservation. She is honest, so honest that the very poor, the down-and-out winos, really believe in her. She doesn't take any money from them, just does her best for the sake of helping them.

I have a nephew, Joe Thunderhawk, who is a healer.

He has the coyote power. On his drum is painted the picture of a coyote, showing Joe's vision. This coyote power has been in the Thunderhawk family for a long time. Many years ago Joe's grandfather traveled in the wintertime. The snows were deep and darkness surprised him in a canyon. He had to hole up in there, trying to keep from freezing to death. In the middle of the night something came up to him, settling down by his legs. He saw that it was a coyote. They gave each other warmth, keeping each other alive, until the next morning. When that man got up to travel again, the coyote followed him.

After that, Joe's grandfather would hear the coyote bark at night, near his home. It would bark in two ways—one bark sounding like a dog, the other like a little boy. One barking meant that something good was about to happen, the other foreshadowed misfortune. Joe's grandfather became a medicine man and a prophet. The coyote told him of things to come. When the old man died, his knowledge died with him. He had not been able to pass it on.

One day Joe Thunderhawk passed through that same canyon where his grandfather and the coyote had warmed each other long ago. My nephew was in a wagon. Suddenly he had a feeling that someone was following him. He looked back and there was a coyote, right behind him. It was kind of lame and very thin. It started to bark in two ways—like a dog and like a child.

That night Joe Thunderhawk dreamed about this coyote and understood that he was meant to be a medicine man, that he would carry on his grandfather's work. He is working now in the Indian way, with his own medicines, curing sick people who would have to undergo surgery otherwise. Thus the coyote power has returned to the Thunderhawk family.

As for myself, the birds have something to tell me. The eagle, the owl. In an eagle there is all the wisdom of the world; that's why we have an eagle feather at the top of the pole during a *yuwipi* ceremony. If you are planning to kill an eagle, the minute you think of that he knows it, knows what you are planning. The black-tailed deer has this wisdom, too. That's why its tail is tied farther down at the *yuwipi* pole. This deer, if you shoot at him, you won't hit him. He just stands right there and the bullet comes right back and hits you. It is like somebody saying bad things about you and they come back at him.

In one of my great visions I was talking to the birds, the winged creatures. I was saddened by the death of my mother. She had held my hand and said just one word: "pitiful." I don't think she grieved for herself; she was sorry for me, a poor Indian she would leave in a white man's world. I cried up on that vision hill, cried for help, stretched out my hands toward the sky and then put the blanket over myself—that's all I had, the blanket and the pipe, and a little tobacco for an offering. I didn't know what to expect. I wanted to touch the power, feel it. I had the thought to give myself up, even if it would kill me. So I just gave myself to the winds, to nature, not giving a damn about what could happen to me.

All of a sudden I hear a big bird crying, and then quickly he hit me on the back, touched me with his spread wings. I heard the cry of an eagle, loud above the voices of many other birds. It seemed to say, "We have been waiting for you. We knew you would come. Now you are here. Your trail leads from here. Let our voices guide you. We are your friends, the feathered people, the two-legged, the four-legged, we are your friends, the creatures, little tiny ones, eight legs, twelve legs—all those who crawl on the earth. All the little creatures which fly, all those under water. The powers of each one of us we will share with you and you will have a ghost with you always—another self."

That's me, I thought, no other thing than myself,

different, but me all the same, unseen, yet very real. I was frightened. I didn't understand it then. It took me a lifetime to find out.

And again I heard the voice amid the bird sounds, the clicking of beaks, the squeaking and chirping. "You have love for all that has been placed on this earth, not like the love of a mother for her son, or of a son for his mother, but a bigger love which encompasses the whole earth. You are just a human being, afraid, weeping under that blanket, but there is a great space within you to be filled with that love. All of nature can fit in there." I was shivering, pulling the blanket tighter around myself, but the voices repeated themselves over and over again, calling me "Brother, brother, brother." So this is how it is with me. Sometimes I feel like the first being in one of our Indian legends. This was a giant made of earth, water, the moon and the winds. He had timber instead of hair, a whole forest of trees. He had a huge lake in his stomach and a waterfall in his crotch. I feel like this giant. All of nature is in me, and a bit of myself is in all of nature.

PETE CATCHES: "I too feel this way. I live in an age which has passed. I live like fifty years ago, a hundred years ago. I like it that way. I want to live as humbly, as close to the earth as I can. Close to the plants, the weeds, the flowers that I use the medicine. The Great Spirit has seen to it that man can survive in this way, can live as he is meant to live. So I and my wife are dwelling in a little cabin—no electricity, no tap water, no plumbing, no road. This is what we want. This simple log cabin knows peace. That's how we want to be for the rest of our lives. I want to exist apart from the modern world, get out, way out, in the sticks, and live much closer to nature, even, than I am doing now. I don't even want to be called a medicine man, just a healing man, because this is what I am made for. I don't ask for anything. A white doctor has a fee, a priest has a fee. I have no fee. A man goes away from me healed. That is my reward. Sometimes I do not have the power—it makes me sad. When I have the power, then I am happy. Some men think of money, how to get it. That never comes into my mind. We live off nature, my wife and I; we hardly need anything. We will somehow live. The Great Spirit made the flowers, the streams, the pines, the cedars—takes care of them. He lets a breeze go through there, makes them breathe it, waters them, makes them grow. Even the one that is down in the crags, in the rocks. He tends to that, too. He takes care of me, waters me, feeds me, makes me live with the plants and animals as one of them. This is how I wish to remain, an Indian, all the days of my life. This does not mean that I want to shut myself off. Somehow many people find their way to my cabin. I like this. I want to be in communication, reach out to people everywhere, impart a little of our Indian way, the spirit's way, to them.

"At the same time, I want to withdraw further and further away from everything, to live like the ancient ones. On the highway you sometimes see a full-blood Indian thumbing a ride. I never do that. When I walk the road, I expect to walk the whole way. That is deep down in me, a kind of pride. Someday I'll still move my cabin farther into the hills, maybe do without a cabin altogether, become part of the woods. There the spirit still has something for us to discover—an herb, a sprig, a flower—a very small flower, maybe, and you can spend a long time in its contemplation, thinking about it. Not a rose—yellow, white, artificial, big. I hear they are breeding black roses. That's not natural. These things are against nature. They make us weak. I abhor them.

"So as I get older, I burrow more and more into the hills. The Great Spirit made them for us, for me. I want to blend with them, shrink into them, and finally disappear in them. As my brother Lame Deer has said, all of nature is in us, all of us is in nature. That is as it should be. Tell me, what are you going to call the chapter of your book in which you put the things we have talked about today? I know, you will call it 'Talking to the Owls and the Butterflies.' "

# 8
# Two in a Blanket

About this men-women business. You tell me one can't have a book nowadays without a lot of sex. That's O.K. with me. Right from the start I'll have to tell you a big secret. I'll just whisper, because I don't dare to say it aloud: We Sioux are real bashful. Boys are shy, the girls even more so. Now the cat is out of the bag!

In the old days the *wincincalas,* the good-looking girls, were pretty hard to get. It takes a good man to find the right woman because they are always looking away, hiding their faces, and you can't tell if they are beautiful or ugly or what. If you talk to them, they don't answer. If you come close, they run away. Some of that shyness remains. Bashful or not, we Indians are no prudes. Looking around you, seeing all these families with eight, ten, twelve kids, you know that the people are busy at night, especially when they don't have that TV to take their minds off more important things.

But at the same time we don't show affection when other people are around, kiss or hold hands. Not only lovers, married people, too, are shy with each other in public.

In the old days it wasn't easy for a boy and girl to meet. There was no privacy in the family tipi, and sneaking off into the sagebrush all by yourselves was dangerous, somebody unfriendly might be lying in wait there, having his knife out for your scalp. And if you were a tipi-creeper you'd find out that mothers had a habit of tying a hair rope around their daughters' waists, passing it through her legs. This was a "No Trespassing" sign. If a boy was found fooling around with that rope, the women would burn his tipi down or kill his horse. My grandmother told me about a certain medicine the Santee boys used when they went tipi-creeping. It was supposed to make everybody blind and deaf to what that boy might be doing. If there ever was such a medicine, it's long forgotten now.

You could, of course, wait for a girl near the river, knowing that she would have to show up with her skin bag every morning to get water for her family. That was one place to get acquainted. But what good did it do? You both were likely too shy to start a conversation. Maybe, to attract attention, you'd shoot an arrow through her water bag. Big deal! There was really only one way for the young folks to get together. The girl had to stand outside her family's tipi with a big blanket. Her lover would come up and she would cover both of them with her blanket. Inside that robe they would put their faces closely together and whisper to each other. The people who saw them standing there respected their privacy and pretended not to see them. If a girl was pretty and popular, there would be a stag line—three or four bucks waiting their turn. It was all very innocent, this old-style dating.

If a boy wasn't satisfied just standing in a blanket rubbing noses with his girl, he could ask an elk-medicine man to make him a flute and to give him a song which would turn a girl's head. The flutes, which always looked like a bird's head with an open beak, could be very powerful. If a girl heard that flute, made by an elk-dreamer, she left her tipi and ran after that sound. She couldn't help herself; the medicine was that strong.

I know quite a few of those elk songs, old and new ones. I'll sing you the song of the ghost lover. There lived a young man, long ago, whom no woman could resist. A conjurer had given him a powerful love medicine, and when he played his flute at night a girl would just get up and go to him. Her mind told her to stay in the tipi, but her feet would just keep going to where he was. He was the kind of man who wanted to conquer women the way a warrior conquers his enemies. He was counting coup on those girls.

One day this young man did not return from his hunt. His parents waited for him day after day, and when he did not come back they asked a medicine man to find him with his searching stones. The medicine man said, "This young man has been killed," and he told the parents where to search. They found the body out on the prairie—dead with a wound in his chest. They put the young man's body on a scaffold and the tribe moved to another place. One evening, when the people were busy eating and talking, the dogs at the edge of the camp started to howl mournfully. Nobody could see what was stirring them up. But one could hear owls hooting softly in a spirit way, and the trees were making a strange noise. The people got an uneasy feeling. They put out all their fires and went into their tipis.

The warriors were listening. They knew a spirit was coming, and finally they made out that young man's voice. It was singing, "Weeping I roam. I thought I was the only one. I thought I was the only one who had known many loves, many girls. Now I am having a hard time. I am roaming and I'll have to wander for as long as the world stands." After that night people heard this song many times. A lone girl coming home too late, a woman getting water too early in the morning, when it was still dark, they would hear this song and see a shape like a man wrapped in a gray blanket. Even as a ghost that young man won't leave the girls alone.

At a time of parting our girls often make up songs for the one they love who has to go to war. When you hear these songs you make the crying sound, no matter how tough you are. At the time of Pearl Harbor a girl made up this song for her boyfriend: "If you leave me, to prove that I love you, the people will hear

Mako Šiča—the Badlands, strewn with the bones of the fabled monster Uncegila; a place to hide yourself, the last refuge of the ghost dancers.

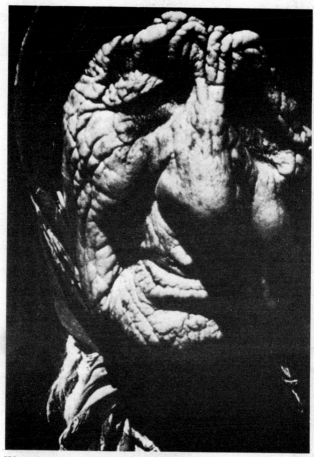

We are a part of the nature around us, and the older we get, the more we come to look like it. In the end we become part of the landscape with a face like the Badlands.

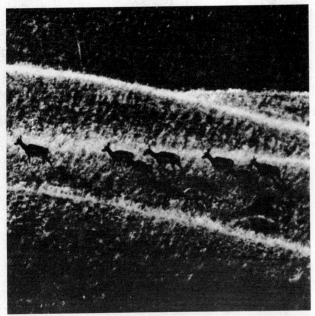

Paha Sapa—the Black Hills—were sacred to us. We used to go there to pray. Here you can still see antelope, at Wind Cave and in Custer State Park. They have been put on a reservation like us Indians, but maybe they don't know it. They are beautiful animals.

I like to watch the long-eared mule deer on a high ridge, outlined against the sky. All living creatures are my relatives —even a tiny bug.

We had no word for the strange animal we got from the white man—the horse. So we called it *šunka wakan*, "holy dog." For bringing us the horse we could almost forgive you for bringing us whiskey. Horses make a landscape look more beautiful.

Forty years ago I went on a vision quest on this hill, staying alone here without food or water, praying, waiting for a dream.

Here is one of our young medicine men, Leonard Crow Dog, about to go down into the vision pit.

My grandfather fought Custer. Some of my people died at the Little Bighorn, but only the white soldiers are buried there. Seeing this old Cheyenne coup stick planted on this battlefield makes me feel good.

Indian gravestones are not made to last. Often they are made of wood, but they reflect our nature and our beliefs. Only the mountains and the stars last forever.

Indian Town, with its tar-paper shacks, rusty house trailers, disintegrating log cabins and toppling privies. Some people live in abandoned auto bodies.

The buffalo is our brother, almost part of ourselves. There is power in a buffalo, but there is no power in an Angus or a Hereford, man-bred animals.

A few years ago a Sioux was killed inside this saloon. "NO INDIANS ALLOWED" signs are supposed to be illegal. The Indian words on the right mean: "Sioux, come here to be merry." I wonder whether the white owner knows this.

Tourists like to photograph this jail in Mission, South Dakota. They never take pictures of the inside, which is less funny.

This is Wounded Knee, the hill where over two hundred Sioux men, women and children—massacred by the soldiers—are buried in a common grave. The sweat lodge and the church are a symbol of two religions, Indian and white, existing side by side.

You white men killed your Jesus; we Indians haven't killed our peace pipe yet.

*Inipi*—the sweat bath—precedes all our important ceremonies. It is also a ceremony all by itself.

At the beginning of a *yuwipi* ceremony, the medicine man has his fingers tied together. . . .

. . . After this, he is wrapped up like a mummy in a star blanket and laid on the floor. Then all lights are put out so that the spirits can come in.

My old war bonnet of eagle feathers would fetch a good price nowadays, but I won't sell it—even when I am broke.

Joy and sadness, the whole history of my tribe, is reflected in the faces of my people.

Pulling away at a thong fastened to a skewer embedded in one's flesh until the skin rips apart—this some of us must endure during the sun dance.

This girl likes to draw her dreams, putting them down on paper. Dreams are important to us.

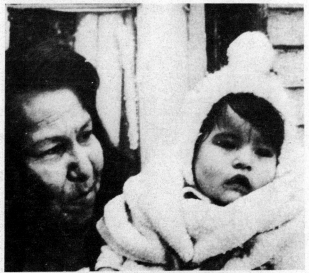
My wife, Ida, and one of our little relatives.

it until a spoon would almost stand upright in it.

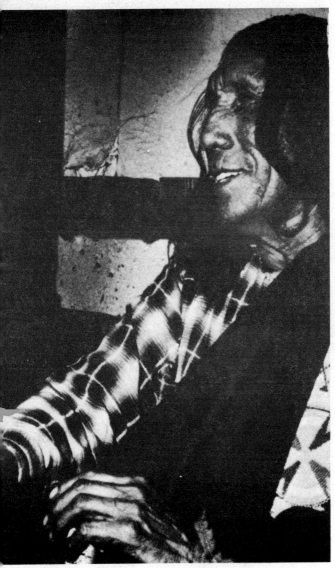

I remember Grandma making coffee on an old wood stove. The stuff got stronger and stronger each time she reboiled it until a spoon would almost stand upright in it.

I like to sing you some of the old Lakota songs. Somebody give me a drum.

A man may live in a big city like a white man, but he will travel hundreds of miles to come to the sun dance and be Indian again.

The pipe—that's us. Its stem is our body, our spine. The red stone of the bowl is our flesh and blood.

The smoke of our sacred pipe is the breath of the Great Spirit. Sitting together smoking the pipe, we form the circle without end, which contains within it every living thing upon this earth.

me cry openly. The day you leave I'll cry for you unashamed. My tears will be seen by everybody. So remember, whatever happens, I'll be waiting for you. You'll see it printed in all the newspapers that I cried for you openly." Our girls know how to love, even though they are usually too shy to show it in public.

Shy or not, that sex was there, but it had to be done with good manners. The aim, of course, was to get married and have children. Even our oldest lady— she's so old she doesn't know when she was born and never got a Christian name, with a face like the Badlands—she told you: "You should have come to take my picture eighty years ago when I was beautiful." She still has that spark in her eye. It never dies.

The right way to go about a marriage used to be for two families to get together and decide on it. You just didn't marry without the parents' consent. It would cost a boy some fine horses to get a wife, to show that he respected her and that he was a good provider. But if he was poor and didn't even have a single horse, there was a way for him, too. We had a ceremony that was called "He wanted her so much, we gave her to him," and that was a fine marriage also.

Sometimes parents wanted to give their daughter to a famous old chief, while the girl had her heart set on some young boy, a nobody. In that case she eloped, took one of her dad's horses and took off with the one she liked best. They stayed out by themselves for a few days and then came back and set up house. Well, everybody knew what went on when these two had been alone. There was no use huffing and puffing. What's done is done. In sex matters we have always been very forgiving, taking pity on the young people, the oldsters remembering the time when they had been cutting up. The families accepted those elopements, and that made good weddings too.

More and more often, young Indian couples who have been married in the white man's way only, in a church, or just in the marriage bureau where they took out a license, feel that something is missing. They don't feel properly wedded until I join them together in the old, Indian way, with a blanket around them, their hands grasping the sacred pipe, their wrists bound together with a strip of red cloth. My ceremonies are very simple, with no trimmings. You have seen me do this in South Dakota and, once, in your own place where I married that beautiful young Navajo couple. Your place is good for that, because you have my buffalo skull from the sun dance, and also because there's always some sweet grass and *kinnickinnick* in your home, you got everything I need.

During such a ceremony, when I want the spirit to affect me, I wear no fancy outfit. I take my shirt off. I want my arms to be bare. I want to get that smoke around me, be touched by it. A ceremony like this is like a dream. I can sense things that I don't notice otherwise. During that rite, when I touched the young couple, I felt a good fortune and it made me glad. On the other side, I had two sad handshakes there from the right. Those people could fall sick, or even be dead in a year or two. I don't even know them, but their handshake told me of a misfortune. I sense this only when the pipe—the stem and the bowl—are joined together, ready for the smoke. The moment I open up the pipe, disconnect it, these feelings of good or bad things to come disappear.

I put a red blanket over this Navajo boy and girl, let them take hold of the peace pipe, tied their hands together with a cloth, sang the old prayers over them. Now this is what I told them: "We are here in the big white man's city. You are supposed to stand on the earth, your mother, but you are in an apartment way up on the eighth floor. I will ask this of you, while I am doing my work, I want you to pretend that you are home. Forget this old city, remember that there's a hill, a spot of earth you feel drawn to which made you feel the presence of the spirits. Pretend that you are standing there on top of the world. A city is not the right place for an Indian ceremony, but our thinking will make it right. Forget about the traffic, the big noise outside, concentrate, hold onto this pipe; that way our ceremony will be good, and from the four corners of the world, from the sky above and from the earth beneath, the blessing of the Great Spirit will be with us.

"The same way, the Indian people who are here with us remember where you are from. Remember your parents at home, remember your grandfathers, remember the hard times you had, and the good times, too. Remember it always. I give you a looking glass, a very small-size looking glass. Now, what do you see? You see an Indian face in there. All the joy and suffering of all of us, the things we did, the things that were done to us, it can be seen in your faces. So before anything else, know what you are—an Indian fighting to survive in a rugged, tough world.

"But you and her alone, the spirit is with you as you stand there under this blanket, and the Great Spirit will give you a little gift, a new life, and only when you get this gift will my ceremony be complete. It's a nest you are building, and I pray to the Great Spirit to help you. And now we are all going to smoke the pipe. *He-hechetu.*"

And that was all, except that I will say that your wife cooked good that day and that there was plenty for everybody. After a ceremony you eat. Good food at a wedding, nobody left hungry, a little morsel left for the spirits—that's a good beginning.

At home, when I marry a boy and girl the Indian way, there's more to it. More talk, more medicine men, a tipi, an altar, a big open space under the sky, singers and drummers, a big feed outdoors, a give-away of presents and afterward, when it gets dark, everybody dresses up for the big dance. But one ceremony is as good as the other. It's only a few main things that count.

And this main thing, in marriage, is children. We Sioux used to deliver our own babies. You want to have a good baby you have to look for the right midwife. We had an old woman who was very good with a birth. This old squaw always got a horse, or its value, for a delivery. When she did her work the baby was always healthy, good-natured, and seldom cried. That woman was busy all the time. She was a good witch.

Having a child was always a great moment, like counting coup for a warrior. Usually there was a stick planted in the ground for the mother to grab hold of. Among our Burned-Thigh tribe a woman was standing up at first, then she knelt down to deliver the baby, kind of squatting, pressing against that stick, then she stood up again waiting for the afterbirth to come out. We have all kinds of medicines to help during a childbirth, but I'll tell you about them when we talk about herbs and doctoring.

Some old women also used a squaw belt to help a mother get the baby out, tightening it over her belly, pressing down, kneading her. A belt of deerskin was also good for the mother's abdomen after the birth had taken place. A newborn baby was put on a clean piece of deerskin and washed with warm water in which the wacanga herb had been steeped. The baby's navel was disinfected with the powder of a puffball and then bandaged. We used a kind of absorbent cattail plant for a diaper.

Before the child arrived a grandmother always made two little doll-like forms in the shape of a turtle or a lizard. The lizard, *manitukala,* is a little guardian spirit. It lives on nothing almost. It gets its moisture just from the dampness of the earth. They are very fast and hard to kill. You cut a leg or tail off and this little creature grows another one. The turtle, too, is very tough. These little animals stand for strength and long life. For this reason they are chosen to protect a

148

baby against evil spirits. Those little turtle and lizard dolls are only about as long as a hand. They are made of deerskin and covered with beads. One puts the child's umbilical cord into one of these charms; the second is stuffed with grass. This one was made to fool evil spirits, attract them. The one which had the umbilical cord in it was sewed to the baby's cradle and later, when it began to walk, on its clothes. After five years the mother kept it.

A young mother's aunt usually made her a fine cradleboard, beaded all over. They were very heavy. If there were more aunts than one on her father's side, she could receive more than one cradle. We don't have many of them left, because they bring good prices from the museum people. They go for as high as 300 or 400 dollars.

I am always hoping that there will be some twins in the marriages which I perform. That would make me happy. You see, love is something that you can leave behind you when you die. It's that powerful. The *nagi*, the soul, it will roam and travel. If two people loved each other very much they come back again as twins. They had a great love, they're whirling around there, and the Great Spirit has pity and lets them come up again. Those little traveling souls come right back in again—twins, triplets, not only lovers but a brother and sister too who were especially fond of each other could come back like this. One reborn this way could carry a memory going way back. I used to know one, a man named Somebody, who remembered part of his former life over 200 years ago.

Some parents, if they had a child who died, a little one they loved above everything, wanted to keep its soul, wanted to "own the ghost." They would keep a lock of the child's hair for over a year, and then they would have a great spirit-keeping ceremony. They'd put up a spirit lodge and a spirit bowl with food for the little soul. For this day you saved up things to give away. You gave up everything, even the shirt off your back, not as the white man means it, as a figure of speech, but you really did this, because such a big give-away often ended with the parents handing out the clothes they wore. You gave till it hurt, till there was nothing left.

Most Indian marriages last longer than white ones because we feel very responsible for the children. Both families, his and hers, want to get into the act and spoil the little ones. That holds people together. But we had our divorces too. A man could send his wife back to her family together with her property if she was no good. He could even perform a *wihpeya,* a "throwing-his-wife-away" ceremony. If she was lazy, or if she was cutting up with another man, he'd get the men from his warrior society together and do a dance and throw a certain stick among his friends, saying, "Who wants her, come and get her. I don't want her anymore."

He'd better have a damn good reason for doing this, or his name would suffer and her relatives would be after him. And would she be mad! That throw-away wife, she'd come at him with her skinning knife and cut him, or, worse, sneak up to his best horse and hamstring it. But it was not all a one-way business. A woman could divorce her husband too, simply by throwing all his things out of her tipi. He'd know what that meant: Get out and don't come back.

When it comes to what you call facts of life we were always very straightforward, didn't tell any fancy tales to the children or lower our voices when we told a sexy story. But we have a great sense of privacy, of pretending not to notice. That's very important, because we have to make our own privacy where it really doesn't exist. In a tipi, where the whole family was sleeping, and today, with often many persons living in the same room, you learn ways to preserve your own privacy and that of the people around you. You don't intrude.

You never hear the whispering, moaning and wrestling, and yet you know Papa and Mama are making love, because every year there is a new little brother or sister as a living proof. So we Indians have learned to make love like the porcupines—very carefully. Not because we want to hide something but because we don't want to show our feelings, troubling somebody else with them, making him a part of it.

We have a special word to express our shyness in sex—*wistelkiya*. That's a bashfulness between male and female relatives. It means that you don't pronounce the names of certain relations, look them in the face, or talk to them directly. It's not because we are ashamed of the sex act but because of our fear of what you call incest. This for us was a most evil thing, so bad you didn't even want to think or hear of it.

Therefore you could josh your sister-in-law, be playful with her, tell her jokes, and she would do the same with you. If you ever stepped out of line with her—well, that could cause a big row, lead to a hell of a fight with her husband, if she was married, but it wouldn't be anything terribly shameful or unnatural. It would just be misbehaving.

But it was different with a man's own relatives, his sisters or female cousins. You don't look them straight in the eye, kid around or touch them. And a girl has to be very reserved with her brothers and male cousins. But between a man and his mother-in-law, a woman and her father-in-law—why, it is just as if there was a brick wall between them. They avoid each other completely. That is because your in-laws are looked upon as real parents. Cutting up with your mother-in-law would be like sleeping with your own ma; you can't even imagine such a thing.

I know of a young man who was friendly with an old lady. He liked to drop in on her for a chat and a piece of pie. Those two really liked each other. After a while the young man fell in love with the old lady's daughter. He lived with her as man and wife and they had kids together, but he would not marry her, because that would have made the old woman he loved so much into his mother-in-law. Then he couldn't have been friends with her anymore.

It's hard to avoid your mother-in-law altogether. If they happen to be in the same room the son-in-law sits in one corner and she in another, fidgety, as far apart as possible. He is hungry and muttering to himself, loud enough for her to hear, "I wish somebody would cook a meal for me." He isn't talking to her, mind you; he's just thinking aloud. But she suddenly gets the idea of putting the kettle on her old wood burner. She is talking to herself, too: "Those lazy so-and-so's; nobody cut wood for me today. I wish somebody had." Well, the young man suddenly gets it into his head to go out and do some chopping. That's one way of communicating. My dad was very old-fashioned. He never talked to his mother-in-law. If he wanted to tell her something, he told his wife, and she told her.

One thing we are particular about in our sex beliefs is when a woman has her period. We call this *isnati*—dwelling alone. Formerly a girl had to stay in a little hut by herself for four days, her mother going there from time to time to feed her. We didn't think that menstruating was something unclean or to be ashamed of. On the contrary, when a young girl had her period for the first time her parents treated the event as something sacred which made her into a woman. After the first *isnati* they gave her a big feast, invited everybody and had a give-away of presents.

But we thought that menstruation had a strange power that could bring harm under some circumstances. This power could work in some cases against the girl, in other cases against somebody else. If a girl was tanning the hides of certain animals during her period she could break out in boils. She had to abstain from a number of things, just as a man had to abstain from sexual intercourse for four days before a vision quest or some other religious ceremony. A woman shouldn't come near a medicine man's holy bundle or take part in a ceremony when she had her time. Our young women don't dwell apart anymore during their periods, but we are still careful that their power shouldn't clash with that of a medicine man. It could harm them both.

We think that if a woman has two little ones growing inside her, if she is going to have twins, sometimes instead of giving birth to two babies they have formed up in her womb into just one, into a half man—half woman kind of being. We call such a person a *winkte*. He could be a hermaphrodite with male and female parts. In the old days a *winkte* dressed like a woman, cooked and did beadwork. He behaved like a squaw and did not go to war. To us a man is what nature, or his dreams, make him. We accept him for what he wants to be. That's up to him. Still, fathers did not like to see their boys hanging around a *winkte's* place and told them to stay away.

There are good men among the *winktes* and they have been given certain powers. As far as I know no white man has ever interviewed a *winkte*. That's why we went to this bar where I knew I could find one. I guess you weren't even sure of whether I was talking to a man or to a woman.

Well, the first thing this *winkte* asked me was "Do you have some wine?" I told him he could have all he wanted if he told me the truth about *winktes*. He told me that if nature puts a burden on a man by making him different, it also gives him a power. He told me that a *winkte* has a gift of prophecy and that he himself could predict the weather. In our tribe we go to a *winkte* to give a newborn child a secret name. Most often this is done for boys, but sometimes he could give such a name to a girl. Ida, for instance, got one. A name given by a *winkte* is supposed to bring its

bearer luck and long life. In the old days it was worth a
fine horse—at the least. The *winkte* told me that these
names are very sexy, even funny, very outspoken
names. You don't let a stranger know them; he would
kid you about it. Having a *winkte* name could make a
man famous. Sitting Bull, Black Elk, even Crazy
Horse had secret *winkte* names which only a few
people know. The *winkte* in the bar does a little
prophesying. He told a woman she would live to be
eighty years old, and she gave him a fine pair of
moccasins for that. He also does certain cures and
uses herbs known to *winktes*. Well, this man-woman
told me that in the old days the *winktes* used to call
each other sisters and had a special hill where they
were buried. I asked him when he died, when he went
south, what he would be in the spirit land, a man or a
woman. He told me he would be both. It was a long
interview, lasting through two bottles of wine.

The anthropologists are always after us, wanting to
know about Mister Indian's sex life. For years and
years it used to be "Who killed Custer?" Now it's
"aboriginal sexual patterns." One middle-aged, white
anthro-lady went so far as to ask an Indian man to
undress and get on top of her. She wanted him to keep
his war bonnet on, though, and arranged for a third
party to take their picture. In the interest of science, I
guess. But the Indian respectfully declined. Some
folks have fun with those anthropologists, telling them
wild stories, playing games with them. The game
works like this:

Anthropologist: "How's your sex life?"

Indian: "Fine. How is yours?"

Anthropologist: "Do you always have the same
position?"

Indian: "Yes, I've been an ambulance driver for
twenty years."

Anthropologist: "You have a taboo about your
organ?"

Indian: "The only guy around here with an organ is the Catholic priest. You should see him working it."

Some of our people are very good at this kind of thing.

I know a very jolly man who was going with a girl and wanted to get married. They were told to get a blood test first. They tried, but always something went wrong. The car stalled, they ran out of gas, or it snowed like hell. At last one day everything worked. The cars ran well and the weather was perfect. He took her parents along for the ride. When they arrived at the doctor's office he was out on an emergency call. They were told to come back the next day. They put up someplace, and that jolly man and his girl had a good time at night. In the morning he was no longer in a mood to get married. But he didn't want to disappoint her parents, who had come a long way. He gave them a big smile. "Say, folks, when you got hitched they didn't have this blood test. That way you are not properly married. I'll give you a treat." So he marched them off to the doctor's office and the *parents* got the blood test.

Years ago I happened to be in the superintendent's office. The door opens and in comes a fat lady pushing a man ahead of her with a big feather stuck in his cap. She was talking a blue streak in Indian: "This man is no good. We been married for two weeks and this man makes love to me all the time. He just loves me to death. You must stop it." The husband says nothing; he just looks sleepy.

We had just got a new young superintendent, and this was his first case to settle. I had to translate. That woman never stopped complaining; she went on and on. "I'm in misery. That old goat is never done. We never sleep. What do you say, Superintendent?" The superintendent blushed. He started to explain: "In our white man's way we call this a honeymoon. That's when we have a big time. Consider yourself lucky. He

has a husband's rights. Give him another try." I'm
trying not to laugh, translating all this. I tell her
"honeymoon," but it means nothing in Indian. She
got real excited: "Honey, the moon, what has it got to
do with me? This white man is crazy." The superintendent got redder and redder. He repeated it over
and over again in English: "Ho-ney-moon, ho-ney-
moon." I told her in Indian: "That's what the white
men do at the start—go at it all the time. That's what
this honeymoon means. You've got to take it." She
gave the superintendent a dirty look and said, "If I die
before my time it will be your fault." Then she pushed
her husband out the door. "O.K., old man, let's go and
*tawiton, tawiton, tawiton* till we drop dead." You have
a word for *tawiton,* but it's shorter.

You see, we don't have great sex problems here.
Maybe the old-timers did, the ones with many wives.
Back in the twenties I asked an old man who at one
time had been living with six wives, "How could you
keep it up?" He told me the secret. He said, "You can't
play favorites. Your number-one wife could be old and
wrinkled, while number six is young and tempting,
but you have to be good to all of them. You give them a
fine time, one after the other, but you don't 'pop' with
the older ones. You save that for the young hot one."

When I was a small boy we still had one old man
who lived openly with two wives. One day the missionaries went to him and said, "Chief, you are looked
up to by the whole tribe, but having two wives is
setting a very bad example. You must tell one of your
wives to go away." The old man looked hard at the
missionary and said, "You go tell her!" And that was
the end of it.

What about sex and the medicine man? Well as I
said before, they don't pay him to be good; they pay
him because he has the power. A medicine man has to
find out about all of life and sex. That's the most
important part of it, and, of course, a medicine man

has to deal with sex in his doctoring. One medicine man whom I taught myself told me he had cured a case of nymphomania with an herb. If she was unhappy, all right, but if she was a happy nymphomaniac, why cure her?

There's a medicine that will stop a woman from giving birth. It's an herb with which a medicine man could flush out a woman's womb without any harm, just like the white man's castor oil. But this doesn't mean that we want to help women from having babies. My doctoring is something I have to do right. On this reservation some people ask me always for this herb, but I don't give it, I don't sell it; it is for the best. If the spirit advises me that a woman better not go through with a birth, when I know that she had a deformed or retarded baby inside her, that's the only time I use this so-called flesh medicine.

What do I think about birth control? I have thought about it and gone to a lot of people. I asked about ten of my best friends personally, and nine of them said, "No good." And one says birth control is good, but he's a wino, an alcoholic. You see, the population explosion doesn't worry us much. All these long years, when the only good Indian was a dead Indian, the bodies at Wounded Knee, the Sand Creek Massacre, the Washita, all this killing of women and children, the measles and small pox wiping out whole tribes— the way I see it, the Indians have already done all the population control one could ask of them a hundred times over. Our problem is survival. Overpopulation —that's your worry.

There are charms that can make a girl fall in love with a man. I could split up a couple, too, make a man leave his wife, and the other way round, make her leave him. There's money in the witch-doctor business, but I leave this to the conjurers. I never do that. I could go into the hills, search for a plant with little seeds all rolled up in a ball that acts like a Spanish fly.

You put two of these tiny seeds into a girl's drink or sandwich and pretty soon she'll scratch and bite you all over in a nice way. It acts on a boy, too. It will make an old man feel young again, real young. But I keep this a secret, too. Well, maybe sometime when you and your wife are old and shriveled up, I'll do you a favor.

# 9
# Medicine, Good and Bad

I am a medicine man—a *wićaśa wakan*. "Medicine man"—that's a white man's world like squaw, papoose, Sioux, tomahawk—words that don't exist in the Indian language. I wish there were better words to make clear what "medicine man" stands for, but I can't find any, and you can't either, so I guess medicine man will have to do. But it doesn't convey the many different meanings that come to an Indian's mind when you say "medicine man."

We have different names for different men doing different things for which you have only that one puny name. First, we distinguish the healer—*pejuta wićaśa*—the man of herbs. He does not cure with the herbs alone; he must also have the *wakan* power to heal. Then we have the *yuwipi*, the tied-one, the man who uses the power of the rawhide and the stones to find and to cure. We also speak of the *waayatan*—the man of vision who can foretell events which will happen in the future, who has been given the power to see ahead. Things that have come true according to such a man's prediction are called *wakinyanpi*. This word also means the winged-ones, those who fly through the air, because the power to foretell the future comes from them.

Then there is the *wapiya*—the conjurer—what you might call a witch doctor. If he is a good man he does the *waanazin*—the shooting at the disease, the drawing up and sucking out of your body evil things which have been put into a person by a bad spirit, such as a particular kind of gopher that will shoot sharp blades of grass and tiny bits of porcupine quills from his hole in the ground into your body, causing it to break out in boils.

If such a conjurer is bad, he himself will put a sickness into you which only he can cure—for a price. There are some fakers among this group of men. They give a little medicine to a soldier boy which is supposed to protect him from harm, make him bullet-proof and ensure his coming home safely. If he comes back in one piece, they collect. If he doesn't—well, that's just too bad.

Another kind of medicine man is the *heyoka*—the sacred clown—who uses his thunder power to cure some people. If you want to stretch the word out like a big blanket to cover everybody, even a peyote roadman could squeeze underneath it and qualify as a medicine man. But the more I think about it, the more I believe that the only real medicine man is the *wićaśa wakan*—the holy man. Such a one can cure, prophesy, talk to the herbs, command the stones, conduct the sun dance or even change the weather, but all this is of no great importance to him. There are merely stages he has passed through. The *wićaśa wakan* has gone beyond all this. He has the *wakanya wowanyanke*—the great vision. Sitting Bull was such a man. When he had his sun-dance vision at Medicine Deer Rock he saw many blue-coated soldiers fall backward into the Indian camp and he heard a voice telling him, "I give you these, because they have no ears." Sitting Bull knew then that the Indians would win the next battle. He did not fight himself, he commanded no men, he did not do anything except let his wisdom and power work for his people.

The *wićaśa wakan* wants to be by himself. He wants to be away from the crowd, from everyday matters. He likes to meditate, leaning against a tree or rock, feeling the earth move beneath him, feeling the weight of that big flaming sky upon him. That way he can figure things out. Closing his eyes, he sees many things clearly. What you see with your eyes shut is what counts.

The *wičaśa wakan* loves the silence, wrapping it around himself like a blanket—a loud silence with a voice like thunder which tells him of many things. Such a man likes to be in a place where there is no sound but the humming of insects. He sits facing the west, asking for help. He talks to the plants and they answer him. He listens to the voices of the *wama kaśkan*—all those who move upon the earth, the animals. He is as one with them. From all living beings something flows into him all the time, and something flows from him. I don't know where or what, but it's there. I know.

This kind of medicine man is neither good nor bad. He lives—and that's it, that's enough. White people pay a preacher to be "good," to behave himself in public, to wear a collar, to keep away from a certain kind of woman. But nobody pays an Indian medicine man to be good, to behave himself and act respectable. The *wičaśa wakan* just acts like himself. He has been given the freedom—the freedom of a tree or a bird. That freedom can be beautiful or ugly; it doesn't matter much.

Medicine men—the herb healers as well as our holy men—all have their own personal ways of acting according to their visions. The Great Spirit wants people to be different. He makes a person love a particular animal, tree or herb. He makes people feel drawn to certain favorite spots on this earth where they experience a special sense of well-being, saying to themselves, "That's a spot which makes me happy, where I belong." The Great Spirit is one, yet he is many. He is part of the sun and the sun is a part of him. He can be in a thunderbird or in an animal or plant.

A human being, too, is many things. Whatever makes up the air, the earth, the herbs, the stones is also part of our bodies. We must learn to be different, to feel and taste the manifold things that are us. The animals and plants are taught by Wakan Tanka what to do. They are not alike. Birds are different from each other. Some build nests and some don't. Some animals live in holes, others in caves, others in bushes. Some get along without any kind of home.

Even animals of the same kind—two deer, two owls—will behave differently from each other. Even your daughter's little pet hamsters, they all have their own ways. I have studied many plants. The leaves of one plant, on the same stem—none is exactly alike. On all the earth there is not one leaf that is exactly like another. The Great Spirit likes it that way. He only sketches out the path of life roughly for all the creatures on earth, shows them where to go, where to arrive at, but leaves them to find their own way to get there. He wants them to act independently according to their nature, to the urges in each of them.

If Wakan Tanka likes the plants, the animals, even little mice and bugs, to do this, how much more will he abhor people being alike, doing the same thing, getting up at the same time, putting on the same kind of store-bought clothes, riding the same subway, working in the same office at the same job with their eyes on the same clock and, worst of all, thinking alike all the time. All creatures exist for a purpose. Even an ant knows what that purpose is—not with its brain, but somehow it knows. Only human beings have come to a point where they no longer know why they exist. They don't use their brains and they have forgotten the secret knowledge of their bodies, their senses, or their dreams. They don't use the knowledge the spirit has put into every one of them; they are not even aware of this, and so they stumble along blindly on the road to nowhere—a paved highway which they themselves bulldoze and make smooth so that they can get faster to the big, empty hole which they'll find at the end, waiting to swallow them up. It's a quick, comfortable superhighway, but I know where it leads to. I have seen it. I've been there in my vision and it makes me shudder to think about it.

I believe that being a medicine man, more than anything else, is a state of mind, a way of looking at and understanding this earth, a sense of what it is all about. Am I a *wičaśa wakan?* I guess so. What else can or would I be? Seeing me in my patched-up, faded shirt, with my down-at-the-heels cowboy boots, the hearing aid whistling in my ear, looking at the flimsy shack with its bad-smelling outhouse which I call my home—it all doesn't add up to a white man's idea of a holy man. You've seen me drunk and broke. You've heard me curse or tell a sexy joke. You know I'm not better and wiser than other men. But I've been up on the hilltop, got my vision and my power; the rest is just trimmings. That vision never leaves me—not in jail, not while I'm painting funny signs advertising some hashhouse, not when I am in a saloon, not while I am with a woman, especially not then.

I am a medicine man because a dream told me to be one, because I am commanded to be one, because the old holy men—Chest, Thunderhawk, Chips, Good Lance—helped me to be one. There is nothing I can, or want, to do about it. I could cure you of a sickness just with a drink of pure cold water and the workings of my vision. Not always, but often enough. I want to be a *wičaśa wakan,* a man who feels the grief of others. A death anywhere make me feel poorer. A young woman and her child were killed the other night on the highway. I feel so deeply about them. At sundown I will talk to the Great Spirit for them. I will fill my pipe and offer it on their behalf. I do this always. Would you believe it, that when Robert Kennedy was assassinated shortly after he had come out here to talk to us Indians, I went into my sweat lodge and made an offering for him. Could you imagine a white man praying for Crazy Horse? I have passed through all the phases, the healing with herbs, the *yuwipi,* the peyote. I just took my pipe and went from this to a higher spot.

I want to speak some more about the ways of our medicine men, those still alive and those who have passed away. I'll close my eyes, thinking while I talk, let the spirit talk through me. This is a remembering. We have a word for this special kind of remembering, *waki-ksuya.* It means to recall, to travel back into the past, to hold communion with the spirits, to receive a message from them, to bring to one's mind the dead friends, to hear their voices once again, even to the point of having a vision. Don't let me spook you. I don't want to do all this now. I just want to lean back, close my eyes, let somebody else do the driving. I'll just keep talking and let the words find their own way.

You become a *pejuta wicaśa,* a medicine man and healer, because a dream tells you to do this. No one man dreams of all the medicines. You doctor where you know you have the power. You don't inherit it; you work for it, fast for it, try to dream it up, but it doesn't always come. It is true that some families produce a string of good medicine men, and it helps to have a holy man among your relatives who teaches you and tries to pass his power on to you. It works sometimes, but not always. Medicine men aren't horses. You don't breed them. You can give a boy a car for a present and teach him how to drive, but if there's no gas in the tank, the learning and the car won't do him any good. Sometimes the power skips a generation and reappears in a grandchild.

A medicine man, when he's old, tries to pass his vision and his knowledge to his son. There's a power line there, but sometimes no juice is coming through. If in spite of all the learning and trying and begging for a vision a man doesn't obtain this power, he'll know it. Most of the time he'll be honest about it and just stop trying. But sometimes a man will fake it, pretend to be something he isn't. In the end it will only bring misfortune on his own home. Trying to trick others, he'll only trick himself. So most men won't try this.

One of our greatest Sioux holy men was old Chips. Without him, maybe our religion would have died out. During the darkest years he kept his vision alive, worked it for the good of the people. He was a real *wičaśa wakan*. If he hadn't taught us, there would be no medicine men left among us now. He did it almost all by himself. Well, he passed his power on to his son, Ellis Chips, and he is a good man. But the real great power of the old holy man has passed on to his grandson Godfrey, who is still only a boy of sixteen. First the power was given to an elder brother. But this young man did not know how to handle it. He was too fond of the hard stuff, liking to have a glass or two now and then. "Take this burden away from me," he said. 'It is no good to me."

But the power turned up in the younger boy Godfrey. Nobody had tried to pass it on to him. The spirits, the *yuwipi*, picked him and talked to him for about three months. He didn't understand them and they scared him at first. He told his father about this. His father said, "Why don't you ask them for something to put in your ear so you will understand them?" Well, he did, and the *yuwipi* gave him something and told him to look for a certain herb. His dad told him to rub it in his ear and right then and there he understood what the spirits were saying. They told him he was going to be their interpreter and he was supposed to relate everything exactly as the *yuwipi* told him. So from that night on he's been their spokesman. He was only thirteen years old when this happened. He is our youngest *yuwipi* man.

Otherwise he is a cheerful, normal boy. He plays the usual boys' games and he likes to take machinery and gadgets apart to see how they work. The only way he is different from other kids is that he will not get into any fights anymore. If another boy hits him, he won't strike back. Also he won't go near a girl who has her monthly sickness, because this could be very bad for both of them. So in everyday life he is just another good-looking kid, but at night he is a very powerful *yuwipi*. The Chips family was related to Chief Crazy Horse, and people say that the spirit of this great warrior is sometimes present during young Chips's ceremonies. One of the spirits there is powerful, all right. It sometimes breaks things, smashes dishes, nearly wrecks the place.

Well, Crazy Horse was a warrior, not a medicine man. He was a man-killer, but he had strange powers, like the pebble behind his ear which made him bulletproof. He also wore an herb—*santu bu,* red grass—as his *wotawe,* his special medicine. Crazy Horse's power is still around, like two flintstones clashing, powerful. I have a son whom you have never met. I sometimes think he got some of that warrior power. For years he used to be an Indian stunt man in Hollywood, doing crazy, dare-devil things. But he was never hurt or even scratched. Like Crazy Horse, he was injury-proof. It gave him a confidence.

When it became clear that young Chips was going to be a medicine man, his parents kept him out of school. We usually do this in a case like Chips's. Going to a white school and walking a medicine man's road, you can't do both. I know one father of a youngster who was showing signs of being *wakan.* The father drove the truant officers off with his shotgun. That boy can't read or write, but he grew up to become a fine medicine man.

In the case of Godfrey Chips, the Indian police came after him and their car swerved and turned over, one officer coming out of it with a dislocated shoulder. After this they never bothered him again. He now has a certificate which says that he is living according to the traditional Indian way and that he doesn't have to go to school.

We all knew right away that his powers were great. One family traveled 200 miles to seek his help. They had lost their little boy, who had disappeared without a trace. They asked young Chips to find him for them. They had this ceremony and Godfrey asked the spirits. He told the parents, "I see your son, and you'll see him too, in seven days, but I don't know whether you'll be happy to see him." And he told them where to find him. Later he took me aside and said, "Uncle, I have seen this boy. I didn't want to tell this to his father, but the child is dead. I saw him. He was still alive, but then, in my vision, I watched him drown in the Missouri River. I could describe him as he is now, but I don't want to. I know I must tell the truth, but maybe not all of it at once." Chips was still so young himself, telling those parents was a great burden to him. It was almost too much. They found that poor boy seven days later, just as Godfrey Chips had foreseen.

So you can become a medicine man in different ways, like Chips, by the *yuwipis* talking to you, or like me, through a *hanblechia*—a vision quest. You could be lucky and have a holy man give you his power. It will soon be time for me to look for a young man to give my power to. When he appears I'll know him. I'll sense: This is the one! This power is something like AC and DC. The white preacher goes on AC. He takes whatever he has and it just goes straight on and vanishes. It never comes back. I'm on DC. The line can be cut, it still comes back, it moves like a circle without end. I'm watching my line to the other medicine men, on the lookout for power breaks. Also I'm watching for my successor.

As I said, most of the time a person becomes a medicine man through his own vision. His dream is his very own; nobody else has it exactly the same.

There'll be a certain something in it which will be just for him—his own special secret. On the other hand, part of his dream he'll share with the other medicine men—a common vision which holds them all together, which comes out of our common blood, out of the prairie itself. Being a medicine man ties a man to his people as with a *yuwipi*'s rawhide.

I respect other religions, but I don't like to see them denatured and made into something else. You've made a blondie out of Jesus. I don't care for those blond, blue-eyed pictures of a sanitized, Cloroxed, Ajaxed Christ. How would you like it if I put braids on Jesus and stuck a feather in his hair? You'd call me a very crazy Indian, wouldn't you? Jesus was a Jew. He wasn't a yellow-haired Anglo. I'm sure he had black hair and a dark skin like an Indian. The white ranchers around here wouldn't have let him step out with their daughters and wouldn't have liked him having a drink in one of their saloons. His religion came out of the desert in which he lived, out of his kind of mountains, his kind of animals, his kind of plants. You've tried to make him into an Anglo-Saxon Fuller Brush salesman, a long-haired Billy Graham in a fancy night shirt, and that's why he doesn't work for you anymore. He was a good medicine man, I guess. As you read it in the Bible, he sure had the power, the healing touch. He was a hippie, too. *Hipi*—in our language that means "He is here, we are here, it is here"—something like that. So I don't mind a young white man with long hair and a beaded headband coming to me, asking to learn about our Indian religion, even praying with us. But I would mind it if he tried to change our beliefs, adapt them to his kind of culture, progress, civilization and all that kind of stuff. I would mind that very much. You can't take our beliefs out of our Badlands and prairies and put them into one of your factories or office buildings.

A big Catholic church is being built for Indians on

one of our Sioux reservations. It is shaped like a giant tipi. Over its altar hangs a huge peace pipe together with the cross. It tries to make you believe that Jesus was a *yuwipi*. It says: Come all you peyote men, medicine men, *heyokas* and elk dreamers, come all you Indians and worship here. This is like a *hanblechia,* or a peyote meeting; it's all the same, there is no difference. I don't like it and many others besides me don't like it. It is dishonest. Because there is a difference, and there will always be a difference, as long as one Indian is left alive. Our beliefs are rooted deep in our earth, no matter what you have done to it and how much of it you have paved over. And if you leave all that concrete unwatched for a year or two, our plants, the native Indian plants, will pierce that concrete and push up through it.

In order to be a medicine man one should find the visions there, in nature. To the west a man has the power from the buffalo. From the north he gets the power from the thunder-beings. From the east his strength comes from the spirit horse and the elk. From the south he has the ghost power. From above, from the sky, he will receive the wisdom of the great eagle. From beneath, from the earth, he will receive the mother's food. This is the way to become a *wićaśa wakan,* to learn the secret language, to speak about sacred things, to work with the stones and herbs, to use the pipe.

Much power comes from the animals, and most medicine men have their special animal which they saw in their first vision. One never kills or harms this animal. Medicine men can be buffalo, eagle, elk or bear dreamers. Of all the four-legged and winged creatures a medicine man could receive a vision from, the bear is foremost. The bear is the wisest of animals as far as medicines are concerned. If a man dreams of this animal he could become a great healer. The bear is the only animal that one can see in a dream acting

169

like a medicine man, giving herbs to people. It digs up certain healing roots with its claws. Often it will show a man in a vision which medicines to use.

The old medicine men used to have bear claws in their sacred bundles. These claws, pressed into the flesh of a sick person, would make the healing bear medicine penetrate into his body. Many songs of the bear dreamers end with the words *Mato hemakiye*—a bear told me this. Then everybody knows who gave this medicine man his powers. One great gift of the bear dreamers was fixing up broken bones. They had a special bear medicine—*huhuwenhanhan pejuta*—which they mixed with fat and smeared on a broken arm or leg. They had a way of setting the bone, pulling it into place, then wrapping the whole up tightly with a moistened rawhide, and in a month that man would walk again on that broken leg, draw a bow with his doctored arm. This the old people told me. It was cheaper than a hospital, too, I tell you.

Those bear medicine men knew how to cure. We used to have people ninety and a hundred years of age and they still had all their teeth left. Now you look around and you see all those commodities-fed young Indians with most of their teeth gone. The modern food, the shiny new hospitals and bad teeth seem to go together. But we used to be a healthy people. Those old men, the warriors who had fought Custer, still used to meet in the 1930s and 1940s. Some were over a hundred years old, still able to sit on a horse, still liking to chew on tough meat. They had their spiritual meetings in the dark. I helped them sing. I learned most of the *yuwipi* songs from a pair of twin brothers. We had to sneak off for these parties because the Government was trying to discourage us so they could take away the power the Indian doctors had.

An elk dreamer was almost as strong as a bear man. The elk stands for many good things—strength, youth, love. An elk is brave; he defends his herd. Elk dreamers, therefore, look out for the womenfolk, for the weak and helpless children. They take pity on the poor. They have a way with the girls, but they are not women-chasers. They treat women with respect and gentleness, but they have the love power. The women know it. When an elk medicine man is near, even before they see him, they feel it. They fidget around, scratch themselves, hitch up their skirts, get restless. Nobody has to tell them. All this comes from the elks. Just watch such an animal, how he protects his harem, always putting himself between his does and the danger.

The elk is an athlete. In spite of his big antlers he can run through a dense forest no matter how close the trees are standing together. You don't quite know how he does it. He lives with the trees, is himself formed like a tree; his antlers are like branches.

An elk master gets his power from this animal. This power turns your eyes inward and penetrates into your mind, filling your whole body with *wakan*. An elk man will have a good voice, be a good musician, a flute player. This flute, the *siyotanka*, it charms, it plays the love songs with which a boy calls his girl. The sound travels far; even the animals in the woods love it. A good spirit comes with it. An elk medicine man grows to be like his animal. He can leave the footprints of an elk behind him to show his power. The elk spirit comes with a foot-click on the ground, like a hoof striking iron. I have experienced this. The elk dreamers used to wear masks when doctoring people. They always wore a special small, quilled hoop in their hair because the circle is one of the elk's symbols.

An elk man is good at treating sick women. He can make powerful hunting charms, and the love charms too. He performs the *hehaka lowanpi* ceremony. He knows the elk songs. He works with the elk medicine —*hehaka tapejuta*—what you call horse mint. It grows in the dry hills. It looks like a drumstick with little blue and purple petals, and it has a good, sweet taste. This mint is a blood medicine. One chews the leaves and puts them on wounds and bad cuts. It stops the bleeding and has a fast-healing power. You can use this medicine also as a tea. You drink it against coughing and fainting. The elk medicine, used in different ways, cures many sicknesses.

We also have buffalo, coyote and badger medicine men using the powers their special animals gave them. I once saw a snake medicine man at work. In 1919 a person I knew was bitten by a big prairie rattler. It stung him twice, on the ankle and then a little higher up. His leg got swollen and discolored. The man was in terrible pain and he was vomiting. His family called for a snake doctor, Black Moon, from Cherry Creek. He could move his body like a snake. His tongue was like a snake's tongue, darting in and out of his mouth, flickering-like. He could make his eyes look hard and flinty, without any expression, like a rattler's. He told the man who was suffering: "The snake is my friend. Rattlers, blue racers, bull snakes, they are all friends. I got the power. If you believe me, you'll be cured in four days. I don't even have to use any medicine on you. I have it here, *zuzeka tapejuta,* the beard tongue herb, but I don't need it."

Black Moon then performed a *kankakpa*. He looked at the punctures from the rattler's fangs where the blood was oozing out. Black Moon took a sharp stick, forked like a snake's tongue, put a dime in the fork, tied a string made of gut tightly around the leg and the stick, then snapped it hard, hit the big vein. I saw that greenish, dark stuff spurt out. As soon as that green is out and the blood turns red again, you tell that snake to go to hell. It was as the medicine man had said: After the bleeding the man got better, and four days later he was as good as new.

This kind of bleeding we do, this *kankakpa,* is used for a number of ailments. You hit that vein and the blood comes out, killing the sickness. If your blood is not too dark the medicine man does this on only one arm. That's good for eczema and sore eyes. Otherwise he does it on all four limbs. Men with high blood pressure, their blood is dark. The medicine man waits until the blood turns light. Afterward he puts some spider webs on the spots where he has done this *kankakpa*. Spider webs are better than iodine, peroxide—all that stuff. After four or five days the sick man feels fine, as though coming out of a sweat house.

The birds, too, give power to a medicine man. Take George Eagle Elk. I think he gets much of his power from the eagle, because when he does his curing you hear and feel the presence of a big bird. It takes four days for old George to cure a person. He uses all kinds of herbs, making them into something like a soup or tea.

Whenever you see me getting ready for a sweat bath in preparation for a big ceremony, look up at the sky and watch. Most of the time you'll see an eagle circling up there, just a tiny black spot going round and round. That eagle power is always there. The owl, too, is very sacred. It is awake when men and animals sleep. It sees in the dark, moves at night, gives us dreams. I respect it. I'll never harm one from the owl nation. The buzzard, *heca*, is a weather forecaster. Once it arrives, that's the end of cold and snow. Another weatherwise bird is the *mastekola*, the lark. There'll be good weather whenever it flies straight up toward the clouds. It sings as it goes: "*Masteko, masteko*—I like the warm air."

The *huntka*, a water bird, if an arrow hits him, he dives and comes back without the arrow, as if nothing had happened. *Wakinyela*—the mourning dove— makes a sound, *m-m-m-m*, that means there's a ghost here. All the time a medicine man has to keep learning from nature, has to listen to its voices.

We have talked of holy men, of healers and prophets. I must also speak of the conjurer, the *wokabiyeya*. He does the *kiyapa*, sucking a disease out of you with his breath, inhaling the sickness, so to say, dragging pieces of porcupine quill or sharp blades of grass out of your body, things which have been shot into it by an evil spirit or by a gopherlike animal, which does much mischief, making you break out in boils. A conjurer is a man who works with *wihmunge*—witch medicine. Anthropologists like to call him a witch doctor.

This type of curing comes from an old belief that a sickness is something put into you from the outside, something bad—sharp objects, worms, stale water, an internal pain, a fire placed inside you by the fever spirits. The conjurer can inhale these ailments, suck them up, bring them to the surface and spit them out.

My uncle Chest, one of the medicine men who taught me, was a conjurer who used a kind of magic in his doctoring. And he was good at it. He had a square of black cloth and an eagle feather. He would pin this cloth to a wall. He also had a special powerful rattle. When he sang his curing song, that rattle would hit the sick person. At the same time the eagle feather would jump onto that black cloth, right in the center of it. You could watch it as often and as closely as you liked. One moment the black cloth was empty and the next, sudden as a flash, there'd be the feather on it. The eye couldn't see it move, that feather was so fast.

To drag a disease out of a man, old Chest would take his little bag and pick a feather or some of his curing stones out of it to send them into a body. They hit a fellow like a shock, disappeared in him. The feather always returned to the cloth with a little blood or mucus sticking to it. People say that the old man cured many bad cases of rheumatism this way. Chest made out well with his doctoring. He always came home with gifts—blankets, food, coffee, everything he needed. He lived in a little one-room cabin with his possessions, but he gave most of these things away, because he was a generous man. He always knew beforehand if someone was coming to seek his help. When he got this feeling he sang a little song: "I am going to get some money today." And he was always right.

Chest was an honest man. He never once misused his power. He was an old-fashioned kind of healer, a man from another age. He was never greedy. But there are some conjurers who are fakes and cheats. Maybe some of them have a little power, but they use it in a bad way. One of them could throw something sharp at you, a quill, a jagged piece of rock, then you'd get sick and only he could cure you. It would cost you. Or he could take your soul away, change a person's mind. He could part husband and wife, make him love another woman, make her go for another man. Then you'd have to pay him to get your mate back. A so-called medicine man may turn witch doctor when he feels that he is failing, slipping, when he can't cure anymore.

But it backfires. A man who misuses his power in this way may see his own children fall sick or even die. The more he gets, the more he loses. You can tell a good medicine man by his actions and his way of life. Is he lean? Does he live in a poor cabin? Does money leave him cold? Does he have a good, loving wife and happy children? Then he is a good medicine man, no matter what methods he uses. It is also a good sign if a man doesn't pretend to be able to cure all sickness. If he tells you: "For your ailment my medicines are no good, but I will send you to somebody who has an herb for you." If he tells you this you know you have spoken to a good man.

I never tried any conjuring of that sort, never wanted to. That's not in my vision. But I once played a trick on some guys, a stunt a witch doctor could have pulled. I was volunteering for the Army, going through my physical test. We were all standing in line

175

being told to make water in a little bottle. There were many draftees there who really wanted out; they didn't want to be taken. They all said, "Oh, what I'd give to have the diabetes or clap. Then I wouldn't have to soldier." I told them, "Boys, you are in luck. I suffer from *both,* a social disease *and* sugar. For a buck apiece, I'll make a little water in all your bottles." Boy, were they eager, waving their green dollar bills at me. Of course there was nothing wrong with me. I was as healthy as a bull. I was very busy the next hour, drinking gallons of water, sprinkling a little drop of comfort here and there, getting more customers than I could accommodate. I made about forty dollars as a sprinkler. Well, that Army doctor was smiling from ear to ear. "I never saw a healthier bunch of guys in all my life. You'll all go into the infantry." I had to take some of these new-made soldiers out for a drink. They were so mad at me, without treating them to a beer they'd have killed me.

There's one thing a medicine man shouldn't try to do: doctor a woman who is *isnati,* having her monthly period. That's a strange and powerful force. A woman who is that way, if she spits at a rattlesnake, that snake will die. If you have a flower in a vase and a lady comes in who has her sickness, the petals will often curl. It is no good if a woman in this state comes to a ceremony. She has this power and it will somewhere clash with the power of the medicine man. It could harm her or him. Maybe with a special feather or a special herb she could come, but why take a chance? It's better if she stays away for four days.

A medicine man has to be of the earth, somebody who reads nature as white men read a book. He should know about food and diets, what to give a sick person to eat. Certain kinds of food make a sick person worse. The old-time Indian food is the best— raw kidney, raw liver, *wasna,* maybe the whole fetus of a cow. Reservations are like bird cages and they make us eat bird food. That's one reason we Indians are not as healthy as we used to be.

Let me tell you about some of the herbs and plants we use in our work. These herbs have their own ways like all living things. We have one, *aunyeyapi,* a kind of sand berry, if you approach it from the wind side it tastes bitter, but if you come from the other direction you'll find it sweet. That's how strange some of these herbs are. I know of some roots which bring on a high wind if you use them right. Sage drives out evil spirits; sweet grass attracts the good ones.

For a stomach ache we use *taku-sasala*—the smart-weed. It's good for cramps and the runs. Red oak also binds you up. Horse mint and verbena tea are good for stomach and abdominal pains. The blossoms of the prairie clover are good for swollen throats, and its roots purge you but good. *Wagamu pejuta* is a melon medicine. Boil the melon and take half a teaspoon. It's an emetic, a hot flush; it cleans out your gall and kidneys. It opens you up. The four-o'clock weed— *huokihe hanskaska*—will open you up if you can't make water.

*Wina wizi cikala* is a kind of licorice. It's bitter when you chew it, but it is good against the flu. *Can makatola* is purple lily plant. A powder made of it is good for lumps and swellings. *Cante yazapi icuwe* makes a fine tea for all kinds of heart trouble. *Sinkpe tawote*—that's muskrat food, sweetflag, one of our busiest medicines. It has bitter roots that are very good against a fever. When you grind them up and mix them with gunpowder they are a help against cramps in arms and legs. *Tate canuga*—a kind of snakeroot—is for treating a poor appetite. But with no jobs and no money on the reservations, that's one herb we don't need right now.

*Taopi pejuta* is our great wound medicine. You have to go into the Badlands, search among those prehistoric monster bones, to find this herb. It is especially good for wounds caused by bullets. *Pejuta wahesa* is good for the same thing. This is the hairy red root. The root looks black, but if you peel the dark outer skin off, it is red underneath. One makes a powder from it for people who are shot through the chest and lungs. There's a story of a girl who was shot right through her body, but when she was given this medicine she was cured. The white doctors had given her up. "It's hopeless," they said. *Winawizi hutanka*—I don't know the white man's name for this—is good for stopping hemorrhages. It grows in wet places along creeks.

The purple cornflower chewed up is good for snakebite. The butterfly plant is good if you want to vomit. Red cedar is used for bad lungs. The great Chief Red Cloud also used it to stop a very deadly cholera epidemic among his people over a hundred years ago. *Pispiza tawote*, the prairie-dog medicine, helps those people who have difficulty in breathing.

We have many herbs that have to do with childbearing, with baby care and with sex. *Hupe stola*—that's the soapweed, a kind of yucca. It is truly a big medicine. Mixed with a certain cactus, *unkćela blaska*, it helps a mother in labor when the baby doesn't want to move down. Used in a different manner, it becomes *hoksi yuhapi sni*—a medicine which aborts. When there is a very good reason for a woman not to have a baby one gives her this and there won't be a birth. One uses this carefully after thinking about it for a long time.

This medicine is *lila wakan*—very sacred, working two ways. It is also good for catching wild horses. Let these animals smell its smoke and they slow up, quiet down enough for you to catch them. This herb also kills lice, if you should have this problem, and makes your hair grow at the same time.

*Itopta sapa tapejuta*—or snow-on-the-mountain— is a milkweed. You pick it in prairie-dog towns. You make a tea of it for mothers who don't have enough milk for their babies. Its crushed leaves are good against swellings. Green milkweed is used for stopping a baby's diarrhea. *Can hlogan wastemna*—a ragweed—helps a woman during a bad child-bearing. It will also make a man fall asleep so that you can steal his horses, but it's no good for stealing cars.

As for sex medicines, the little female wild sage helps a woman during her menstrual cramps. A certain kind of skunk cabbage, if you make a liquid of its boiled roots, is a birth-control medicine. It has to be taken with some care. Too much of it and you can't have any children. But some tribes use it. If a man is weak and can't get it up, a certain snakeroot could be a big help. One plant, if just one tiny seed of it is given an old man, can keep him going the whole night through. I won't describe or name it, otherwise the whole place would be overrun by white men from the big cities looking for these seeds. They'd go crazy with this herb, and I'd catch hell for telling about it.

Finally there are some herbs that are not used on men but just to cure horses and cattle. Those ecology people should know about *hante*—a certain cedar. It's a natural, harmless bug spray. It will drive the potato bugs away if you crush and boil this plant and use the liquid. Other herbs are just for food, such as prairie apples, wild turnips, which we call *tinpsila* and use like bread. The dried-out bush is your tumbleweed. We even have herbs that are used neither for curing nor for food, such as *pejunige tanka*. In the old days, before we had matches, when you lit this herb it would keep smoldering for months. It used to be hung up before the tipi. If you needed a fire you just blew on it until it glowed, then you hung it up again to smolder some more. Some things you use aren't herbs at all. Badger fat is not a plant but what its name says it is. It's a good medicine against baldness. And I told you about giving somebody a turtle heart to eat to make him brave and strong. I could add some more plants and medicines to this list, but I think we have more than enough here.

I would like to talk about one more thing. I have been to New York, Chicago and some other big places, stayed in your house many times, met a lot of people and kept my eyes open. So I know a little about what you call psychology. I have heard about group therapy and encounter meetings and found out that some white people have a way of acting out their troubles as in a play. Well, I must tell you that we Indians knew about these things a long time before you did. For longer than anybody can remember, many Sioux ceremonies always ended with a kind of Indian "group therapy"—with everybody taking his turn in a circle, talking about his problems, about what's wrong with him. And a *heyoka,* a thunder-dreamer and clown, always has to act out his dreams in public, no matter how embarrassing that may be. At least it doesn't cost him thirty-five bucks an hour.

I also think that it is a very wise sort of Indian psychology that a medicine man doesn't dress up fancy with feathers and war bonnet when he performs a ceremony. You have seen me praying, performing a wedding, or running a ceremony in an old sweat-shirt and patched pants. There's a purpose in this, a certain humbleness in the presence of the spirits, but not of men. It means a medicine man should be stripped down to the bare essentials when he does these things. It's not the package and the wrapping which counts but what is inside, underneath the clothes and the skin.

As I get older I do less and less curing and ceremonies and more and more thinking. I pass from one stage to another, trying to get a little higher up, praying for enough gas to make it up there.

I haven't told you all I know about the herbs and about the ways of our holy men. You understand that there are certain things one should not talk about, things that must remain hidden. If all was told, supposing there lived a person who could tell all, there would be no mysteries left, and that would be very bad. Man cannot live without mystery. He has a great need of it.

# 10
# *Inipi*—Grandfather's Breath

In speaking of sacred things I will tell you first about the *inipi*—the sweat bath. I do this because we always purify ourselves in the sweat house before starting one of our ceremonies. Whether we celebrate the sun dance or a vision quest, the *inipi* comes first. It could be that the *inipi* was our first rite, that all the other ceremonies came later. We have an old tale which makes many of us believe that this is so. It is the story of Inyan Hoksi—the Stone Boy.

The tale begins with a young girl who had five brothers. They lived together. The girl did the cooking, made robes out of hides and stayed with her brothers all through the seasons. Each day the five brothers went out to hunt. They followed the game. As soon as one place was hunted out they moved their tipi to another one. One day they came to a creek which flowed through a canyon. This place made them feel strange and uneasy, though they did not know why. The brothers went out to hunt in the morning, each one choosing his own path, but when night fell only four came back. They did not know what had happened to the one who did not return. Four went out the next day, but only three came back. They were scared, but still they had to hunt if they wanted to eat. Every time they went out one brother failed to come back.

And so the girl was left alone. She did not know what to do. She had nobody to bring her food or to protect her. She didn't even know how to pray to the spirits for help, because this happened long ago, before the people had ceremonies or ways of worshiping. They did not dance or have a pipe then.

The girl did not want to go on living alone. She went to the top of a hill and cried. She picked up a good-sized, round stone and swallowed it, thinking: "This will kill me." As soon as she had swallowed that rock she felt at peace. She drank a little water and at once the stone began to move within her. It made her feel happy. She was pregnant, though she did not know what child-bearing was. After four days she gave birth to a boy.

This Stone Boy, Inyan Hoksi, grew fast. In one week he grew as much as others do in one year. His mother would not let him go far, because she did not want to lose him as she had lost her brothers. They lived on herbs and roots. One day Stone Boy made a bow and arrow. He took a sharp stone and chipped it into a barbed point, which he fitted to the arrow shaft. This was the first stone arrow point. Up to then hunters had used only pointed sticks hardened in fire.

When Stone Boy's mother saw this bow and arrow she started to weep. He asked, "Why do you cry?" She told him, "I do not like these things, because now you will go out and hunt and never come back," and she told him of his five uncles who had not returned. He said, "Fix me a pair of moccasins and some food, I must go and find them." She cried, "But if you don't come back, what will I do?" He only smiled at her. "I will come back with my uncles."

He started out early next morning. In the evening he smelled smoke. He followed the smoke and came to a tipi before which an old, huge and ugly woman was sitting. Next to her, propped up against her tipi, were five large bundles. She invited him to stay and gave him some meat to eat. When it was dark he wanted to lie down and sleep, but the old woman said, "I have a backache. I wish you would rub my back or, better still, walk on it. That will make me feel better." Stone Boy walked up and down on the huge woman's back and felt something sharp sticking out of her backbone like a spear. He told himself: "This is what she used to kill my uncles." He jumped high into the air and came down hard on the old woman, breaking her neck.

He built a big fire, threw the old witch in and burned her to ashes. He looked at the five large bundles and thought: "Could these be the bodies of my uncles?" He felt the presence of spirits, heard their voices. They told him to build a little lodge of willow sticks and hides and put the five bundles inside in a circle, to put red-hot stones from the fire into the middle of it, to take water in an animal skin bag and pour it over the rocks.

He thanked the rocks. He said, "You brought me here." He covered the lodge up so that no hot air could escape. It was dark inside. Stone Boy saw something moving in the darkness. The souls were returning to the bodies in their bundles. When he poured water over the rocks for the fourth time, his uncles came alive again. They started talking and singing. He told them, "The rocks saved me, and now they saved you. And from now on this sweat house shall be sacred to us. It will give us good health and will purify us." That was the first *inipi*.

This story gives us a hint of how old the sweat bath is, that it was the first of our many rites. It tells us about the sacredness of the stones which were the first things we worshiped. A sweat bath can serve as the first part of a larger ceremony, but it can also stand as a sacred rite by itself. There should be no Sioux family without their sweat lodge.

There is something holy and uplifting about the building of a sweat house. When two enemies participate in the putting up of the little beehive-shaped lodge, their old hatreds are forgotten. Envy and jealousy disappear. The two men laugh and josh each other; they joke about the fights they have had.

You start by looking for the right kinds of rocks. You find them on the prairie and on the hills. They are earth turned into stone, solid, dull. They are not shiny and sparkling. They are firm and hard, not brittle. They won't burst and hurt the people inside the sweat lodge when they are red-hot. They are called bird stones—*sintkala waksu*—stones with "beadwork" on them. If you examine these rocks closely you will see fine designs and tracings on them, greenish, like moss. They don't last long, just about four days, then the designs fade and disappear. It is thought that some birds put them on a stone. You can see the future in these designs. Once I heard an old man say, "I see a river here and a broken bridge. The water is overflowing. A flood is coming here." And so it happened. Besides the rocks you collect firewood for the sweat bath. You use only cottonwood for this, because it is our most sacred tree.

You go down to the creek and cut twelve white willow trees. We peel these sticks and plant them in the ground in a circle. They are easy to bend. We form them like a beehive and tie them together in this shape. The sticks form a square at the top, representing the universe, the four directions. In some cases sixteen sticks are used. These willow wands form the skeleton of the hut. They are like the bones of our people. They are covered up. In the old days we covered them with buffalo hides; nowadays we use tarps, blankets or quilts. For the sun-dance sweat lodge we choose the best of our blankets with the most beautiful patterns. The finished sweat lodge reaches about as high as a man's ribs.

The sweat house is small, but to those crouching inside it represents the whole universe. The spirit of all living things are in this hut. This we believe. The earth on which we sit is our grandmother; all life comes from her. In the center of the lodge we scoop out a circular hole into which the stones will be put later. We pray to the Great Spirit as we do this. His power will be there in this little pit, which, when it is used in a sacred manner, will become the center of the whole world. We save the scooped-out earth carefully and form it into a little ridge, a path for the spirits, leading about ten steps out of the sweat house. At the end of it we make a little mound, called *unci*— grandmother—because this is what the earth means to us. The center pit also represents *wakicagapi*—the beloved, dead relative who has returned to the earth. You have to remember him when you put the rocks into that hole. This pit is a circle within the circle formed by the hut. This symbol, a circle within a circle, stands for life, for that which has no end. Plants, animals, men are born and die, but the Indian people will live.

A little farther out from the *unci* mound, following the line of the sacred path, we make the fire in which we heat the stones. This is the flame which is passed on from generation to generation. Everything we do during our ceremonies has a deeper meaning for us and, in one way or another, symbolizes the universe, the powers of nature, the spirits, all of which are ever-present in our minds. So when we build this fire we first put four east-west sticks down and then lay another four north-south sticks crosswise over them. Upon these we build up logs as if we were making a small tipi. All this, once again, represents the four directions, the earth beneath us and the sky above. The logs of wood also represent us, the tipi with the Indians inside. It means that we are part of the universe, that it is part of us, that it is present in our houses, in the sweat lodge, in our hearts.

The entrance to the sweat lodge faces west, toward the setting sun. I know that most of the anthropologists have written that it faces east, but this is true only for the sweat houses of the *heyoka,* the clowns who do everything different from anybody else. Before the lodge we plant two forked sticks and place a third one horizontally across. This makes a rack against which we lean the sacred pipe. This is an altar too. Some people also put a buffalo skull there with six tobacco offerings tied to the horns. Others put a black-and-white stick there representing day and night. We also keep a pail of water handy. This must be fresh and from a running stream, and it represents the water of life. In former days we filled the skin of an animal with water, but the old, beautifully decorated skin bags are all gone now. For us an ordinary pail must do.

The man who acts as the leader first goes into the hut with his pipe. He covers the ground with sage, which is sacred. It means that the green living things, the spirits of trees and plants, are with us in the sweat house. The leader then burns some sweet grass. It is braided like a woman's pigtail. One end is lit and the smoke and sweet smell are whirled around so that it gets into every part of the sweat lodge. Thus everything is made sacred and all bad feelings and thoughts are driven out. Now all is prepared and the sweat house is ready for the people to go in. Usually six or seven people will purify themselves. These are good numbers. If there are seven, one is the leader, one represents the earth, one the clouds, and the others the four directions. Up to seven people can sit crosslegged. On rare occasions as many as twelve try to get in. Then they have to sit on their knees.

When you enter, don't come in shorts or with a towel around you. You are going to be reborn. You'll be like a baby coming out of your mother's womb, our real mother, the earth. You'll come out with a new mind. You don't want to be reborn with a pair of shorts on. If you come with that people will think maybe you have something wrong with your dick. So don't be bashful. Some white men have a guilty mind—that's the towel. There is a change, though. Friends of mine had a young white lady staying with them and she took all her clothes off when she went into their sweat house with them. That was a good, natural thing to do. It's not only men who purify themselves through the *inipi;* women do this too, but usually they go in a group by themselves. Men take a sweat bath more often, because a medicine man has to purify himself before each doctoring. As you stoop to crawl into the sweat house you are like an animal crawling into his den. That should remind you that you are a relative of all four-legged creatures. As we go in, counterclockwise, the leader will sit at the entrance on the right and his helper on the other, the left side. The others seat themselves wherever they want to. We also need one man to help us on the outside.

This man now brings in the heated rocks, one by one. While he is doing this no one is permitted to cross his path and come between him and the sweat house. If the leader is very particular to do this ceremony right, a forked stick should be used to bring the rocks in; otherwise a pitch fork or other suitable tool could do the job. As the first rocks are passed through the entrance we say, *"Pilamaye*—thanks." The first rock is put right in the center for grandmother earth. Then we place four rocks around the first one—west, north, east and south—one each for every direction from which the wind blows. Finally you place one rock on top of the first one—for the sky and for the grandfather spirit. After these first six you can pile on the rocks as you please. For a curing ceremony, when medicine is given, you put in twelve more, or eighteen altogether. For special occasions you can have as many as fifty rocks. These extra stones represent the trees, the plants and the animals.

The man who puts on the ceremony now lights the pipe and passes it around. It makes us holy and links us as brothers. You grab hold of that smoke, rub your palms with in, rub it all over your body. You pray to the Great Spirit, to the sacred rocks, the *tunka*, the *inyan*. They have no mouth, no eyes, no arms or legs, but they exhale the breath of life. The helper on the outside now closes the flap over the entrance and makes sure that no light comes into the hut.

The leader now pours, or sprinkles, water over the glowing rocks. If he does this in the old way, he uses a sprig of sage or sweetgrass, otherwise he takes a dipper. The water is ice-cold and the stones red-hot, so here is a unifying, the earth and the sky, the water of life and the sacred breath of the spirit, grandfather and grandmother coming together. There is a great surge of power. You inhale that breath, drink in the water, the white steam. It represents clouds, the living soul, life. The heat is very great. Your lungs are breathing fire, and if you can't stand it you can say, *"Mitakuye oyasin—all my relatives,"* and somebody will open the flap and let the cool air in for you.

You sit there quietly in the dark, thinking what the *inipi* is for. You close your eyes, listen to the hiss of the icy water on the heated stones, listen to what they have to tell you—a little spark coming into your mind. The sweat house shakes and trembles as the men sing *"Tunka-shila, hi-yay, hi-yay."* The heat, the earth-power, it hits you. You inhale it, get filled with it. That power penetrates into you, heals you. That steam stops at the skin, but that earth-power penetrates your body and mind. It cures many sicknesses —arthritis, rheumatism. It heals the wounds of your mind. This *inipi* is our little church. It is not like some white churches where people sit in pews, showing off their fine clothes. The *inipi* is different. There is no bragging and impurity here. Just naked humans, huddling in the dark, close to the earth and to the spirit. If the spirit is with you, you could pick up the glowing rock and it would not hurt you.

We open the entrance four times and let the coolness in and the light. Always we sing two songs before we open the entrance again. Four times we pour the water, and four times we smoke the red willow bark tobacco, the smoke of which goes up to the Great Spirit. When the flap is open, you might want to talk about something, a sickness you want to have cured. Or you might just have to say something good about sitting here with us in the sweat house. Or some of us will tell you that we are glad having you here with us. Maybe somebody will talk about a drinking problem in his family and ask for help and prayers. It all depends on the reason for which the sweat bath is performed.

After we smoke for the fourth and last time, we say, "All my relatives," and the ceremony is ended. The last man to smoke takes the pipe apart and carefully cleans the bowl. We leave the sweat house the way the sun travels, counter-clockwise. We drink cold water and rub down our bodies with dry sage leaves. We come out with a feeling of well-being, lightheaded and happy. We know that we have done something good which will benefit not only us but all people, all living things.

The little beehive hut, which is so simple to make and which doesn't cost a penny to build, can be used over and over again for this ceremony, until it falls apart or the willow sticks which hold it up finally break. In that case you burn it down, bury the rocks, smoothen the ground and make the earth whole again. Then you start a new sweat house in another place. I hope the day is coming soon when every Indian will once again have a sweat lodge standing near his house.

# 11
# *Yuwipi*—Little Lights from Nowhere

Imagine darkness so intense and so complete that it is almost solid, flowing around you like ink, covering you like a velvet blanket. A blackness which cuts you off from the everyday world, which forces you to withdraw deep into yourself, which makes you see with your heart instead of with your eyes. You can't see, but your eyes are opened. You are isolated, but you know that you are part of the Great Spirit, united with all living beings.

And out of this utter darkness comes the roaring of drums, the sound of prayers, the high-pitched songs. And among all these sounds your ear catches the voices of the spirits—tiny voices, ghostlike, whispering to you from unseen lips. Lights are flitting through the room, almost touching you, little flashes of lightning coming at you from the darkness. Rattles are flying through the air, knocking against your head and shoulders. You feel the wings of birds brushing your face, feel the light touch of a feather on your skin. And always you hear the throbbing drums filling the darkness with their beating, filling the empty spaces inside yourself, making you forget the things that clutter up your mind, making your body sway to their rhythm.

And across the black nothingness you feel the presence of the man lying face down in the center of the room, his fingers laced together with rawhide, his body tied and wrapped in a blanket, a living mummy, through whom the spirits are talking to you. This is what you experience during a *yuwipi* ceremony.

*Yuwipi* is one of our most ancient rites. Some

191

people say that it is not so old, but they are wrong. Their belief stems from the fact that *yuwipi* is never mentioned by name in the old books about Indian religion and because it has remained hidden from outsiders. I am an old man now, but my grandmother told me about this *yuwipi* when I was still a small boy, just as she had been told during her childhood. In this way the knowledge of it goes back through the generations, and nobody knows its beginning.

I believe *yuwipi* to be as old as our people, because its symbolism, the whole thinking behind it, goes back to our earliest times. The sacred things used in this ceremony are ties that bind us to the dim past, to a time before the first white man set foot on this continent. Even though it is not mentioned by name, one book describes *yuwipi* as it was practiced long ago, before we had houses to live in. This book was written by a woman who lived for a number of years among us, when I was a small boy, before the First World War. She got her stories from the white-haired, holy men who still remembered the days before the reservations. Here is a page from this book*:

When a man skillful in the use of the sacred stones was called to attend a sick person he was expected to give a demonstration of his supernatural power. Many were invited to witness this exhibition, and it is said that harm would come to those who did not "believe in the sacred stones." The sick person filled a pipe, which he gave to the medicine-man. After smoking it the man was tightly bound with thongs, even his fingers and toes being interlaced with sinews like those of which bowstrings are made, after which he was firmly tied in a hide. The tent was dark, and the medicine-man sang songs addressed to the sacred

*Frances Densmore, *Teton Sioux Music*.

stones; he sang also his own dream songs. Strange
sounds were heard in the darkness, and objects
were felt to be flying through the air. Voices of
animals were speaking. One said, "My grandchild,
you are very sick, but I will cure you." Frequently a
buffalo came, and those who did not believe in the
sacred stones were kicked by the buffalo or struck
by a flying stone or bundle of clothing. At last the
medicine-man called, "Hasten, make a light!" Dry
grass, which was ready, was placed on the fire. In its
light the man was seen wedged between the poles
near the top of the tipi, with all the restraining
cords cast from him.

All the main features of today's *yuwipi* ceremony
are described here—the stones, the darkness, the
tying up. *Yuwipi,* like all our sacred words, has many
meanings. *Yuwi* means to bind, to tie up. *Yuwipi* is our
word for the tiny, glistening rocks we pick up from the
anthills. They are sacred. They have the power. We
put 405 of these little rocks into the gourds which we
use in our ceremonies according to the number of our
green relatives, the different trees in our Sioux universe. *Yuwipi wasicun*—that is the power of the sacred
rocks. It is also another name for Tunka, our oldest
god, who was like a rock, old beyond imagination,
ageless, eternal. The ancient ones worshiped this god
in the form of a huge stone painted red. The old word
for god and the old word for stone are the same—
*tunkashila,* grandfather—but it is also a name for the
Great Spirit. The word *tunka* is in there.

A more modern word for rock is *inyan.* Inyan
Wasicun Wakan is our Indian name for Moses. Indian
medicine men, too, find round stones on the hilltops,
which they bring down with them and use to cure
people. And these stones bear a hidden message,
which they sometimes reveal to us, invisible writing
for those who read with their hearts. The old medicine

men used to talk to the stones and were able to communicate with them.

*Tunka, inyan,* the rock, has always been sacred to us. The story of our greatest mystery, the story of the peace pipe, also tells us that when White Buffalo Calf Woman gave us this sacred pipe, she also gave us a rock, round and red as the earth, made from the life-blood of our people. Inscribed upon it were seven circles, the seven campfires of our nation, the seven ways to worship with the pipe. Long ago this stone was kept in a special sacred *oinikaga* tipi. The bowl of the pipe and this sacred stone were made from the kind of rock which we dig out from the Minnesota pipestone quarry, the only place in the world where it is found. In this way the sacredness of the rock is linked to the sacredness of the pipe.

In the old days one man had a stone which he sent out to look for buffalo. He always spread a red-painted buffalo skin for the stone to return to. One moment the hide would be empty and then, suddenly, the stone would be there in the center of it. Sometimes the stone brought back a pebble or a sprig of some medicine plant. The owner then questioned the stone and would make known to the people what it had told him. One Sioux tribe had a scouting stone which they would send out to see what their enemies were up to. This stone also had a returning place, a square earth altar made of fine red powder.

The ancient *yuwipi* men unloosed rocks to search for lost objects. The farther such a stone had to travel, the longer it needed to return. Some medicine rocks don't like to be alone. They have helpers, smaller pebbles. Some rocks are used for curing and are kept wrapped carefully in a piece of buffalo skin lined with the down of eagle feathers. The stones like to stay in there. You don't lose them this way.

A medicine stone is a perfect work of Wakan Tanka, the Great Spirit. It is made up of one kind of matter only. Its surface has no beginning and no end. Its power lasts forever. Such stones should not be dug out from the ground. Stones thus embedded have been put there by the lightning, by the thunder powers. A *yuwipi* man, unless he is also a *heyoka,* a contrary, does not use them. He finds his stones on the surface of high buttes. To white people this kind of talk seems strange. They have short memories. I have heard that in all the prehistoric caves the world over one finds painted pebbles used in religious rites. Your Bible is full of stories of sacred rocks set up in high places. Think of the Rock of Ages, of St. Peter, whose name means rock. Think of Stonehenge. White people have forgotten this and have lost the power which is in the rocks.

In a *yuwipi* ceremony the spirits and the lights dwell in the stones. The bright spark which you see in the dark, that light is *inyan*—the round pebble. It controls our mother, the earth. It has the power; a soul goes into that rock and starts talking to you. It might say, "I am your grandfather. Do you recognize me? I am his soul. I have come to help you." So listen carefully. During a *yuwipi* ceremony everybody puts a sprig of sagebrush behind his ear so he will understand the spirit when it comes to him. Men and women do this. So you see how ancient the *yuwipi* is. But there is much more to it than the lights and the stones. Let me describe a *yuwipi* ceremony from the beginning to the end. You have seen it; you are about to experience it again. I shall try to make you understand it fully.

A *yuwipi* ceremony starts when someone, a man or woman, has a problem and needs help. That someone could be sick, or he could be looking for a lost relative. He sends a peace pipe, loaded with Bull Durham, to a *yuwipi* medicine man. If he does this in the right way the medicine man cannot refuse to help him; he must perform the ceremony. Not all medicine men are *yuwipis;* some don't want to be. Being a *yuwipi* involves finding something. This could be a missing person, dead, drowned at the bottom of a river. If the *yuwipi* finds him, he brings grief to the family. Or the something could be a stolen article. The *yuwipi* finds it and everybody is embarrassed, the thief as well as the medicine man and the man who asked him to search for it. Some medicine men shy away from this. I myself used to practice *yuwipi,* but I don't do it anymore. I have passed beyond this stage. But I have taught a number of men to become *yuwipis,* and I will teach more.

You need a sponsor and a medicine man to have a *yuwipi* ceremony. The sponsor is the one with the problem, the one who needs help. There's no real fee for a medicine man's services, but the sponsor is expected to provide the food. When many people come to a ceremony, this can run into money, as much as twenty dollars, maybe, because everybody is welcome. During a meeting not only the sponsor but everybody can ask for help and all will be fed. This brings us to the dog, a young and plump one. It is marked with a dab of red paint and quickly strangled. A woman will singe its hair off, cut it up, put it into a kettle over an open fire and boil it. You can't have a *yuwipi* meeting without dog meat. You must eat of it, at least one small piece. We Sioux are fond of our dogs, but killing one for this ceremony is regarded as a sacrifice. The dog dies so that the people may live. His flesh helps to cure the sick, gives them a special strength. The dog is not killed for nothing.

Any large room can serve as a good place to hold a *yuwipi* meeting, but some medicine men keep one permanently fixed up for this ceremony. As a start, one must remove all furniture and cover all windows and doors with blankets. Not the smallest flicker of light is allowed to penetrate from the outside, even though the ceremony always takes place at night. Even the faint glow of the moon would spoil the total blackness which we want. We go so far as to remove all mirrors and glass-covered pictures or, at least, turn them against the wall. Nothing shiny which could reflect light should be in the room. Because eyeglasses and wrist watches reflect light, people will remove them before a ceremony and put them in their pockets. Otherwise the spirits which love the dark might become angry and knock their glasses off or yank the watches from their wrists.

Next, the floor is covered with sagebrush. There are several kinds of sage and all of them are sacred to us. It is our "first aid" plant and we use it in all our ceremonies. It represents the powers of nature. A sage stem in our hair will make the spirits come to us, helps us to understand them.

All through the afternoon before the ceremony, two girls have been busy making tobacco ties, little bundles of Bull Durham about the size of a hazelnut. They start by cutting cotton cloth into squares about an inch long and wide. They use cloth of four different colors for the four directions of the universe. They make 405 of these little squares, putting about a thimbleful of tobacco on each. They make these squares into tiny bundles, which they tie into a long, thin string. When they have done this, some men take the string with its many tobacco ties and form it into a large rectangle on the floor of the room. This rectangle leaves just enough space between the string and the wall for a person to sit down with his legs stretched out. In this space, between the string and the wall, sit all those who wish to take part in the ceremony. The inside of the rectangle is sacred. In its center the medicine man will lie wrapped up like a mummy. Nobody is supposed to step inside this rectangle except the two men who will tie up the *yuwipi* man, and they will step outside again and sit with the others after they have done their work.

In the old days we had only four large bags of deerhide filled with tobacco instead of the string with the many little bundles, and we used *kinnickinnick*— our own red willow bark tobacco—instead of the Bull

Durham. After laying out the string we put up four flags of colored cloth at all the corners of the rectangle—a black, red, yellow and white flag, in that order. The black stands for the west, the night, darkness, and contemplation. The red represents the north, the pipestone, the blood of our people. Yellow stands for the east and the rising sun. White is the south, the sun at its zenith. The south also represents death. "Going south" in our language means dying, because the soul travels from north to south along the Milky Way to the Spirit Land. Some *yuwipis* are also using green and blue flags these days. The green stands for our mother earth. The blue is the sky above us, the clouds.

The four directions of the winds are also represented by a black, a red, a yellow and a white horse. A fifth horse, which is spotted, represents the up-and-down direction, the link between the sky and the earth which is also symbolized by the stem of our sacred pipe and the smoke rising from it. Some medicine men also explain that the four colors represent mankind—the black, red, yellow and white race—the unity of all human beings.

Besides the four staffs which hold up the colored flags there is one more stick. This is the really important one. It stands in the middle between the black and the red flags. This staff is half red and half black, with a thin white stripe separating the two. In this case the red stands for the day and the black for the night. To the top of this staff is tied an eagle feather. This represents the power and the wisdom which comes from above, because we Indians believe that the eagle is the wisest of all living creatures. *Wanbli galeshka,* the spotted eagle, is the great power from the north.

Halfway down the staff hangs the tail of *taha topta sapa,* a special kind of deer with a black streak across its face. This deer is very sacred. To kill it is an unlucky deed. It represents the unity of the universe. Early in the morning, before anybody goes to the

brook for water, this deer has already drunk it and
blessed it. We use its hide for our sacred gourds. We
put up these five staffs by filling big empty tin cans
with earth, planting the sticks in them. Some people
don't like this. They don't want to see a Maxwell
House coffee can or an empty can of Hawaiian Punch
used for this. It is a little thing, maybe, but understandable. It is better to cut a round tree trunk into
short sections, making a hole in the middle, planting
the sticks in there. About these staffs, we don't use just
any kind of wood for them. They are *wo-wakan*,
supernatural. They are branches of *canunkcemna*,
skunkwood, a kind of sumac. Why do we use this?
There is a power in this wood. Those strange bushes
have always twelve limbs on the west side and seven
limbs on the south side. We do not know why. The
seven limbs are watching the south and east wind; the
others—six for the west and six for the north—watch
the universe. The moment when you pull that stick
out of the ground is most important. Looking into the
hole in the earth where it grew, you will see what kind
of sickness is troubling the person you will try to cure
during the ceremony.

Now we will speak about the altar, which is situated
right behind the red and black center staff. It is
formed of powdered earth made smooth with an
eagle's feather. It stands for *maka sitomni*—the all-
over earth, the universe. Through it the whole world is
in that room during the ceremony. In this sacred
square of earth the medicine man traces a design with
his finger. Some of these designs are well known and
used by all *yuwipis*. Others are special, belonging to
one man alone, according to his vision. I myself use
mostly four altar designs though I know many, many
more. My chief design represents the Great Spirit, and
one uses this to doctor a sick person. I have already
drawn and described this design in the chapter about
the circle and the square, about Indian symbolism.

Another design comes from drawing a circle in this

earth and it represents the "without end." The man who makes this design also puts himself in there through the picture of an animal, a woodpecker, a bear, an eagle—that's up to him. He also makes a lightning sign to get the thunder power.

A design representing *iktome,* the tricky spider-man, would not ordinarily be used by a medicine man, but by somebody who wanted to perform some magic, a *heyoka* perhaps. This spider design could be used like a love charm. With this powerful design one could take the souls of a boy and a girl and tie them together. Then they couldn't help finding each other, falling in love. You don't have to believe this, but it really works.

The gourds, the rattles called *wagmuha,* are most important for the ceremony. You put them at the sides of the altar. There should be two of them, though some medicine men use four for the different directions. In this case you put the one in the east last. The east side works with *tunkashila,* the Great Spirit, and with the morning star. The rattles are made of deer hide, some old ones of buffalo hide. I know some that are made from a buffalo's scrotum. As far back as people can remember rattles have been used to cure the sick. Long ago we even had men who were specially designated "keepers of the gourds." Inside the gourds, as I already told you, are the sacred, tiny *yuwipi* stones. In some cases, men or women cut little squares of skin from their arms and put these into the rattles to help a relative to get well.

The sound from the rattles is not music, and it does

not represent a rattlesnake as some white men believe. These rattles talk to you. If the man who is putting on the ceremony gives you some of the holy herb and puts it in your ear, you will understand what the rattle is saying. This herb has no name in the white man's language. It has no green stuff at the top; it is just a root. When a spirit enters the room during the ceremony, he picks up the rattle and makes a noise with it and he may hit the body of a sick person to make a cure. That rattle travels so fast nobody could ever catch it. This has to do with *takuskanskan*—the power which moves.

All these things I have mentioned—the tobacco knots, the colored flags, the staff, the altar—the gourds are holy things, and no *yuwipi* ceremony can be performed without them, but the most important thing I have left to the last. We must also have the holy pipe, which plays a big role in all our rites. All these things we must have. Other objects a *yuwipi* man might use from his own medicine bundle—eagles' heads and claws, bear paws, special stones, antlers, animal and plant things, according to his vision. These he will use every time he performs a *yuwipi* ceremony, but the tobacco ties and the flags will be used only once. They can be burned afterward, or be given away for a keepsake, but one can never use them again in the spiritual way.

Besides all these sacred things we have also waiting the kettle with dog meat and a pot filled with cold, clear water from a spring. These, too, are placed within the rectangle of tobacco ties, near the red flag. Elsewhere in the room are pots and plates with bread and soup, corn and berry *wasna*, the pudding called *wojapi* and a special kind of mint tea we drink on this occasion. All this food will be distributed after the ceremony is over.

All is now ready for the *yuwipi*, for the skull practice, as they used to say in the old days. Before the tying up the room is purified with sweetgrass. We call it *wacanga* and it is braided like a woman's pigtail. We burn it at one end, walking around with it, waving it so that the scent spreads through the room blessing it with its fragrance. It smells so good; it swirls around us and makes us all relatives. With it we purify all the things we use in the ceremony. It drives out evil influences. It counteracts the effect of a woman having her monthly time. When she has her period she is not supposed to take part in a ceremony because being *isnati* is having a great nature power which could spoil the medicine and undo the curing. If a woman is *isnati* one can't doctor her. Women know this and stay away from a ceremony when they have their time, but in case there should be one who doesn't know, well, the smoke from the sweetgrass will neutralize this power. For some ceremonies one uses cedar smoke, which gives a man the power to dream, but for *yuwipi* we prefer the sweetgrass.

We also use *wahpe-wastemna*, Indian perfume. The Great Spirit told me to use these things. We pass a bag around to put on ourselves, rub our bodies, our clothing with it to smell like nature. Now the spirit comes through the house. Everybody puts a sprig of sage behind his ear or in the hair. Now the spirit can work well.

The medicine man stands before the altar. He is ready to be tied up. We use rawhide for this, the same as our bowstrings. We start with his fingers, put his arms behind his back, tie each finger to the other. The finger tying represents the *wakinyan*, the thunder-birds, the lightning. This finger is also symbolized by the bowstring. The spirit strikes as with a bow, quickly.

Then we wrap the *yuwipi* man up like a mummy. In the old days we used a buffalo hide for this, but now we make do with a large star blanket, a quilt with many colored pieces of cloth forming the design of a morning star. The background is usually white. These blankets are beautiful. Some people are buried in them. They are big enough to cover the whole man, including his head. Next we tie man and blanket into a bundle with a long thong of rawhide. We have to tie him up in the right way, with seven knots. We cannot afford to make any mistakes because this could endanger his life. We make that rawhide tight so that the man will sense with his body how the people feel.

The tying up, the thongs, the string of tobacco ties have a deep meaning for us. This is tying us together, ending the isolation between one human being and another; it is making a line from man to the Great Spirit. It means a harnessing of power. The man is tied there so that the spirit can come and use him. It pulls the people together and teaches them. It is not only during a *yuwipi* ceremony that this tying up with rawhide occurs. In the old days a man vowed to become a *kola*, a friend, to another. "Friend"—white people use this word lightly. Maybe you don't know what real friendship is. The young men who vowed to be a *kola* to each other would almost become one single person. They shared everything—life and death, pain and joy, the last mouthful of food, even their women. They had to be ready at all times to give their lives for each other. In the same way an older man could adopt a younger one by becoming his *hunka*. By this the younger man became the son of the older, even if only a few years separated them in age. Men sealed these special friendships with a ceremony. Covering both of them with a buffalo robe, the medicine man tied them together with thongs, announcing to the people that these men were now tied to each other as *kolas* or as *hunkas*. In the same way of thinking we had an "untying" ceremony—*kici yuskapi*. By this a man who had killed another could untie himself from the blood guilt. After this ceremony the families involved had to forgive each other.

The *yuwipi* man has to be tied up to make the spirits appear. You unloosen him, and they go away. Sometimes they don't come at all. Sometimes you just feel a furry hand, soft as a kitten, on your shoulder and neck.

When the tying up is finished, two men lift up the *yuwipi* man and place him on the floor, face down, his head lying near the altar. He is now as one who is dead. He does not exist anymore. We were never buried in caskets; like the *yuwipi* man our dead were tied up in a blanket. They were placed on a scaffold, left to the winds and the rains until nature swallowed them up. While the *yuwipi* lies on the floor in his star blanket, his spirit could be hundreds of mile away in the far hills, conversing with the ancient ones. He has ceased to be. It is up to us to bring him back. We must concentrate on this, help him through *wace iciciya*—through praying within ourselves.

Now the kerosene lamp is extinguished. Total darkness will help you to concentrate. The medicine man and all of us present have to use our powers the right way. Otherwise he could be killed, helpless as he is. Lightning could strike him dead. Now the spirits are reaching us. They may touch you, but you can't touch them. We are ready for the drums, the songs and the prayers.

The words of my first song are: "Where is that sacred spirit that is fated to be with me tonight?" The second song means: "I have done wrong. I have hurt the vision of the spirit. But I will change. I will be different. My life will change. I have four lives from the four directions of the wind. From above coming down to the earth I have been promised a power to use among the people." In my third song I call for the spirits to appear. I am singing, begging them to come. I am calling the spirits of the west, the black power, the red power, the yellow power and the white power from the south. I beg the power from above, the eagle power, to make itself felt here. I pray to the powers below, to our mother, the earth, to be with me, to help me, to make our wishes come true.

My fifth song says: "Upon this rock I have laid my sacred pipe. This rock is me, I am the rock. Therefore the wisdom of the Great Spirit will be with me at this moment." The sixth song is addressed to the lady spirits. It says that four of them are present, two women with wings above me in the sky and two women spirits upon the earth, helping me, honoring me with their presence. They guide me so that I can understand their language; they make me understand the spiders and the ants. The Great Spirit has blessed these tiny creatures. Through his blessing I can speak to them and to the winged ones, the fowls in the air. Thus the spirit is with me.

My seventh song says: "Here come the dancing spirits. They are praising the mystery power with songs and gourds. They are dancing and they are happy." My last song starts: "You hear my voice, I hear your voice; the voice of the spirit is coming to me now. What I am hearing tonight, about sickness, about a person's need, the spirit will now talk to me and through me to all of you."

And so the spirits come, from the west and from the south, coming in the shape of bright sparks of light, coming in the soft touch of a feather. They come from above and beneath, making the walls and the floor shake and tremble. They come as voices, little voices without bodies or mouths, nonhuman voices which we can understand all the same.

The ceremony lasts a long time, but finally the lights are rekindled and we see the medicine man sitting with the string of tobacco ties around him, unwrapped and untied, existing once more among us. Each of us, in turn, now has something to say, something good, about how he feels and what he has experienced. Or we can ask questions, about our health, about family problems, about somebody or something which has been lost. And the *yuwipi* will answer each one of us. If he is good, if he has the power, he already has been told the answers while he was lying in the dark inside the blanket.

The medicine man lights the sacred pipe and raises its stem in prayer. The pipe then goes around, clockwise, from hand to hand and from mouth to mouth. Its stem, its smoke is a link between earth and sky, between man and man. We each take four puffs, the pipe going around in a circle without beginning or end, coming back to the medicine man.

Now, tonight, we want you to taste the dog. You are going to take this medicine. It is sacred. Don't say, "I don't want to taste this old thing, brrrh!" That's what we don't want to hear from you. Be happy if you wind up with the dog's head, because this will bring you luck. There is good food for all of us here—bread, sweet *wasna* and sweet *wojapi*. All our ceremonies end with a feast. Filling one's belly—that is sacred, too. Eating together like this, sitting on the floor, our backs resting against the wall—that's another thing which ties us together as with rawhide. At last a boy comes around, walking clockwise, carrying a dipper and a bucketful of pure, cold water, a sacred thing without which there would be no life. Let's hope there still will be some pure water left when our boys have become old men. The boy who gives the water to each of us is very young. We give him this important job to make him feel like a man, to show him that we believe that it is a great thing—his being here, forming a link to the next generation, passing on our old beliefs to the ones who will be coming after us. Without such a feeling of continuity life would make no sense.

The medicine man now carefully empties the ashes from his pipe and parts the stem from the bowl. With that action he breaks the tie which binds earth and sky together, which has been keeping us bound to one another. Separated like this, the pipe is no longer sacred. Opened up this way, it is just a thing.

And now we all have to say certain words, each one of us in his turn. Learn to say the words right. They are

*mitakuye oyasin*—all my relatives, all of us, everyone.
This means all human beings upon this earth, all
living things down to the tiniest insect, the tiniest
plant. After this we don't say anything anymore. We
just get up and leave, because this *yuwipi* ceremony is
over.

# 12
# Looking at the Sun, They Dance

Staring open-eyed at the blazing sun, the blinding rays burning deep into your skull, filling it with unbearable brightness . . .

Blowing on an eagle-bone whistle clenched between your teeth until its shrill sound becomes the only sound in the world . . .

Dancing, dancing, dancing from morning to night without food or water until you are close to dropping in a dead faint . . .

Pulling, pulling away at a rawhide thong which is fastened to a skewer embedded deeply in your flesh, until your skin stretches and rips apart as you finally break free with blood streaming down your chest . . . This is what some of us must endure during the sun dance.

Many people do not understand why we do this. They call the sun dance barbarous, savage, a bloody superstition. The way I look at it our body is the only thing which truly belongs to us. What we Indians give of our flesh, our bodies, we are giving of the only thing which is ours alone.

If we offer Wakan Tanka a horse, bags of tobacco, food for the poor, we'd be making him a present of something he already owns. Everything in nature has been created by the Great Spirit, is part of Him. It is only our own flesh which is a real sacrifice—a real giving of ourselves. How can we give anything less?

For fifty long years they jailed us if we danced the sun dance, calling it a crime, an "Indian Offense."

Freedom of religion doesn't always include us Indians.

The sun dance is our oldest and most solemn ceremony, the "granddaddy of them all," as my father used to say. It is so old that its beginnings are hidden as in a mist. It goes back to an age when our people had neither guns, horses nor steel—when there was just us and the animals, the earth, the grass and the sky.

Nowadays clever people study sun spots through giant telescopes, and your man-made little stars zoom around the earth as if they were late on a job. You have even landed on the moon and left a few plastic bags of urine there and a few chewing-gum wrappers. But I think the Indians knew the sun and the moon much better in those long-forgotten days, were much closer to them.

Huddling in their poor shelters in the darkness of winter, freezing and hungry, hibernating almost like animals, how joyfully, thankfully they must have greeted the life-giving sun, let it warm their frozen bones as spring returned. I can imagine one of them on a sudden impulse getting up to dance for the sun, using his body like a prayer, and all the others joining him one by one.

So they made this dance, and slowly, generation after generation, added more meaning to it, added to its awesomeness. My father taught me, as he had been taught by his father, the learning and teaching going back to the beginning of time.

*Wi wanyang wacipi*—the sun dance—is our greatest feast which brings all the people together. I told you of *hanblechia,* the vision quest, one man, alone by himself on an isolated hilltop, communicating with the mystery power. Well, the sun dance is *all* the people communicating with *all* the mystery powers. It is the *hanblechia* of the whole Sioux nation.

The sun dance is the most misunderstood of all our

rites. Many white men think of it as an initiation into manhood, or a way to prove one's courage. But this is wrong. The sun dance is a prayer and a sacrifice. One does not take part in it voluntarily but as the result of a dream, or a vision.

The sun dance you are about to witness is sponsored by someone who dreamed that he must undergo this ordeal to bring his son back from Vietnam, to bring peace to the people of this world so that they can understand one another. We will dance for this.

The dance is not so severe now as it once was, but even today it asks much of a man. Even today a man may faint for lack of food and water. He may become so thirsty blowing on his eagle-bone whistle that his throat will be parched like a cracked, dry riverbed. He may be blind for a time from staring at the sun so that his eyes see only glowing spirals of glaring whiteness. The pain in his flesh, where the eagle's claw is fastened in his breast, may become so great that a moment arrives when he will no longer feel it. It is at such moments, when he loses consciousness, when the sun burns itself into his mind, when his strength is gone and his legs buckle under him, that the visions occur—visions of becoming a medicine man, visions of the future.

Insights gained at such a price are even greater than those that come to a man on a hilltop during his vision quest; they are truly *wakan*—sacred.

One thing makes me sad. Here in the town of Winner live hundreds of Indian families eager to keep the old ways, but we are surrounded on all sides by white cattle ranchers. The only place we can hold our sun dance now is on the old fairgrounds where the local cowboys used to have their rodeos. It's not good enough for them anymore; they've built a new one and we have kind of taken this one over. The old grandstands are peeling and full of splinters, but they are still safe enough to sit on. You can still see the fading signs: "Drink Pepsi-Cola," "See Your Local Ford Dealer." Pretend not to see them.

Some communities are luckier, not so fenced in. They can still hold their ceremonies out on the open prairie, on whatever is left of it, but we will have a good sun dance here all the same. We will do it right, in the sacred manner of our forefathers, as our elders have taught us—at least as far as this is possible at this time and in this place.

We want you to understand and to watch, but not with your eyes only. This is a good hour to relate to you how we celebrated the sun dance in days long past, to make you see it in your *mind* in all its ancient awesomeness.

Just telling about it makes me a little uneasy. Formerly we didn't talk much about it even among ourselves, and then only on solemn occasions, when twelve old and wise men were present to make sure that what was told was right, with nothing added and nothing left out.

I have said much about the pain of the sun dance, little about its joys. We Sioux are not a simple people; we are very complicated. We are forever looking at things from different angles. For us there is pain in joy and joy in pain, just as to us a clown is a funny man and a tragic figure at one and the same time. It is all part of the same thing—nature, which is neither sad nor glad; it just is.

Thus in the old days the sun dance was not all sacrifice but also a happy time when the choke cherries were ripe, the grass was up and the game plentiful—a happy time for meeting old friends.

We were spread out then in small hunting parties from Nebraska to Montana, like pebbles flung in the sagebrush. But nobody would miss the sun dance, even if he had to travel hundreds of miles. At the sun dance you came across relatives whom you had not seen for a year and swapped stories with them of all the bad and good things that had happened to you in the meantime. Here boys met girls they could court and make love to. We Sioux have such a fear of inbreeding, with so many rules which forbid you to marry within your clan, that I think the sun dance was for many a young man his only chance to find the right girl.

Every family put up their tipi in the place that was proper for them, with the herald riding around the camp circle telling everybody what to do. These were days of visiting back and forth between tents, of good food, good talk, good company. This was a time for begging songs, the singers going from tipi to tipi collecting gifts and food for the poor. It was also a good time for girls to look for a special kind of herb with four buds which acted as a love charm—an herb that would make their lovers faithful. There aren't too many of these herbs around now, the women tell me.

The sun dance lasted for twelve days: four days for preparing the campsite, four days for the medicine men teaching the participants the many things they had to know, four days for the dance itself.

The sun dance really began with the choosing of the *can-wakan*—the sacred pole. It was always a cottonwood, our sacred tree. If you cut off the top branches, make a clean cut with your knife, you will find a design resembling a star at the core of each branch. In making their choice men were not looking for just the first, good-sized cottonwood they might come across. The most perfect of all trees was just good enough. To find it the tribe sent out four scouts, brave men of blameless character. It was a great honor to be selected for this task. The scouts rode off as if going on the warpath—painted and armed. They were looking for an "enemy" to capture—a wooden enemy, a forked cottonwood. When the scouts had found a worthy tree they returned at a dead run and made their report to the medicine men.

On the morning after the camp was filled with

excitement. The drums throbbed. Everybody sang brave-heart songs, black-face-paint songs. You know, a warrior who had distinguished himself in battle had the right to paint half of his face black upon returning to the camp.

The whole tribe rode out following the four scouts —the young men and women on their best horses decorated with trailing vines and leaves. The scouts rushed up to the tree, counting coup upon it as if striking an enemy. They told the tree: "You are lucky to be chosen from among all others. It is a great honor!"

The "killing" of the tree was done by four young women who had never been gossiped about, who had never been with a man. They were proud to be chosen for this. If a girl had been so foolish as to pass herself off as a virgin when she was not, the man who had lain with her would have spoken up at once and shamed her forever, but this never happened.

The ax used to fell the tree had to be brand new—never used before, never to be used again. Each of the young women took her turn, at first only feigning, giving the young men a chance to tell about their brave deeds. Often this was done by way of a song. My grandfather used to sing these words:

> In a fight,
> I yield first place to none.
> Black face paint
> I strive for.
> Unafraid
> I live.

When the women at last cut the tree down they made the shrill, spine-tingling killing sound which honored a brave enemy. As the tree fell, it was not allowed to touch the ground but was caught by the twenty pole bearers. After that no one was permitted to touch the tree, walk before it or step over it. A man who once carelessly jumped across it had his neck broken the next day when his horse threw him. You might call this an accident, but we old full-bloods know better.

There are so many things to do, or not to do, during a sun dance that we always put one medicine man in charge of the ceremony to see that everything was done right, that all the things used were new and specially made. This man was the intermediary between the people and the mystery power. At times I have been this man.

The dance also must have a sponsor, a man who is responsible for putting it on, because a vision has told him to do so and he has made a vow. Such a person will give away most of what he owns to provide food and gifts for the poor.

I am not so young anymore and my head is so full of thoughts and memories that it is hard to keep this story from wandering. My talk is like the sun dance—so many things going on at one and the same time.

When the tree was down four medicine men who had been chosen earlier cut off all the lower branches and covered the "wounds" made on the trunk with vermilion paint. The fork of the sacred tree and the topmost branches with their leaves were left untouched. A buffalo robe painted red, or a scarlet cloth, and a weasel skin were tied to it together with the figure of a man and a buffalo made of rawhide. These small images had large male parts on them, ready for action, you might say. These had a deeper meaning. Among other things the sun dance also stood for the renewal of life—new plants shooting up, mares foaling, babies being born. Those stiff male parts stood for the renewing force in nature. The tree was then brought to the dancing place with its top pointing toward the front. Special sticks were used to carry it, as it should not be touched. Four times on the way the bearers stopped to rest.

One thing we shall perhaps never see again: the mad

rush of the young warriors on their horses after the last rest of the pole bearers, every rider trying to be the first at the pit where the tree would be put up. What a sight it must have been, the strong young men milling in the dance circle, the horses prancing, kicking up dust, their coats painted, their tails tied up, the neighing, the snorting, and yelling. War bonnets streaming, the loose hair flying, riders knocking each other from their horses in their eagerness to be the first to touch that spot and win red-coup-stick honors. Those strong-hearted young men on their brave ponies, where are they now?

When the tree finally arrived in the camp circle a great shout of joy rose from all the people. Buffalo fat had been placed inside the pit which was waiting to receive the sun-dance pole. The fat was an offering to the Buffalo nation asking their help to feed the tribe in the coming year. A cross-bar was fastened to the fork of the tree. To this were tied the rawhide thongs, one for each man who had made the vow to undergo the ordeal of "piercing." The top of the pole was decorated with strips of colored cloth, one each for the four corners of the earth. To the cross-bar was also tied the sponsor's offering—a large bag beautifully decorated with bead and quill work around which branches of the choke cherry had been wound so that the bundle blended in with the leaves at the top of the tree. Inside the bundle was a choice hunk of buffalo meat with an arrow stuck through it. This ensured good hunting. The tree was also painted a different color on each side.

All this time the medicine man in charge was talking and praying to the tree and the pit in so low a voice that nobody could make out the words. At last the pole was raised. This was done in four stages. I guess by now you have caught on to this: that four is our sacred number, that we do everything by fours. While the tree was being raised the people were silent and not a sound was to be heard, but once it stood upright everybody raised a great cheer and the men fired their guns in the air.

For a short while there was some horseplay as men and women shouted jokingly at Iya and Gnaske—the two little figures with the big male parts. This banter had all to do with sex; it was what you might call "talking dirty." Ordinarily women would have been ashamed to speak this way, coarsely, with all the people to hear them, but at this one time it was all part of a rite and therefore good.

Now that the tree was up it was supposed to "speak" to the people. These words were sung in its name:

> I am standing
> In a sacred way
> At the earth's center
> Beheld by the people,
> See the tribe
> Gathered around me.

Around the pole the sun-dance lodge was erected. Also called the "shade house," it was a circle of poles holding up a roof of pine boughs. From here the people could watch the dance. A little way west of the pole they made a square of earth—*owanka wakan,* the sacred place. It contained a measure of power given by the Great Spirit to be used for the people. Two lines traced within the square, small ditches, really, were filled with tobacco, covered with vermilion powder, silvery mica dust and downy eagle feathers. The cross symbolized the four directions of the wind. Nobody was allowed to step between the pole and the *owanka wakan.*

A tipi was then set up for the dancers, and a sweat lodge was prepared for them. Now everything was ready for the actual sun dance, which lasted for four long days. There was no merry-making, no visiting back and forth on the night before it. The medicine men prayed as the people stayed quietly in their lodges. For the first three days the men danced from dawn to sunset, blowing on their eaglebone whistles, their bodies moving as one until they were faint with weariness. And then came the fourth, the most solemn day.

Before dawn on the last day the medicine men would go up a hill to catch the first rays of the rising sun, to welcome it, to ask for good weather and strength for the dancers. Those who had made the vow purified themselves in the sweat lodge and were painted, each in a different way according to his vow. They wore wreaths on their heads and wrists and long kilts of red cloth from their waist down. They all had their medicine bundles hanging from their necks. Women did not pierce like the men, but they, too, could make a sacrifice by having many tiny squares of flesh cut from their arms.

Led by the medicine men, the dancers made a solemn march from the sun-dance tipi to the dance circle. The medicine man who acted as intermediary to the Great Spirit walked ahead along a marked trail carrying a painted buffalo skull. This was placed upon the altar facing the sacred pole together with a loaded peace pipe. Before the men underwent their ordeal it was the babies' turn to have their ears pierced. A space had been covered with sage, and here the mothers sat with their little ones calling to this or that brave and wise man to perform this task. While the men pierced the tiny earlobes with an awl they told of their brave deeds and reminded the parents to bring up the children in the right way—the Sioux way. This was supposed to influence the minds of the children, but not right away, I think, because there was much crying and squealing among the little ones.

At last it was the men's turn, and that was no child's play, believe me. Nobody had been forced or talked into this, but once he had made a vow, he had to go

through with it. You can't break your word to Wakan
Tanka.

The piercing could be done in four different ways.
For the "Gazing at the Buffalo" way the flesh on the
dancer's back was pierced with skewers. From these
were hung up to eight buffalo skulls. Their weight
pulled the skewers through the flesh after a few hours.

The second way was "Gazing at the Sun Leaning."
This was the one most used. The flesh on the dancer's
breast was pierced about a hand's width above each
nipple and a wooden stick or eagle's claw stuck right
through the muscle. At the end of the dance each man
had to tear himself loose.

The third way was "Standing Enduring." The dancer was placed between four poles. Thongs were fastened in his flesh—two in his chest and two in his back
underneath each shoulder blade. The loose ends were
tied to the poles and the dancer had to struggle bravely
to free himself.

The last way was "Gazing at the Sun Suspended."
In this case ropes were tied to skewers in a man's chest
and back and he was pulled up into the air with his
feet above the ground. This was the most severe test of
all, as the dancer could do little to hasten the end of
his ordeal by pulling or jerking but had to wait until
his own weight finally ripped his flesh open. Some just
kept hanging there until friends or relatives pulled
them down.

Usually a man had his friends by his side, encouraging him, cleaning his wounds and wiping away the
cold sweat with a bundle of soft sage leaves. Plants
used in this way made a powerful love charm prized
by women. The skewers of sagewood, too, are sought
after. The dancers present them to their friends, who
use them to tamp down the tobacco in their peace
pipes. A girl might also quench her lover's thirst by
bringing him a little water to drink if thirst threatened
to overcome him.

Some white men shudder when I tell them these

things. Yet the idea of enduring pain so that others may live should not strike you as strange. Do you not in your churches pray to one who is "pierced," nailed to a cross for the sake of his people? No Indian ever called a white man uncivilized for his beliefs or forbade him to worship as he pleased.

The difference between the white man and us is this: You believe in the redeeming powers of suffering, if this suffering was done by somebody else, far away, two thousand years ago. We believe it is up to every one of us to help each other, even through the pain of our bodies. Pain to us is not "abstract," but very real. We do not lay this burden onto our god, nor do we want to miss being face to face with the spirit power. It is when we are fasting on the hilltop, or tearing our flesh at the sun dance, that we experience the sudden insight, come closest to the mind of the Great Spirit. Insight does not come cheaply, and we want no angel or saint to gain it for us and give it to us secondhand.

Well, my friend, it is good to sit here and watch another sun dance come to its high point. It is good to see our people hold onto their Indianness. Some of the outward splendors of the sun dance are missing these days, but the essentials remain untouched. Sure, we no longer have the *Ucita,* the grand parade, men and women riding side by side in all their finery. Many of our people no longer have horses. Still, it is good that so many have come on their real-live hay burners instead of in their skunk wagons with their stink of gasoline. Yet that man over there with the old Buffalo headdress came from as far away as Denver, and the family next to him with the beautifully painted tipi which would have made a Sitting Bull proud traveled all the way from California to be here today. You can't hold it against them that they came by car. They came from Chicago, from Milwaukee, from Canada, from the East Coast. They are here—that is the main thing. The sacred pole has been chosen in the ancient manner, the buffalo skull is in its place and the suffering is as real as ever. That sacred cottonwood means so much to me. Its leaves are shaped like a heart. When they are twisted they look like a tipi, and when they are flat they symbolize a moccasin. The trunk of this tree represents the Milky Way. The fork, where a limb branches off, symbolizes the place where an old woman—*hihan kara*—sits in the Milky Way. When we die we have to pass her on the way to the spirit land. If we have a tattoo on our wrists *hihan kara* lets us pass. Our tattoo marks represent a kind of baptism. Without them we could not go to the spirit land but would have to walk back to earth as a ghost.

The last few years I have been in charge of the sun dance, acting for the people, but this time I asked a younger medicine man whom I taught to take over for me. Maybe this is my sacrifice today, to give up my power, hand it on, let the honor go to someone else. We Sioux haven't got your generation gap. We believe in bringing the young along to take our place because this is nature's way. It's maybe this, our willingness to share power with the young, which makes our old people loved and respected, which makes talk easy between the generations.

It means I can sit back and explain things to you today. I have fasted and abstained from tobacco and other pleasures and this will be my offering. Before the dancers enter the sacred grounds the singers take their places on the outside. They have been practicing the seven sun-dance songs. They beat their drums with unwrapped willow branches. The dancers are coming in a line. They walk slowly around in a circle. They stop four times before they enter. They are barefoot, because the earth on which they are about to step is sacred. The main dancer puts his head against the cottonwood pole and embraces it; they are crying, because this is a great moment.

There are about a dozen dancers, a few women among them. Some have cut their arms, but only four have made the vow to be pierced. Two of them are

medicine men—Bill Eagle Feathers and Pete Catches.
It is Pete's wife who holds the sacred pipe, symboliz-
ing the White Buffalo Calf Woman. Earlier this morning Pete told me, "Today I want to pierce deeper,
suffer more, to bring peace in Vietnam, to preserve
life." He has stuck eight eagle feathers deep into his
flesh and let me tell you, they hurt him badly every
time he moves.

It is time for the piercing now. Maybe you cannot
see clearly what happens down at the ground near the
pole. Pete is lying on a buffalo hide on his back with a
piece of wood clenched between his teeth. Bill is
kneeling over him, taking Pete's flesh above the heart
between his teeth, biting hard, making the flesh go
white and numb, so that the piercing won't hurt so
much. Did you see the flash of the knife? It is done
and Bill is putting a strong sage stick and an eagle's
claw through the wound. Pete gets up, and the rawhide
cord hanging down from the pole is attached to the
stick. Bill now pierces the other two men in the same
way. I shall now leave you for a moment and do Bill's
piercing for him. I'll do it swiftly, gently, like a feather
on a wound, because I have much practice.

Did you look at your watch? I am sure it took no
longer than a minute. The dancers are helped to stand
up. Each one has a wreath of sage on his head. Once
they are bound to this pole, the medicine man who
runs the dance no longer has pity on the men. He pulls
the dancers backward until the flesh stands out on
their chests. When this is done the singers sing the first
song: "I offer myself to you, Great Spirit. Have me for
what I want. Pity me, for I want to live."

The dancers are now raising their arms in prayer,
blowing on their eagle-bone whistles. They will stay in
one place, turning always to the sun, always facing it
as it travels, their eyes gazing steadily into its brightness. Everybody is silent, except for the singers. No
baby squalls; even the dogs have stopped barking.

Do you get tired from just watching? Is the sun too

bright for you today, sheltered as you are under the pine boughs? Does the throbbing of the drum, the never-ending sound of the whistles send you dreams?

There are some old-timers among us, pointing to the deep scars on their chests, scoffing at the dancers of today.

"They don't go underneath the muscle," they say. "It's only the flesh," and "The young men have gone soft." They complain that nobody hangs suspended anymore, or drags eight buffalo skulls after him till his flesh is stripped from his shoulder blades.

I don't know where anybody would get eight buffalo skulls nowadays, and as for tearing out their muscles . . . These dancers work for a living. They must earn dollars to buy food for their families. No matter how deep their wounds, in a few days they must be fit again to pitch hay, drive a tribal ambulance or pick beets.

One did not need money in those old days. While a dancer's wounds healed, the hunters brought him all the meat he and his family could eat.

No, in many ways the dancers of today are braver than those of days gone by. They must fight not only the weariness, the thirst and the pain, but also the enemy within their own heart—the disbelief, the doubts, the temptation to leave for the city, to forget one's people, to live just to make money and be comfortable.

It is time for them to break free. Pete has torn loose and now Bill. That young man over there is having his troubles; it's his first time. They are bringing him a stick, plant it in the ground before him so that he can push himself away. He has done it. *Hehetchetu*—it is finished.

There is a man lying down by the center pole. He is suffering from an illness and wants to get cured. This is the time and place to be healed. Under the cotton-wood, during the sun dance, healings occur suddenly, in a few seconds. It happens with great power, with a spirit force, something like an electric shock. It is up to a person; if he wants to be cured, he will be cured. Last year, Pete Catches was suffering from a sickness, something inside him, and he had a dream that he would lie underneath the sun-dance pole and get cured. But his vision also told him that nobody was to come near him at this time.

He told me later what happened. As he was stretched out on the ground, believe it or not, in a few minutes there was somebody down in the earth, about twenty feet beneath the surface, walking around there, roaming. Pete could hear him, see him, feel him. There was somebody down there and pretty soon he was coming up, breaking through the earth and rock, hitting his round belly, stretching out his arms, looking at Pete. He was coming to doctor him.

And just at this moment one of the dance leaders took it into his head to show off before the tourists and cameras, waving his eagle fan above Pete, pretending to do a medicine ceremony, wanting to give the spectators their money's worth. Pete had told everybody to keep away from him, but maybe this man forgot, and that being beneath the earth went away, backed down. It didn't like all that tourist stuff. Pete was so sad he could have cried.

But I know of a man who was cured underneath the center pole. This guy had a bad case of arthritis. He could hardly walk or bend over anymore. And when he was stretched out underneath the cottonwood he had a vision. He saw a rider coming on at a dead run between the white flags wearing a single feather in his hair. He was gliding in from the west between the white flags, skimming in over the sun shade, astride a gray horse whose hoofs never touched ground. That sick man was stiff with terror seeing the horseman come at him full speed. And he could feel the rider touching him with his lance and disappear. And that man got up and he could walk. His sickness was gone. There is a great power near the altar and the sacred pole during a sun dance.

The people are lining up to thank the dancers and shake their hands. They are bringing the large root from the foot of the pole, a root as big as a child, shaped like a human being, with arms and legs. They are chopping it up. It is a powerful medicine, and Pete and Bill will give a piece of it to each person. Come and join the line-up. You too have taken part in the sun dance, watching, listening, learning. You too must thank the medicine men, get a hunk of that root. It's good against rheumatism.

The sun-dance pole, the gift offerings, the tobacco bundles we shall leave to be blown over by the winds, the rains and the snows, leaving them to nature, to the sky, to the earth from which they came. Here, take an extra piece of medicine to take home with you. And now, as we Sioux always say after a ceremony—even the most solemn, sacred rite—*wa uyun tinkte,* let's go and eat! I haven't had a bite since yesterday.

# 13
# Don't Hurt the Trees

I've been waiting for you to ask me about the peyote church. Often that's the first thing a white man asks: "Hey, Chief, got any peyote?"

We have many visitors, young people wearing fringed rawhide shirts and beaded headbands made in Hong Kong. The men usually have long hair—sometimes in braids, Indian style—and beards. It's like being invaded by so many Jesuses and Saint Johns the Baptist—I don't know which.

They are nice kids, most of them, looking for something, hoping to find it here with us. We try to help. First we feed them. They are always hungry, hungry like Indians, hungry for a meal, for new ideas, for the truth. There's a feeling of friendliness, of kinship between us and them—they are gentle, try to get back to nature—but we don't always understand one another. They come and go fast, it takes more time than that to know one another.

Maybe understanding comes hard, because we speak a different language. Two of those young Jesuses from the University of Minnesota turned up here some time ago. They called themselves "White Panthers."

"Chief, we've come with a message," they told me, very solemnlike, "we bring you the truth."

"What's the message," I asked.

"Get rid of the mother-fuckers!" they said.

"We have no men here who do *that* to their mothers," I told them.

You see, that's one of our troubles. We can't curse. We have no four-letter words. Sure, we have a word for intercourse; it means just that—a man and a woman making love. That's hard to understand for us—using a word that really means bodies coming together in joy—using that for a curse.

Anyhow, it's peyote which attracts many of our young visitors. It creates some problems for us. It is legal for us Indians to use peyote in our religious ceremonies, if we are members of the Native American Church. But what about our white guests? One man in our tribe is under indictment on a drug charge for letting a white man eat a few buttons during a peyote meeting. We don't know how it will turn out in the end.

Another member of the peyote church—an old man—was given a bottle of little pills by some white students. "Here, Chief," they told him, "eat this. It's peyote—modern-day peyote. You don't have to gag anymore swallowing those big, bitter cactus buttons which constrict your throat. Get with it, Chief, turn on the modern, easy way, just take a few of these."

Well, the old man happily started popping those pills into his mouth, and, I tell you, they nearly drove him out of his mind. For two, three months he was confused, couldn't get rid of the noise in his ears. He said it was like a big powwow going on in his head day and night. He had eaten up all the little pills at one sitting. He said they had tasted good—like candy. Now he wonders what was in them.

Well, my friend, as you can see I am slow getting around to the real meat of this peyote story, like a dog circling a boiling kettle of stew. The reason is that I'm of two minds about this—wanting to talk about peyote but also not wanting to.

I was a member of the Native American Church for five years, went to their meetings every week, ate the peyote. You know us Sioux—when it comes to religion, to visions, we want to try everything.

Even the famous Black Elk, who was so set in his old Sioux ways, when he was an old man he got so interested in the Christian religion that his granddaughter had to get up on his horse behind him and read to him from the Bible while he was galloping back and forth all over the prairie.

Well, I once was part of the peyote cult, but I stopped a long time ago. A man cannot be forever two things at one and the same time. At least I can't.

I am a medicine man in the old Sioux way, believing in Wakan Tanka and in the sacred pipe.

The peyote religion is something new. It is not one of our ancient, native beliefs. It came to us about fifty years ago, spreading from tribe to tribe, always traveling north. It must have started way back before Columbus, somewhere in Mexico, maybe among the Mayas and Aztecs, and then slowly came up to the Pueblos, to the Navajos, to the Kiowas and Comanches, to the Oklahoma tribes and, finally, to us. The peyote plant doesn't even grow anywhere near here. The Sioux church members have to get it from Texas.

In a way the peyote cult, as it is practiced by many Sioux, is a perfect marriage of Indian and Christian beliefs. That part is all right. We believe all religions are really the same—all part of the Great Spirit. The trouble is not with Christianity, with religion, but with what you have made out of it. You have turned it upside down. You have made the religion of the protest leader and hippie Jesus into the religion of missionaries, army padres, Bureau of Indian Affairs officials. These are two altogether different religions, my friend.

The young people somehow sense this. That's why they come to us—looking for a spiritual experience their churches can no longer give them. That is good—as far as it goes. The blending of beliefs, the best of yours and ours—maybe that's one answer. The Pueblos are quite happy being Catholics and Kachina worshipers at one and the same time. I know of one Catholic saint whom they made into a Kachina rain god, and they tell me he's doing fine at that job.

Many of us Sioux go to a church on Sunday, to a

peyote meeting on Saturday and to a *yuwipi* man any day when we feel sick.

At Pine Ridge they are building a new Catholic church in the shape of a tipi with a peace pipe next to the cross.

All this confuses me. I am getting too old for it. I have my hands full just clinging to our old Sioux ways—singing the ancient songs correctly, conducting a sweat-lodge ceremony as it should be, making our old beliefs as pure, as clear and true as I possibly can, making them stay alive, saving them from extinction. This is a big enough task for an old man.

So I cannot be a *yuwipi,* a true Lakota medicine man, and take peyote at the same time.

It is also that my ideas about drugs have changed. Not that peyote is a drug—it is a natural plant. If it were a part of my native belief, such as the peace pipe, I would cling to it with all my heart. But as I see it now, as I feel it, I want my visions to come out of my own juices, by my own effort—the hard, ancient way.

I mistrust visions come by in the easy way—by swallowing something. The real insight, the great ecstasy does not come from this.

Instant light by flicking on a switch, instant coffee, instant TV dinners, instant visions through pills, plants or mushrooms—that's what I want to get away from. To my thinking that's part of the white "instant" culture.

Of course I can—and I do—argue against myself. Peyote is a natural part of the religion of many Indian tribes. At the core of all Indian beliefs are visions gotten in various ways. The Christian and Jewish religion, the great religions of the East, are based on the same thing, only white people have forgotten this. It's no longer important to them.

It is a good thing for Indians to look upon all Indian religions as a common treasure house, as something that binds us together in our outlook toward nature, toward ourselves, making us one, no longer just Sioux,

Cheyennes, Navajos, Pueblos, Iroquois, Haidas—but something much bigger, grander—*Indians*.

One of my young brothers, Leonard Crow Dog, is a *yuwipi* and a peyote priest at one and the same time. He is practicing the old Sioux ways but also visits the tribes in Arizona and New Mexico learning their ways. He is an Indian first—and then he is a Sioux.

I am still first of all a Sioux, a Minneconjou Sioux, and after that an Indian. I have fewer years left than my young friend here and must confine myself to a narrower, simpler circle.

I could tell you all about peyote. I took it for many years. But now I think it is no longer fitting that I should speak of it. Listen to Crow Dog here. He will explain it to you. Even better—go with him, take part in a peyote meeting. It will be a good thing. Then you can come back and tell me for a change.

LEONARD CROW DOG: "I am a road man in the Native American Church—the peyote church. I am also a *yuwipi*, a medicine man in the old Sioux tradition. I can neither read nor write. My father Henry drove off the truant officers with a shotgun. He didn't want a white school spoiling me for becoming a medicine man.

"When I was about thirteen years old I started out with four peyote buttons. Two years later I ate twelve buttons during a meeting. I have no book learning and don't speak good English, but I'll explain it as well as I can.

"Peyote power is the knowledge of God with peyote. God—Wakan Tanka—the Great Spirit.

"We have a Bible here and the peace pipe. Some of the people coming here for this meeting are Catholics, others belong to Protestant churches, some are not even Christians and you, my friend, we haven't asked you what you believe. Because in the end, it is all the same. Jesus and Wakan Tanka are the same. God and the White Buffalo Calf Woman, yes, Christ and this stone here in my medicine bundle, the light from that kerosene lamp and the holy spirit—it's all one and the same. You get it? Eat the peyote, then you'll understand.

"That peyote is holy. It's not a chemical gimmick but a sacred herb—our sacrament. That peyote took me a lot of good places, brought me to some good people. I got married with it; my children got baptized in the Native American Church.

"That peyote, it's opening three doors to me: makes me recognize myself, makes me understand the people around me, makes me understand the world.

"We have to go to Texas for our peyote, go a long ways to get it. The state of Texas made a bill outlawing peyote as a dangerous drug. It's all right to kill ourselves with whisky, or murder each other with drunken driving. It's all right getting cancer from cigarettes—most of us Indians don't live long enough anyhow to get cancer—but peyote is dangerous. Do you get it, my friend? Because I myself do not understand this. They tell me we have freedom of religion. It is guaranteed by the Constitution, but then we have a whole trunkful of treaties guaranteeing us the sacred Black Hills for as long as the sun will shine. Well, you know what happened to our Black Hills. Maybe the same thing happened to your Constitution. It's bad, not only for us but for you too, friend. I know, even though I can't read or write.

"We are ready for the meeting now. This is just an ordinary home, as you can see. We don't need a church house. Take all the furniture out of the room and you have a place of worship. We all sit on the floor. Lean your back against the wall. This will last from sundown to sunup, so make yourself comfortable.

"This is a cross-fire ceremony. We also have a moon-fire way of conducting a peyote meeting—Navajo style. The difference is that in the moon-fire we have a woman acting a big part—the water-woman, standing for the earth, for all growing things. The moon-fire is more Indian, has less of the Bible in it. Pretty soon we'll have some Navajo friends visiting us. Then we'll have a moon-fire ceremony in a tipi with a big half moon made of sand.

"That's funny. We Sioux have our peyote meetings in each other's homes. The southern tribes have theirs in a tipi. But it was us who invented the tipi. Now it takes a visit from the Navajos for us to put one up.

"We are setting up a square of sheet metal and asbestos now in the middle of the room. That's for the fire. The fire chief will bring it inside. We have five men running the meeting. The road man—he runs the meeting like a priest—the fire chief, the drummer, the cedar chief, the helper who serves the holy sacrament, the holy peyote. Red Bear is our road man today, so I am free to explain things to you.

"I guess Chief Lame Deer let you know how for us everything has a symbolic meaning.

"First we set up an altar—a Mexican rug and on it a Lakota Bible in our own language. We use only the revelations of St. John in our meetings. It's very Indian—full of visions, nature, earth, the stars. Something we understand very well, maybe better than you do.

"Across the Bible we put an eagle feather—it stands for the Great Spirit, for the Holy Ghost. That holy spirit is like an eagle with sharp eyes. You can't fool him.

"On the left is a rawhide bag with cedar dust to sprinkle on the fire. That's our incense. It stands for the plants, the green things of this earth, whatever has not yet been paved over with your highways. Those green things want to live, so that we the people can go on living.

"To the right is the peyote fan made of feathers. That fan catches good songs from out of the air, good peyote songs. It stands for all the winged creatures that fly through the air.

"There's also the peyote staff and the gourd, the sacred rattle. The staff represents authority given from above to hold the meeting. It's also the staff of life. Our prayers travel up along this staff.

"The beadwork on that gourd is something special —seed beads, Kiowa work. We can't get these tiny beads anymore. The designs mean visions, dreams, clouds and rainbows. The stones inside the gourd— the sound they make—that's prayer, talking to God. The tuft of horsehair at the top, those are the rays of the sun, the life-giving sun.

"Maybe you are wondering what that white man's alarm clock is doing there by the altar. Well, you'll see. The night is divided into four parts—every two hours the meaning and the symbols will change. That's what we need the clock for.

"You also notice the empty tin cans. Take one and keep it near you. Some people, the peyote makes them retch and throw up. If it happens to you don't be embarrassed. It's natural. Use the tin can. Nobody will pay it any attention.

"Now the fire chief comes in with the glowing embers. Never walk between a man and the flames. The fire stands for the generations. Pass fire to fire. Pass the flame to those who come after you. Pass along the spirit.

"We shape the glowing embers into a half moon— *hanhepi wi,* the night sun. It stands for the night, darkness. Time to think, concentrate, contemplate, with yourself. The peyote unites us all in love, but first it must set everybody apart, cut us off from the outside, make us look inside ourselves. There will be a prayer now.

> And he said to him, give me the little book.
> Take it, and eat it up;
> And it shall make thy belly bitter,
> But it shall be in thy mouth as sweet as honey.

"The helper is bringing the holy peyote now. We have chopped it up like relish. That makes it easier to swallow it. Take four spoons. I hope you didn't have any salt today. The peyote doesn't like salt. There—it didn't even make you gag. Now crawl into yourself. Let it work on you.

"It takes time for the peyote to have its way. For an hour or two there is maybe nothing. Suddenly you notice a change. Things are no longer what they were. The man sitting next to you may suddenly seem to be a million miles away, or the drum across the room may seem to be in your lap. The dividing line vanishes between what is physical and what is of the spirit. Lights, voices, sound blend into one another.

"A new understanding dawns upon you—joyful and hot like the fire, or bitter like the peyote. People tell me they get out of themselves, far away, high up in the air, seeing their bodies way down there on the floor. You'll see people drawing themselves up into a ball, like they were still inside their mothers' bellies, remembering things from before they were born.

"Time, like space, grows and shrinks in unexplainable ways—a lifetime of being, learning, understanding, pressed together in a few seconds of insight, or time standing still, not moving at all, a minute becoming a lifetime. Think what you can do with such a minute.

"I don't know how it will be with you. Wait, and let it happen.

"The drum will go around now—together with the gourd, the staff and the fan as everybody sings four songs.

"Long ago the drum was no brass kettle. Long ago the hide was buffalo hide. Now it is moose. The hide is Jesus' skin as he was beaten by the soldiers. It's Indian skin, beaten by police during a drunk arrest. The hide is all the four-legged creatures who give us food.

"The drumstick is the stick they whipped Jesus

with. The big stick the Government uses on the Indians. It is carved from cedar. It stands for all the trees who are also our friends.

"The rope which is wound around the drum is like a crown of thorns. If you turn the drum upside down and look at its bottom you will see that the rope there forms a morning star. The seven marbles which make up the nobs around the drum stand for the seven sacraments—or for the sacred rites of the Sioux nation. That's up to you.

"The drum is filled with water. As you shake it, breathe into it through the skin; it changes its pitch from a dull to a high ringing sound. We need both sounds. The throb of the drum is your heartbeat. Let it fill your being. Go with it. Don't resist it.

"It is time for some songs now. I shall sing for you. Just pass the holy things along.

*He yana yo wana hene yo*
*He yana yo wana hene yo*
*He yana yo, wani hiyana*
*He ye ye yo wai.*

"Now, let it be now, right now. That's what it means. . . .

"I haven't spoken to you for a while, left you alone with a blanket around you. It is midnight. The fire chief is bringing in another load of embers. We shape them into a heart. Do you see it throb? Peyote is the heart. What's inside ourselves. Makes us feel as one.

"You are putting your hand on your chest. You look scared. I know what it is. It happens to all the first time. The drum is inside you. Your heart is drumming and it goes so fast—like a peyote song. You're afraid your heart can't keep up and will burst. Don't be afraid. It won't. It will feel good after a while. Just give yourself up to the rhythm. There, now you smile. *Washtay.* Time for another four spoons, time for another prayer.

And there appeared a great wonder in heaven;
A woman clothed with the sun,
And the moon under her feet,
And upon her head twelve stars!

"The Virgin Mary, or the White Buffalo Calf Woman, or our own Water Woman here with her pail—it does not matter. Here comes the drum and the gourd again, the song and the fan that catches songs.

"If you'd ever wanted to get baptized, we'd shape the fire into a bird—the dove of peace, the Holy Ghost, the Thunderbird.

"But it is time to shape the fire into a cross. That's for the four corners of the earth. Angels stand in each corner with their wings spread out. Any time they want to, they could destroy this world, but they are here to protect it with their wings. They don't want it destroyed. What they are saying is 'Don't hurt the trees, nor the sea, nor the earth!' Heed these words. Maybe these are not angels, but the *wakinyan,* the sacred thunder beings. Who knows? Maybe you can see them now, with lightning coming out from their eyes. I can.

"We are changing the fire into a star now. Christ said, 'I am the Morning Star.' According to our Indian ways the first people came from the stars. Here come another four spoonsful. Do you have trouble with your camera? Does it jump and wiggle? Does it have fur? Everything is alive—the fire, the water, grandfather peyote—why not the camera?

And I saw a new Heaven and a new Earth!
For the first Heaven and the first Earth
Were passed away.

"That is still the Bible, but it could be a ghost-dance song, couldn't it?

"This is the last prayer. I guess it's getting light now outside. We have been praying for health, yours too.

Here comes the woman with the water. It sure tastes good. Take four swallows. Now everybody has something good to say about this night, just a few simple words—and now we eat together. There's two kinds of *wasna,* beef mixed with berries, and sweet-corn *wasna.* Doesn't it taste good?

"And now let's go out and watch the sun come up, a new kind of sun like you never saw before. Come, it has been a long night. *Hihani washtay*—good morning!"

# 14
# Roll Up the World

The other day I went to Rosebud and saw a group of about twenty Indians I know. They were sitting in the hallway of the council house. You can always find a crowd there, sitting and waiting, sitting and waiting, for lease money, for a job, for some kind of red tape to be cut. They let them wait. Indians have got so much time. Everybody knows that.

Well, those men gave me a big smile and I had to do a lot of handshaking. There was one old man from Norris. He had once been a medicine man but had given up on it many, many years ago. He said, "Say, John, you are a medicine man. I have been out of the Indian religion for a long time, but lately I feel bad about this. I want to tell my grandchildren, teach them the old way, but there is so much that I don't understand, that I have forgotten."

So I asked him what he wanted to know, and people were gathering around to hear what I had to say. The old man told me, "I want to know about the ghost dance."

"Well, there are too many people walking here," I tell him, "too much green frog-skin business and standing in line. How about going to the council hall and thresh things out there?"

"Okay, let's go, *hiyupo,*" he said and followed me in there, and more people followed him. It was like a tribal meeting, with everybody grabbing a chair, and I started to tell them what I know about the ghost dance. And from my vision, my dream, from what the Great Spirit and the little spirituals have shown me, from what I had heard from the old people when I was a small boy, I try to form the story.

Somewhere between 1880 and 1890 there was an eclipse of the sun. Many Indians felt the earth tremble and thought that the sun had died. They felt that a great misfortune was upon them. They had been put on the reservations to farm. They didn't know how, but that didn't matter. They had years of drought. The wind blew their land away in clouds of dust. Even the white farmers, who had better land and the know-how, were having a hard time. The Indians had been given some cattle for the land taken from them and they were supposed to breed them. But as the crops failed and the Government-issue food was late, the Indians ate the cattle. After that they starved. They had measles, whooping cough, lung trouble. It wouldn't have killed strong people, but it killed those who were weak from hunger. The Indians said, "We might just as well lie down and die." They were hoping that some help would come before it was too late.

The ghost dance started in the Southwest among the Utes. When the sun was darkened, one of their holy men heard a loud noise, like many thunders. He fell down dead, but an eagle carried him up to the sky. When he came back to life again he told the people that he had seen God, or the Great Spirit. He had been shown a new and beautiful land which the Great Spirit had prepared for his Indian children. It was covered with lush, high grass. It was as the land had been before the white man came, full of buffalo, deer and antelope. It was dotted with many tipis. In it lived all the Indians who had been killed by the white man or by his diseases. They were all alive again in that beautiful land. No white man's things were allowed among them, no guns, no pots and pans, no whisky.

That Ute holy man came back to earth with a sacred knowledge. He had been taught things in that new land—a few songs and a dance. By singing and dancing the dead Indians could be made to return to the earth together with the buffalo. That Ute medicine man began to teach the dance to his people. He had five songs. The first brought on mist and cold, the second brought snow, the third brought a gentle shower, the fourth brought on a big rainstorm, the fifth made the sun shine again. That man also had received a holy feather and some sacred, red face paint. He told everybody, "Don't hurt a human being, don't fight. My ghost dance is a dance of peace."

It seemed to be the message, the help, the people had been praying for. One tribe after another took up the dance. When the Sioux heard about it they sent four trustworthy men to the south to talk to this Ute holy man. They were Good Thunder, Cloud Horse, Yellow Knife and Short Bull. They had a hard, long time traveling. Most of the land was already occupied by the whites. They had roads, fences and railroad tracks to cross. Indians were not allowed off the reservations without a special permit. They had to travel by night and hide in the daytime. When these four men came back they said, "It's all true, what you have been told about this new belief." One said, "I fell down as dead. I WAS *dead*. I found myself on this new earth, and I saw my relative there who died last year, I saw him as I see you now. And I saw his wife, who was killed by white soldiers a long time ago. They were living in a big tipi and they gave me some meat. I have saved it, this meat from another world. Here it is."

The second man said, "This Ute holy man let me look into his hat and I saw the whole world in there."

The third man said, "This prophet told us, when we killed a buffalo, to leave his head, his tail and his four legs, and it would come alive again. You don't see many buffalo anymore, but we came across a lonely survivor. We killed it, ate its meat and did what the Ute had told us. As we watched from some ways off, the head, tail and hoofs formed themselves up into a new buffalo who walked away."

The fourth man said, "This new religion must be good, because now, when we meet men who used to be our enemies—Crows, Assiniboines, Pawnees—that ghost dance has made us into friends and brothers. Now we are just one big tribe—Indians."

These men brought an eagle feather, some special herbs and sacred red face paint which the Ute holy man* had given them.

Still, the Sioux didn't take up the ghost dance at once. It first came up to the Arapaho, the cloud people, and to the Hole-in-the-Nose people, the Nez Perces, to the Cheyennes and Crows. That's what my grandfather told me. One man in the Arapaho tribe sacrificed himself in a vision quest and he had a dream which instructed him to start the ghost dance. And that dream also gave him the herb that went with the dance. It was really no herb at all. It was a flesh, the flesh of a bird, an owl they say. This Arapaho made different designs which traveled from tribe to tribe, ghost-dance dresses, shirts and robes with pictures of birds and animals, the sun, the moon and the morning star painted on them.

Some of the Sioux were traveling some more to get the full story on that dance, men like Short Bull, who had already visited the Ute prophet, and Kicking Bear, a fierce, scowling warrior from Cheyenne River. These two became leaders of the ghost dance. They told the people that they could dance a new world into being. There would be landslides, earthquakes and big winds. Hills would pile up on each other. *The earth would roll up like a carpet with all the white man's ugly things—the stinking new animals, sheep and pigs, the fences, the telegraph poles, the mines and factories. Underneath would be the wonderful old-new world as it had been before the white fat-takers came.*

They said, "The spirits of the dead will live again on this earth. The ghost dance will bring back our dead relations. It will bring back the buffalo. Everything

---

*The prophet, Wovoka, was actually a Paiute, but the older Sioux always talk about him as the "Ute holy man."

will be good and pure again. There will be no killing.
The white men will be rolled up, disappear, go back to
their own continent. There might be a few good ones.
One could give them an eagle feather to stick in their
hair, then they could come too, be a part of the new
world, live like Indians. Only a very few could make it.
The earth will shake and a big storm will come up.
Then we'll be reborn. Men and women will take their
clothes off at that time and not be ashamed, coming
again from the womb of grandmother earth."

The dancers believed that by their actions they were
bringing about a happy hunting ground for the living,
right down here. There were some good words in their
ghost-dance songs. In one song it says:

> They are butchering cows there,
> They are killing cows,
> So make your arrow straight,
> Make an arrow, make an arrow.

They didn't mean real butchering or real arrows. The
song meant: If you want to go to the new earth you
have to make an arrow, and it has to be straight. It has
to be perfect. And that arrow, that's yourself, and you
have to be straight, be on the good side. For this
reason bows and arrows were made for the dance and
hung up on a pole in the center of the dance ground.
Sometimes the dance started with a woman shooting
an arrow into each of the four directions from which
the wind blows. These arrows were made in the old
way—with stone points.

The dance started with a sweat bath and the burning of sweetgrass. The dancers had their faces painted
red, with a black half moon on their cheeks or
foreheads. They wore nothing made of metal, no
knives, no silver ornaments, nothing that came from
the white man, except that many of the ghost-dance
shirts were made of cotton when the buckskin gave
out. Sometimes a sacred place was made in the form

of a square. On the west corner was placed a sacred pipe—this stood for us, the Sioux nation. At the north they placed an arrow—that meant the Cheyennes, the Shahiyela. At the south they put a feather for the Kangi Wicasha—the Crows. At the east we placed hail marks representing the Arapahos. They did this to show that the dance united the tribes, even those who had been enemies before.

The dance lasted four days. Often they danced at night, until daybreak. The dance leader had a big stick, and on top of it he had a little medicine bag and one eagle feather. If they fanned somebody with this eagle feather it made him swoon. The leader swung this staff with the feather around. And while the people were dancing, hand in hand, joined together, a power came from someplace, and a man or woman grew dizzy and fell down. They looked as if they had died, except that their skin was shivering. Well, they let them lay there, let them be, sprawled in the center of the circle formed by the dancers. The others kept going.

After a while those people came to and got up. Then the dancers stopped for a while, and whoever had a spell or had fainted told what he had seen. Some said, "I was dead and have come to life again." Others said, "An eagle took me up there to see my dead mother." Sometimes they found a piece of meat in their hands, or some choke cherries, some feather or beadwork, something from the other world. The leader, if he brought a handful of corn back, passed it around to every dancer, and that was supposed to come from the ghosts, the spirit land. So they honored this corn, put it in a bag and tied it to their necklaces.

One time a young man had a spell and he came up with some dirt in his fist, a kind of white, grayish earth, and he told the people, "I got a piece from the morning star here, and I was up there. There are people there, but you can't see them, and they can't see you. No man will ever see them, but here is this earth and it is human. We come from the earth, we are part of it, so this earth from the morning star must be a living being in a way."

Another time, during a ghost dance up in Montana, they had a beautiful gathering there, with many dancers. They were all singing in their own, tribal languages and one old man fainted away in a trance. When he came to he said, "I got a piece of the moon here." He repeated it over and over again: "This is a piece from the moon. It looks like earth, but it is flesh." He opened his hand and they saw a strange, powdery, shiny dirt. This was not the only time one of the people who had lost consciousness had woken up clutching some earth they said came from the moon. Some of it was preserved in several old medicine bags by the families of these ghost dancers. I got hold of one of them and sent some of this strange dirt to the University of South Dakota in Vermillion to analyze it. They told me later, "This dirt is really very much like a moon rock, but don't talk about it."

A man from another tribe took part in a ghost dance of ours, an Arapaho, I think. He said, "We are going to make all the ghost-dance robes bulletproof. The designs I taught you to put on the shirts have made them bulletproof already. This ghost dance tells me we must do away with the whites. They must go. We can make them go away, because we have these bulletproof shirts. We can do it." He held up one of the robes and made somebody fire a rifle at it. He picked up a few bullets from the ground and said, "Look, these shells can't penetrate our shirts; they just fall down harmlessly on the earth. The white soldiers can't hurt us."

One man saw and heard this and he went and told the Government people. That's where the trouble started. This was a peaceful dance, a vision dance, communicating with the dead relatives, but somebody had the wrong vision, and some white men misunderstood. The man who carried the tale was a jealous man, telling lies to the Government out of spite, how the Indians wanted to kill all the whites. He carried a grudge because his girl friend had left him to join the ghost dancers. So this jealous man betrayed his own people, and the Government, instead of stopping them in a peaceful way, came to stop the ghost dancers with guns and cannons.

First they killed our holy man, Sitting Bull. McLaughlin, the agent at Standing Rock, knew very well that Sitting Bull was not a ghost-dancer leader. He also knew, in spite of all the talk about a big Indian uprising, that the ghost dance posed no threat to the whites. The old chief was living peacefully in his little cabin. He had made friends with some whites. He liked to talk about the little white children in New York to whom he had given candy when he was in the Buffalo Bill show, saying that children were all alike, whether white or red, that people could get along if they kept a child's mind. He also said, "I want the white man *with* me, but not *over* me." But as long as Sitting Bull was alive the people listened to him rather than to the Government agent who wanted to "civilize" them and make them into white men. Sitting Bull was in the way and he had to die.

About thirty Indian police surrounded the little cabin in which the old man lived. At first he came peacefully, but then he heard somebody in the crowd singing: "Sitting Bull, you were a warrior once, what are you going to do?" He pushed the men away who were trying to handcuff him and said, "I won't go." At once the fight between the police and Sitting Bull's followers started. They always say that if you want to see a real battle you have to watch Sioux fighting Sioux. All other battles are tame compared to this. When it was over fifteen men were lying dead in the snow, among them the old chief. Buffalo Bill had given Sitting Bull one of the circus horses from his show as a gift, and as soon as the shooting started that horse began to dance. He thought he was back in the Wild West show at the circus. But unfortunately this was no make-believe fight.

As long as Sitting Bull and his closest friends, the men who had been with him through thick and thin, were still alive, Standing Rock had held out against this so-called "civilization." It was a place where the Indians clung stubbornly to their old ways and beliefs. But once Sitting Bull was gone, the people gave up and the missionaries had a big time. That's why Standing Rock has fewer medicine men now than the other Sioux reservations.

At Pine Ridge the white agent was so sure that the ghost dance was the start of a big uprising that he called in the Army. Soon the whole place was swarming with blue coats. There were more soldiers than Indians. Some ghost dancers got scared and ran away to the Badlands, holing up there where they were hard to find. We have an old man here whom everybody knows, Mr. Fool Bull. He can still remember the ghost dance. He watched it when he was a little boy.

FOOL BULL: "I don't know how old I am. The Government gave me a birthday according to the fiscal year July 1, 1887. But that's only when they got around to taking a census of our family. I was already maybe four years old when they said I was born. In those days the Government didn't have birth records like they do now. I am told I was born in Oklahoma. So that's all I know about this.

"To start with I'll tell you what I remember of what started the trouble, terrible trouble. We happened to be at Rosebud, camping under guard—soldiers, cavalry. They rounded up all the fathers and grandfathers and made sure they didn't get away and mix up with a 'hostile' bunch. My father was hauling freight from Valentine with an ox team. He went down there early in the morning and was back at night to unload. We heard there was a ghost dance going on north of us at an Indian village called Salt Camp. My mother's youngest brother took sick and he wanted to see the dance so that he could be cured, and they hooked up the buckboard and we drove up there, my uncle, my mother, my sisters and me.

"When we arrived we could see a big, level ground near the village and a lot of commotion, people on horseback, or on foot, running around. We saw a big circle of men and women holding hands, just as they do now in a round dance. They all sang ghost-dance songs and went round and round, round and round. They had no drum, just their voices to keep time. I remember one man. He acted like he was drunk, swaying back and forth. Then he fell on his face. Then he turned over, lying on his back. He was stretched out there and two dance leaders came with fire and a big eagle-wing fan. They put some herbs on the fire and fanned the flame. It woke up this dancer and he got up. They asked him what he had experienced.

"He told them: 'I was on a road from here over there. I couldn't see it, but I walked on it. It went up a hill upon which a lone man was sitting. I went up to him. He said: "There is your people, over this way, a big Indian camp, tipis, buffalo, horses—that's where you are going to be. Now you go back. Teach your people."' This man had come back from the other world with a new song which he taught the people.

"There was this man from another tribe and he fell down in a trance. When he came to he gathered up a few ghost shirts and hung them on poles. These shirts were made out of canvas and they had a sun and a half moon painted on the back. Some men were firing their rifles at them and the Indian from the other tribe said that the bullets could not go through these shirts but were dropping to the ground. My uncle didn't know whether to believe him.

"Some of my uncles—I had seven of them—went

up to Pine Ridge, near Wounded Knee, and influenced my father to join them. My father got a twenty-day pass to go up there and after that time the Indian police told us that we would have to go back. Pine Ridge was just a few buildings then, a couple of offices and a stockade. The tipis were all pushed together and crowded; they were guarded day and night, but some people got away to the Badlands.

"We went up there with a team and covered wagon. My father was a medicine man and he taught me some ghost-dance songs—'*Maka Sitomni ukiye,* the whole world is coming,' and 'I love my children, you shall grow to be a nation, says the father.'

"The soldiers came up to our camp and told us that if we would give them all our bows and arrows, our knives and guns, they might let us go visiting our people. So we put all our weapons on a pile. We had hardly anything left by then which you could call weapons, and the pile was very small. We had already been through this before. I guess we were someplace between Pine Ridge and Wounded Knee. We were staying inside the lodges by the fire as much as we could, because this was December and it was very cold, way below freezing. The earth was covered with snow. Nobody knew what would happen, or what the soldiers were up to. Everybody was scared; even we children could feel it. Suddenly we heard the guns. It made a noise like ripping a blanket apart, one continuous sound, I knew that something very bad was happening by watching my parents' faces. That's when the soldiers killed Big Foot's people—killed everybody, men, women and children. We couldn't have been very far, because we could hear the firing so clearly. They left the bodies lying on the ground overnight, frozen, arms and legs sticking out every which way. In the morning they threw them into wagons, dug a long trench, tossed them in and covered them all up. Our camp was lucky. It could have happened to us. These shirts turned out not to be bulletproof after all."

When the people dared to go there and look for survivors, they found four babies still alive. Their dying mothers had carefully wrapped them in their shawls. Their last thoughts had been for the little ones. One or two women were also still alive. They had lain there bleeding, in the open snow, for three days, in a blizzard and without food. These were strong women. One of the babies who survived was a little girl, Sintkala Noni, or Lost Bird. They say that she had a tiny American flag made of beads on her baby's bonnet.

I am trying to bring the ghost dance back, but interpret it in a new way. I think it has been misunderstood, but after eighty years I believe that more and more people are sensing what we meant when we prayed for a new earth and that now not only the Indians but everybody has become an "endangered species." So let the Indians help you bring on a new earth without pollution or war. Let's roll up the world. It needs it.

# 15
# The Upside-Down, Forward-Backward, Icy-Hot Contrary

I am going to tell you a story about clowns, but it won't be a funny story. For us Indians everything has a deeper meaning; whatever we do is somehow connected with our religion. I'm working up to this part. To us a clown is somebody sacred, funny, powerful, ridiculous, holy, shameful, visionary. He is all this and then some more. Fooling around, a clown is really performing a spiritual ceremony. He has a power. It comes from the thunder-beings, not the animals or the earth. In our Indian belief a clown has more power than the atom bomb. This power could blow off the dome of the Capitol. I have told you that I once worked as a rodeo clown. This was almost like doing spiritual work. Being a clown, for me, came close to being a medicine man. It was in the same nature.

A clown in our language is called *heyoka*. He is an upside-down, backward-forward, yes-and-no man, a contrary-wise. Everybody can be made into a clown, from one day to another, whether he likes it or not. It is very simple to become a *heyoka*. All you have to do is dream about the lightning, the thunderbirds. You do this, and when you wake up in the morning you are a *heyoka*. There is nothing you can do about it. Being a clown brings you honor, but also shame. It gives you a power, but you have to pay for it.

A *heyoka* does strange things. He says "yes" when he means "no." He rides his horse backward. He wears his moccasins or boots the wrong way. When he's coming, he's really going. When it's real hot, during a heat wave, a *heyoka* will shiver with cold, put his mittens on and cover himself with blankets. He'll build a big fire and complain that he is freezing to death. In the wintertime, during a blizzard, when the temperature drops down to 40 degrees below, the *heyoka* will be in a sticky sweat. It's too hot for him. He's putting on a bathing suit and says he's going for a swim to cool off. My grandma told me about one clown who used to wander around naked for hours in subzero weather, wearing only his breechcloth, complaining all the time about the heat. They called him Heyoka Osni—the cold fool. Another clown was called the straighten-outener. He was always running around with a hammer trying to flatten round and curvy things, making them straight, things like soup dishes, eggs, balls, rings or cartwheels. My grandma had one of those round glass chimneys which fits over a kerosense lamp. Well, he straightened it out for her. It's not easy to be a *heyoka*. It is even harder to have one in the family.

The no-account people and winos make fun of the *heyokas,* but the wise old people know that the clowns are thunder-dreamers, that the thunder-beings commanded them to act in a silly way, each *heyoka* according to his dream. They also know that a *heyoka* protects the people from lightning and storms and that his capers, which make people laugh, are holy. Laughter—that is something very sacred, especially for us Indians. For people who are as poor as us, who have lost everything, who had to endure so much death and sadness, laughter is a precious gift. When we were dying like flies from the white man's diseases, when we were driven into reservations, when the Government rations did not arrive and we were starving, at such times watching the pranks of a *heyoka* must have been a blessing.

We Indians like to laugh. On cold and hungry nights *heyoka* stories could make us forget our miseries—

like the *heyoka* who pretended to understand no English. In a cafeteria he points to a sandwich: "Give me this ham and cheese son of a bitch." Or a sister gives her brother a fine pair of moccasins. "Ohan," she says, "put them on." That brother is a *heyoka*. Pretty soon he comes back with a boiling pot of soup. Inside are the moccasins, all cut up. He is eating them. "What are you doing with these moccasins?" cries the girl.

"You told me to *wohan*—to cook—them," answers the fool.

Maybe you heard about the *heyoka* who goes to a store to buy canned goods. He can't read or write. He looks at the pictures on the cans—beans, chickens, peas. Whatever he sees that he likes, he buys. He discovers a can of dog food with the picture of a fat puppy on the label. He buys this and eats it. "Boy, that puppy tastes good," he says.

Or we talk about the *heyoka* turtle and his friend the *heyoka* frog. They are sitting on a rock by a lake. It starts raining. "Hurry, or we'll get wet," says the *heyoka* turtle to his buddy. "Yes, let's get out of the rain," says the *heyoka* frog. So they jump in the lake. Maybe these stories do not sound very funny to a white man, but they kept us laughing no matter how often we heard them.

A clown gets his strange powers from the *wakinyan*, the sacred flying-ones, the thunderbirds. Let me tell you about them. We believe that at the beginning of all things, when the earth was young, the thunderbirds were giants. They dug out the riverbeds so that the streams could flow. They ruled over the waters. They fought with *unktegila*, the great water monster. It had red hair all over, one eye, and one horn in the middle of its forehead. It had a backbone like a saw. Those who saw it went blind for one day. On the next day they went *witko*, crazy, and on the third day they died. You can find the bones of *unktegila* in the Badlands mixed with the remains of petrified sea shells and turtles. Whatever else you may think you know that all this land around here was once a vast ocean, that everything started with the waters.

When the thunder-beings lived on earth they had no wings, and it rained without thunder. When they died their spirits went up into the sky, into the clouds. They turned into winged creatures, the *wakinyan*. Their earthly bodies turned into stones, like those of the sea monster *unktegila*. Their remains, too, are scattered throughout the Badlands. There you also find many *kangi tame*—bolts of lightning which have turned into black stones shaped like spear points.

High above the clouds, at the end of the world where the sun goes down, is the mountain where the *wakinyan* dwell. Four paths lead into that mountain. A butterfly guards the entrance at the east, a bear guards the west, a deer the north and a beaver the south. The thunderbirds have a gigantic nest made up of dry bones. In it rests the great egg from which the little thunderbirds are hatched. This egg is huge, bigger than all of South Dakota.

There are four large, old thunderbirds. The great *wakinyan* of the west is the first and foremost among them. He is clothed in clouds. His body has no form, but he has huge, four-jointed wings. He has no feet, but he has claws, enormous claws. He has no head, but he has a huge beak with rows of sharp teeth. His color is black. The second thunderbird is red. He has wings with eight joints. The third thunderbird is yellow. The fourth thunderbird is blue. This one has neither eyes nor ears.

When I try to describe the thunderbirds I can't really do it. A face without features, a shape without form, claws without feet, eyes that are not eyes. From time to time one of our ancient holy men got a glimpse of these beings in a vision, but only a part of them. No man ever saw the whole, even in his dreams. Who knows what the great thunder-beings look like? Do you know what God looks like? All we know is what the old ones told us, what our own visions tell us.

These thunderbirds, they are *wakan oyate*—the spirit nation. They are not like living beings. You might call them enormous gods. When they open their mouths they talk thunder, and all the little thunderbirds repeat it after them. That's why you first hear the big thunder clap being followed by all those smaller rumblings. When the *wakinyan* open their eyes the lightning shoots out from there, even in the case of the thunderbird with no eyes. He has half moons there instead of eyes, and still the lightning is coming out.

These thunderbirds are part of the Great Spirit. Theirs is about the greatest power in the whole universe. It is the power of the hot and the cold clashing way above the clouds. It is lightning—blue lightning from the sun. It is like a colossal welding, like the making of another sun. It is like atomic power. The thunder power protects and destroys. It is good and bad, as God is good and bad, as nature is good and bad, as you and I are good and bad. It is the great winged power. When we draw the lightning we depict it like this,

as a zigzag line with a forked end. It has tufted feathers at the tips of the fork to denote the winged power. We believe that lightning branches out into a good and a bad part.

The good part is the light. It comes from the Great Spirit. It contains the first spark to illuminate the earth when there was nothing—no light, just darkness. And the Great Spirit, the Light God, made this light. Sometimes you see lightning coming down in just one streak with no fork at the end. This light blesses. It brightens up the earth; it makes a light in your mind. It gives us visions. This lightning is still another link from the sky to the earth, like the stem and the smoke of our sacred pipe. That light gave the people their first fire. And the thunder, that was the first sound, the first word, maybe. Long before the first white man came, we had this vision of the light and knew what it represented.

The lightning power is awesome, fearful. We are afraid of its destructive aspect. That lightning from the south spells danger. It heads against the wind. If it collides with another lightning—that's like a world-wide car smash-up. That kills you. A lawyer, a judge or preacher can't help you there. That flash from the south, that's *tonwan*, the thunderbolt—the arrow of a god. Sometimes it hits a horse. You see all the veins burn up, like an X ray. Afterward you find one of these black stones embedded in the earth where the lightning struck. The old people used to say that the damage caused by the lightning was done by the young, inexperienced thunderbirds. They did all the mischief. They were like pranksters, clowns. The old thunderbirds were wise. They never killed anybody. At least that's the story.

We swear by the thunder powers, by the *wakinyan*. You tell a story and somebody doesn't believe you, doubts your words. Then you say, *"Na ecel lila wakinyan agli—wakinyan namahon."* That settles it. Everyone knows then that you are telling nothing but the truth. Otherwise lightning would strike you dead. Likewise, if you swear by the sacred pipe, holding it in your hands, you cannot lie, or the thunder-beings will kill you.

If the thunder-beings want to put their power on the earth, among the people, they send a dream to a man, a vision about thunder and lightning. By this dream they appoint him to work his power for them in a human way. This is what makes him a *heyoka*. He doesn't even have to see the actual lightning, or hear the thunder in his dream. If he dreams about a certain kind of horse coming toward him, about certain riders with grass in their hair or in their belts, he knows this comes from the *wakinyan*. Every dream which has some symbol of the thunder powers in it will make you into a *heyoka*.

Suppose you have such a dream. What happens then? It is very unpleasant to talk about. What I mean is that a man who has dreamed about the thunderbirds, right away, the next morning, he's got a fear in him, a fear to perform his act. He has to act out his dream in public. Let me tell you one aspect of it, why we fear it. Indians are modest. In the old days, to expose a leg—say, to the knee—for a girl this was improper. We are a bashful race, and the poor *heyoka*, in his dream he would probably be stark naked without even a G-string on him. And he would have to go before the people like this and it would not be easy for him.

Now we have come to an age when we don't have this shame anymore. Look around you, go to the movies, all that nakedness; you can do mostly anything now. So we don't have these dreams about being nude anymore, because it wouldn't be such a terrific thing. I am joking, but if I had a *heyoka* dream now which I would have to reenact, the thunder-being would place something in that dream that I'd be ashamed of. Ashamed to do in public, ashamed to own up to it. Something that's going to want me not to perform this act. And that is what's going to torment me. Having had that dream, getting up in the morning, at once I would hear this noise in the ground, just under my feet, that rumble of thunder. I'd know that before the day ends that thunder will come through and hit me, unless I perform the dream. I'm scared, I hide in the cellar, I cry, I ask for help, but there is no remedy until I have performed this act. Only this can free me. Maybe by doing it, I'll receive some power, but most people would just as soon forget about it.

Let me tell you a story of a *heyoka* who performed

his act the way he dreamed it. It happened in Manderson, back in the 1920s. It happened on a Fourth of July, and this man was real lively the way he acted. He turned somersaults, and there was a bunch of young cowboys chasing him on horseback. They couldn't catch up to him. They were trying to lasso him, but they never came close. He was running in front of them, and sometimes he would turn somersaults. Sometimes he would turn around and run backward, and when they got near him he'd turn around once more and get away. When he was through, when he took off the ragged sack cloth he had on him, with holes for the eyes to look out of, we saw him. He was an old man in his seventies. What was his name? I can't recall it. And old, white-haired grandfather, but the thunder-beings had given him the power to run fast.

A *heyoka,* if he follows his dream to the letter, has to dress up as he saw himself in his vision. Now, here is something strange. The people he saw in his dream, if he saw you, you would be there, at the time and place where he would put on his act. You'd be there to witness it, regardless of whether you had planned to be there or not. You couldn't help being there. It's hard to believe. Some people say it is fantastic; others say it is ridiculous, but it is so.

If you are a *heyoka* you usually don't want to continue being one for the rest of your life, doing everything backward, acting the fool, be a permanant contrary. You'd want to cleanse yourself, be rid of it. Acting out your dream, undergoing the shame, being humiliated so that you don't dare uncover your face, that is one part of freeing yourself from this, but it is not the whole part. The ceremony which must be performed is awesome in some of its aspects.

The dreamer asks the medicine men and all *heyokas* for their help. A horse or a wolf dreamer will make the rounds and announce that a man has dreamed of the thunderbirds and must fulfill his vision. The *heyoka* could also be a woman, but this does not happen often. The dreamer invites all who are, or have been, *heyokas* to join in the ceremony.

First they have a sweat bath, make themselves holy with the smoke of sweetgrass. The Great Spirit wants a man clean and purified for this ceremony. It is the same as with all our ceremonies which start in the sweat lodge. The steam bath is the same as always except that those inside are singing *heyoka* songs. Also, a *heyoka*'s sweat lodge is always sited facing east instead of west. I know that all the books say that a sweat lodge always faces east. Whoever wrote this must have been describing a *heyoka*'s place, or maybe he just got it wrong and everybody copied him afterward. All our sweat lodges face west toward the setting sun.

A *heyoka* ceremony starts with a dance. I want you to know that our dances are not just powwows, having a good time, hopping from one foot to the other. All our dances have their beginnings in our religion. They started out as spiritual gatherings. They were sacred. Clowns are part of this. Many, many ages ago, before people knew how to dance, the thunder dreamers had a vision to run and jump around a buffalo stomach in which some meat was boiling. We had no iron pots in those days. They call this the "Around the Bucket" dance. It is performed in honor of the thunder-beings, the lightning spirits. This is our oldest dance together with the sun dance.

The bucket is there, all right, full of dog meat boiling over an open fire. For this dance all the *heyokas* get together to help one another. You have to have four leaders and four assistants, men who know the *heyoka* songs. All these should be *heyokas,* but these days there are not enough of them, so we have to put somebody in there willing to fill the vacancy. The real *heyokas,* those who are or have been thunder clowns, wear special bustles made of eagle feathers with a tail on them. They also wear crow belts made out of the feathers of all kinds of birds—eagles, owls, crows or woodpeckers. They also have some rattles made from rows of deer hoofs. We honor these things. They are *wakan*.

The substitute dancers who are not *heyokas* don't wear these things. They put grass in their belts and in their hair. From these men come our social dances—the grass dance, the Omaha dance, the good-time dances. They grew into our modern dances, which we do to enjoy ourselves, but all started in our religion. Dancing and praying—it's the same thing. Even at our powwows, with everybody laughing and kidding, we first introduce and honor the *heyokas*. We combine the powwows with our give-aways by which we honor our dead, with the consoling of those who mourn, with aiding each other. It is more than just hopping around.

Well, the *heyokas* dance around that steaming kettle, sing and act contrary. If the dreamer says, "A good day tomorrow," well, it will be a hell of a day next day. And if he says, "Tomorrow will be a bad day, thunderstorms from morning to night," why, you can leave your umbrella at home. You won't need it, because it will be beautiful. And if the *heyoka* sees a sick person and says, "He's going to die," that sick person will be all smiles because he knows he's going to live. But if the *heyoka* says, "You are going to get well," the poor thing, he might as well start writing his will.

And all the time the water is boiling in that pot, which is red-hot, glowing brightly. It's just bubbling up and down. The dog is in there, head, spine and tail together in one piece, the rest in little chunks, swirling around, bobbing to the surface. The medicine man is singing a special song which he has made up for this *heyoka* to dance to. Three times the thunder dreamer dances toward the bucket and each time he comes near it that dog's head pops up by itself, as if it wanted to come out.

The fourth time around the *heyoka* runs up to the

bucket and at the precise moment plunges his whole bare arm into that boiling water, searches around in there and comes up with the head, holding it up to the four winds. He will run with it, and he is guided in this by the spirit, by what he has dreamed, to whom to give this dog's head. He will give it to a certain sick man or woman. That person will be scalded. He will quickly throw it to another man, and he will get burned, and he will throw it to the one next to him and so on. Five or six people will throw that head, because it is too hot for them to hold. And this comes from the thunder power; it is not a cheap, magic trick.

After this the other *heyokas* charge that bucket, put their arms in and get the rest of the meat out. They don't care how hot it is. They give this meat to the poor and the sick. Their dreams told them whom to give it to. That's a good medicine and a hundred times better than all your pills and antibiotics or whatever you call them, because it cures all their sicknesses right there, during the ceremony. This happens every year and I have witnessed it many times.

What is it that makes a *heyoka* not get scalded? You can go up to him and examine his hands and arms. There's not a blister on him. It wouldn't even show color as when you dip your hand in really hot water and it gets red. It's not even pink. There is a special herb that I know of, a kind of grayish moss, the root of it, called *heyoka tapejuta*. When you chew that and smear your arms with it the boiling water won't burn you. But you have to be a *heyoka* for that herb to do you any good. A man who isn't a *heyoka* could never stand that boiling water. He'd have no arm left. He hasn't got the dream and the power. After the meat has been passed to the sick, a man with a special forked stick will get all the rest of the meat out and give it to anybody who wants it, and this ends the ceremony.

We call the *heyoka* a two-faced, backward-forward, upside-down contrary fool, but he is an honest two-faced. He works backward openly. He says "god" when he means "dog" and "dog" when he means "god." You know what is in his mind. He doesn't say, "If I get elected to be a congressman, I will do this or that." He makes no promises. He has the power. He has the honor. He has the shame. He pays for all of it.

I think clowns are holy to all Indians, not only to us Sioux. I have heard about the "Mudhead" clowns in Zuni, way down in New Mexico. I was told they ran around with a big wooden male part and had some grotesque dummy of a woman and all the clowns pretended to have intercourse with her. Only not one of them made it; none of them knew how to. And the whole village looked on and smiled, the old ladies and the young children, because this too was holy, part of a sacred dance for the renewal of all greens things, a prayer for rain. It is very different from us Sioux, yet it is the same. Different but the same—that is real *heyoka* business. I think when it comes right down to it, all the Indian religions somehow are part of the same belief, the same mystery. Our unity, it's in there.

Well, it's late, time to go to bed. Don't dream about the thunder-beings now, Richard. The way your mind works, the stories you tell, if you had to act out your dreams in public, it could be very embarrassing.

# 16
# Blood Turned into Stone

An old tale among our people, passed on from grandparent to grandchild over a span of many generations, tells of an immense flood which at one time engulfed the prairies like an ocean. Some of the people who inhabited this land ages ago tried to save themselves by taking refuge on top of a high hill; but the flood rose and washed over them, overturning the earth and crushing all living beings underneath its weight. The flesh and bones of the people were turned into a large pool of blood. The blood jelled, grew solid and, after a time, turned into red pipestone. It is still there, in the southwest corner of Minnesota, the only place on earth where you can find this sacred, blood-red rock.

One young, beautiful woman survived the flood. As the waters swirled around her a huge eagle swooped down from the clouds and carried her to a high mountain where she was safe from the raging flood. There she gave birth to twins who grew up to be the ancestors of the Sioux nation. This the old people told us.

This pool of blood figures in a few other tales which are so old that there is nobody left now who can remember them in their entirety. My grandfather told me the tale of the rabbit boy. Once upon a time the rabbit came across a pool of blood. The rabbit made it congeal by rolling it around, giving it the shape of a human being, resembling a dwarf. It was still raw blood, not flesh. The rabbit kicked it around until it formed a little gut. He kept moving this around until it grew bones. Still the rabbit kept playing with it until it became a human—a boy. The rabbit dressed this new human being beautifully—in red-painted buck-skin decorated with porcupine quills. And he called him Rabbit Boy.

Rabbit Boy started walking until he came to a village of other human beings where he saw many boys like himself. They asked him where he came from. He said, "I come from another village," but there was no such village. The village he had come to was the only village on the whole earth. Rabbit Boy added, "That place is so beautiful, I couldn't take you there. Your clothes are not good enough."

There was a young virgin in the village. The people thought it would be a good thing to marry her to the Rabbit Boy, because he seemed to have strange powers and it would benefit them to make him their relative. But Iktome, the spider-man, a trickster and schemer who is always waiting to turn somebody's misfortune to his own advantage, wanted this woman for himself. He worked on the minds of the people, turning them against the Rabbit Boy, making them jealous of his fine clothes. One village boy said, "I have a power to work on that Rabbit Boy. I'm going to throw a hoop over him." They also robbed him of his beautiful red-painted robes. When the Rabbit Boy resisted they tied him up. The two-faced spider egged them on: "Let's cut him up with a butchering knife." The Rabbit Boy was still standing, tied with rawhide. He said, "If you are about to kill me, I will sing my death song.

> Friend, friend,
> I have fought the sun.
> He tried to burn me up,
> But he couldn't.
> Even in battle
> With the sun,
> I was not killed."

They cut up the Rabbit Boy into a pile of meat chunks for soup. But that Rabbit Boy was hard to kill.

A great storm arose, floods, rain, hail. A cloud came down, making everything disappear. When that cloud was gone, those chunks of meat were gone, too. But there were some who had seen that the chunks of meat had joined together again, forming themselves up into the Rabbit Boy once more. He had come to life again, but gone up with the cloud.

Again there were voices: "The Rabbit Boy is *wakan* —sacred—full of power. Let us marry him to this girl." The tricky spider said, "Let's forget about him. I am just as powerful. Tie me up. Cut me up." Iktome remembered the words the Rabbit Boy had sung. He thought the power was in those words. Iktome sang:

> Friend, friend,
> I have fought the sun.
> He tried to burn me up,
> But he could not do it.
> Even battling the sun,
> I was not killed.

They cut Iktome up, but he never came to life again. All that was left of him was some chunks of meat.

In very much the same way as the Rabbit Boy, known as Weota-wicasa or Much-Blood-Man, other beings were made, such as the elk and the buffalo whom we hold sacred, because they offered themselves up as food for our people. I will not tell the whole story here, because in order to tell it, or even listen to it, a person ought to have fasted for two days and purified himself in the sweat lodge. But this much can be told.

That pool of blood comes up a third time in our tales. Howard Red Bear, a man from Allen who lived to be almost a hundred years old, used to relate a story his own grandfather had told him. According to this there once was a young man, many lifetimes ago, one of the first to pray with the sacred pipe on behalf of the tribe. At this time there was only this one pipe which the holy White Buffalo Woman had brought us. The young man went to a lone, towering rock; the rest of the people stayed behind, waiting for him to finish his prayers. They waited in vain, because he never returned.

After four days they went to look for him, and at the foot of the distant rock, where they had last seen him, they found a pool of blood and the calf pipe. They camped there for four more days, mourning him. One man prayed for him, leaning his head against the rock, and he heard a voice from deep within the earth answering him: "This is my blood which you are going to use." And again the blood turned into red pipe-stone.

It is good that these ancient legends, passed along from generation to generation, all tell us that it is our blood, the blood of the Sioux nation, which turned into the stone from which the sacred pipe is made. Because this pipe is us. The stem is our backbone, the bowl our head. The stone is our blood, red as our skin. The opening in the bowl is our mouth and the smoke rising from it is our breath, the visible breath of our people.

As we stand on grandmother earth, raising our sacred pipe in prayer, its stem forms a bridge from earth through man through our own bodies, to the sky, to Wakan Tanka, the grandfather spirit. As the pipe is filled with our sacred red willow bark tobacco, each tiny grain represents one of the living things on this earth. All of the Great Spirit's creations, the whole universe, is in that pipe. All of us is in that pipe at the moment of prayer. Often we are so overwhelmed by this that we cry and burst into tears as we raise the pipe toward the clouds.

Our sacred pipe—I have left speaking about it to the very last, for two reasons. This pipe is our most sacred possession. All our religion flows from it. The sacred pipe is at the heart of all our ceremonies, no matter how different they are from each other. Crying for a vision, suffering at the sun dance, in the darkness of a *yuwipi* night, in the sweat lodge, the pipe is always there, right at the core. It is as sacred to us as the holy bundle of arrows is to the Cheyennes. Even more sacred, because the arrow bundle is for the Cheyennes only, while we hold the pipe on behalf of all the tribes of this turtle continent, on behalf of all living things upon this earth.

It is because of this sacredness that one should speak about the pipe at the very end, after everything else has been said. But there is still another reason why I have waited so long to talk about the pipe. It scares me. If an Indian tries to talk about it, he is easily lost. Our minds are not good enough to understand all of it. It is so sacred that it makes me want not to tell all I know about it. No matter how old I am, how long I have thought about it, how much I have learned, I never feel quite ready to talk about the pipe. Sometimes I dream of our writing a book about nothing but the pipe, because all Indian wisdom can be known through the pipe. But, as I say, it scares me and overwhelms me with its greatness.

Our grandfathers told us how the sacred pipe was brought to our tribes. One summer, untold lifetimes ago, our different bands gathered for their yearly get-together. The earth was beautiful, covered with high grass and flowers, but the people were hungry. This happened long before we had either guns or horses, and the life of a hunter was hard and uncertain. Among the Sioux, the Itazipcho—the "Without Bows" tribe—had not had any meat for days. They decided to send out two hunters to scout for buffalo.

The two men searched a long time for game without finding any. At last they came to the top of a hill from which they had a good view, and they saw something moving toward them. At first they thought that it was a buffalo, but as it came nearer it turned out to be a beautiful young woman, the most beautiful they had ever seen. She wore a finely made dress of white buckskin so wonderfully decorated that no human hands could have made it. She wore her hair loose, except for a part of it on the left side which was tied together with buffalo hair. She wore a bundle on her back and carried a fan of sage leaves in her hand.

The beautiful woman spoke to the two hunters: "Do not be afraid. I have come from the buffalo nation with a message for your people, a good message." As he looked upon her, the older of the two hunters was overcome with a desire to possess her. He stretched out his hand to touch her, but she was *lila wakan,* more than human, and had not come to gratify the lust of a man. It is sometimes said that as soon as the hunter reached out to seize her a cloud descended and enveloped him. After it dissolved, a heap of dry bones was all that was left of this man. This is not the only way the story is related, and it is not quite as the spirits have told me. When the right time comes and I feel able to do it, I shall talk more about this. But one thing is certain—desire killed that man, as desire has killed many before and after him. If this earth should ever be destroyed, it will be by desire, by the lust of pleasure and self-gratification, by greed for the green frog skin, by people who are mindful only of their own self, forgetting about the wants of others.

So there was only one young hunter left, and the White Buffalo Woman told him to go back to his people and tell them to prepare for her coming. She explained what she wanted them to do. They were to set up a large tipi and make an *owanka wakan,* a sacred earth altar, inside it. She also wanted them to place a buffalo skull and a rack made of three sticks inside the tipi.

The young man went back to his people and told them what had happened to him and to his companion. He told them that a sacred woman was coming to see them the next morning with a message from the buffalo nation. He made known what she wished them to do, and it was done as she had instructed him.

The next day the crier called upon all the people to assemble around the sacred tipi, and, as the sun rose, they saw the White Buffalo Woman coming toward them in a sacred manner. Instead of the sage fan she carried the holy pipe. She was holding the stem with her right hand and the bowl with her left, and that is how we carry the pipe to this day.

The White Buffalo Woman entered the tipi where the old men of the tribe awaited her. They said, "Sister, we are glad that you came. We have had no meat for some time and all we can offer you is water." They dipped some *wacanga*—sweetgrass—into a skin bag of water and gave it to her in this way, and to this day we dip sweetgrass or an eagle feather into water and sprinkle it on those we wish to cure or purify during a ceremony. Most of our rites end with the drinking of water, and all this constantly reminds us of the White Buffalo Woman.

She then instructed and showed the people how to use the pipe. She filled it with red willow bark tobacco. Then she walked sunwise, clockwise, around the altar. This represented the circle without end, the road of man from youth to age, from ignorance to knowledge. It stands for life. So if we have a ceremony now, we also circle around like this before beginning to smoke. The White Buffalo Woman then placed a dry buffalo chip on the fire to light the pipe with it. For many generations this was the only right way to do this, but now we must take matches most of the time.

The White Buffalo Woman then showed the people how to pray with the pipe, lifting it up to the sky, lowering it toward the earth, pointing it in the four directions from which the wind blows. This lifting up of the pipe we call *hupa gluza*. "With this holy pipe you will walk like a living prayer," the White Buffalo Woman told the people, "your feet resting upon the grandmother, the pipe stem reaching all the way up into the sky to the grandfather, your body linking the Sacred Beneath with the Sacred Above. Wakan Tanka smiles on us, because now we are as one, earth, sky, all living things and the *ikce wicasa*—the human beings. Now we are one big family. This pipe binds us together. It is a peacemaker. There is a pool of blood somewhere, a place you came from. You will find this blood petrified into stone and it is red. It comes from a sacred spot common to all people, where even enemies are turned into friends and relatives." And it is probably from this time onward that the Sioux people started the custom of ending all important ceremonies with the words *mitakuye oyasin*—all my relatives—plants, animals, humans, all one big universal family.

The White Buffalo Woman then addressed the women, telling them that it was the work of their hands and the fruit of their wombs which kept the tribe alive. "You are from mother earth," she told them. "The task which has been given you is as great as the one given to the warrior and hunter." And therefore the sacred pipe is also something which binds men and women in a circle of love. It is the one sacred object in the making of which both men and women take part, the men making the bowl and the stem, the women decorating it with their best quillwork. During an Indian wedding both the man and his bride take hold of the pipe at the same time, and red cloth is wound around their hands, tying them together for life.

The White Buffalo Woman then turned to the children, because they have an understanding beyond their years and, among Indians, the right to be treated with the same respect which is shown to grownups. She told the little children that what the grown men and women did was for them. That the children were the greatest possession of the nation, that they represented the coming generations, the life of the people, the circle without end. "Remember this and grow up, and then teach your children," she told them.

After she had finished speaking, the White Buffalo Woman wrapped the pipe in the bundle she carried on her back and gave it to the old-man chief of the Without Bows for safekeeping. The name of this man is sometimes given as Standing Hollow Horn and sometimes as Buffalo Standing Upward. Together with the pipe the White Buffalo Woman gave the people a round, blood-red stone. On it were the marks of seven circles—the seven campfires of the Lakotas, or the seven ceremonies which go with the pipe. So here again the stone represented the whole universe to those who could read its signs.

After the White Buffalo Woman had done all this she took leave of the people, walking in the same direction from which she had come. She was singing: *"Niya taniya mawani ye,"* which has been translated as "With visible breath I am walking." This has a deeper meaning if one thinks about it for a while. First, *niya taniya* means not only breathing and breath, but also being alive and life itself. It means that as long as we honor the pipe we will live, will remain ourselves. And the thought of "visible breath" can be taken as the smoke of the pipe, which is the breath of our people. It also reminds us of the breath of the buffalo as it can be seen on a cold day. It underlines the fact that for us the pipe, man and the buffalo are all one.

As the people watched, the beautiful woman turned into a white buffalo. It kept on walking toward the horizon until it finally disappeared. This too is good to think about, easy to understand. The buffalo was part of us, his flesh and blood being absorbed by us until it became our own flesh and blood. Our clothing, our tipis, everything we needed for life came from the buffalo's body. It was hard to say where the animal ended and the man began. Ever since that time a white buffalo robe has been the rarest and most valued

thing a tribe could own. A tribe would give all its
wealth for such a white-haired hide. When the buffalo
disappeared, the old, wild Indian disappeared too.
There are places set aside for a few surviving buffalo
herds in the Dakotas, Wyoming and Montana. There
they are watched over by Government rangers and
stared at by tourists. If brother buffalo could talk he
would say, "They put me on a reservation like the
Indians." In life and death we and the buffalo have
always shared the same fate.

The pipe the White Buffalo Woman gave to us is
still kept by the tribe as its most sacred heirloom. It is
called *Ptehincala Huhu Canunpa*—Buffalo Calf Bone
Pipe. It is unlike any other pipe. Its stem is made of
the lower leg bone of a buffalo calf. It is wrapped into
buffalo wool and red flannel cloth. Red eagle feathers,
four small scalps and bird skins are tied to it. It is now
brittle with old age. It has been kept by the Elk Head
family of the Itazipcho tribe of the Sioux nation for
fourteen generations. Since we were put on reservations it has always been kept at Green Grass, north of
Eagle Butte, on the Cheyenne River reservation. It is
said that the old pipe keepers always lived close to a
hundred years of age.

Beside the *Ptehincala Huhu Canunpa* this family
also kept a second, very sacred tribal pipe, one among
the first made from red pipestone in the way the White
Buffalo Woman had taught the people. This old pipe
served as a model after which all our other pipes are
made. It has the feather of a red eagle tied to its
handle. This brings to mind the eagle which rescued
the only survivor from the flood, who gave birth to
twins who, in turn, grew into the Sioux nation. It also
reminds us that the eagle is a symbol of wisdom,
almost as important to us as the buffalo. Many of our
medicine men therefore have an eagle feather tied to
their pipes. For a curing ceremony it is fastened way
up on the stem. If the pipe is used for straightening
out some family trouble, the feather is attached to the

middle of the stem. If one wants to gain knowledge, the feather is placed on the spot where the handle and the bowl touch. The shape of the pipe's head is like this,

the shape of a "T" standing on its head. But this is the pipe of a father, a man who has already founded a family. A bachelor's pipe is just shaped like an "L" with the extra piece at the end missing.

Nothing of importance, good or bad, takes place among us without the pipe. If a man killed a tribal brother, be it through anger or through accident, then the sacred circle was broken and a wound had been inflicted on the whole people. The killer would see his victim's face reflected in the water every time he drank. When there was a shedding of blood only an untying ceremony with the sacred pipe could bring peace to the minds of the people and reconcile the families involved.

If a person's word was doubted, he might offer to "bite the knife." If he did this people would know that he had spoken the truth, because misfortune would be his part if his lips touched iron after having said something which was not true. For many years I haven't heard of anybody biting the knife; people don't seem to believe in this anymore. But the pipe is another matter. Nobody would be foolish enough to tell a lie while the pipe was being smoked. That would surely kill him. And this we believe, even now.

And the pipe has to be properly smoked, every person sitting in his right place, in a circle, the pipe being passed back to the dark from the light in a sacred manner, because it is our altar, while in a white church it is every man for himself, here and there, cafeteria style. My grandfather used to say, "The earth is red, blood is red, the sun is red as it sets and rises, and our bodies are red. And we should be walking the Red Road, the good north-south road, which is the path of life. Thus the Indian and the red pipestone belong to each other."

The pipestone quarry in Minnesota is the only place where this sacred stone can be found. It is now a national monument, but we Indians can still go there and dig out the red rock from which we make our pipe bowls. The quarry is right in the heart of the old Sioux country. Our eastern tribes—the Wahpeton, Sissetons and Wahpekute—held this land until 1851, when they were forced to give it up to the whites. But we got a treaty under which we can still go there to obtain the sacred stone.

In the old days you made a pipe the right way. You purified yourself and made tobacco offerings to the spirits. There are three large, upright boulders there, said to be ancient Indian people turned into stone, and you put tobacco ties there and maybe a feather, too. Right when you dug the stone out, you started with a prayer. The designs carved into a pipe bowl, these were prayers, too. A pipe made like this had the power.

Nowadays pipes are made commercially, with a machine and electric drill. They are easy to make, too easy. There is little power in these pipes. The quarry is all prettied up now, with lawns and lawn sprinklers and a museum. As you come in a loudspeaker tells you about the White Buffalo Woman and other Indian legends, getting it all mixed up, and there is a whirring sound as the slides come on. There are uniformed guides to take you around, explaining the meaning of the peace pipe to the tourists. Only how can they explain something which they don't know themselves? It is all very neat with water coolers and flush toilets, but I close my eyes and try to think of this place as it was before all the landscaping and prettifying was done to it.

A friend of mine, a young medicine man, went to the quarry and a park ranger there told him that he could take out a pound of stone for a dollar—as a special favor, because he was Indian. My friend got angry. It wasn't the money, you understand, but he told them: "I am a Sioux, this is my land, my pipestone. I will take it out and I *will not pay!*" There was another guy who looked like an Indian himself. He said, "Right on," took my young friend to a place where the vein of pipestone lies in the rock like a long red snake and told him to take as much as he liked, courtesy of the National Park Service. My friend came out with a barrelful of stone. It is small victories like this which have to keep up our morale nowadays.

I found an old book by George Catlin in your library which was printed over a hundred years ago. I like to leaf through this book of yours and look at its faded, yellow and brown speckled pictures. I ran across a part where he describes his visit to the pipestone quarry in the 1830s. I think he must have been the first white man to see it. In a way he was also the first tourist and he had to talk to us through an interpreter. He got a few things wrong; maybe the interpreters weren't up to their jobs either. But Catlin was an artist, and he kept his eyes open, and some things he got at least nearly right and somehow it ties in with what we Indians know. Catlin's details could be all wrong, and when he is not sure of a fact he hides this behind a mass of words, but underneath it all, very faintly, you can see the main idea of the pipe coming through.

He knew, for instance, that the stone was the flesh of the Indians. He had heard about the flood which had turned the blood of the people into pipestone. He was also told that in ancient times buffalo were driven over these cliffs and that their blood, too, turned into pipestone. I have never heard this mentioned among our people, but whoever said this to Catlin 140 years ago had a sense that the Indian, the buffalo and the pipe were one.

One Sioux warrior told Catlin that this red stone was part of their flesh and that it would be bad for a white man to take it away; a hole would be made in their flesh and the blood could never be made to stop running.

Another Indian told him, "This red pipe was given to the red men by the Great Spirit; it is part of our flesh and sacred. We know that the whites are like a great cloud that rises in the east and will cover the whole country; we know that they will have our lands; but we want to keep this place." I might have spoken this way if I had lived then.

Catlin also mentions some fabulous birds which at one time were supposed to have been nesting in the quarry, and the way he describes them it sounds as if he meant the *wakinyan,* the thunderbirds. Again, the way I know it, the thunderbirds are not part of the pipe, but it all goes to show that there were many legends about this place in the old buffalo days. Some old people among us are still saying that there are little ghostlike human spirits in the rock, just about a finger long, very fast and hard to see.

The Omaha tribe had a legend about the pipestone quarry. They say that long ago there was an Omaha woman called *Wahegela.* She was married to a Sioux warrior. One day she found herself face to face with a white buffalo. She followed this sacred animal as if in a trance. She watched the buffalo kicking loose large chunks of red stone and knew right away that these were the petrified bodies of her forebears. In this way she discovered the quarry. The Sioux and the Omahas were enemies, but they agreed that they would never fight each other at this sacred place. The land belonged to the Sioux, but the stone belonged to all Indians who honored the pipe.

This is different from what we believe but, again, it ties in with our White Buffalo Woman story, because all the main parts are there, even if they are jumbled up: the woman, the white buffalo, the Indians' blood turned into stone, the pipe as a peacemaker. These many stories show that, no matter what the differences are, the pipe is sacred to all tribes.

A year ago I went to a convention of many tribes which was held to work for unity among us Indians. I had my old pipe with me which I have used for more than thirty years. We had a good ceremony during the night, just before daybreak, and fifty-four tribes smoked my pipe. I lit it for them, and 161 people smoked my pipe and it never went out. It kept on glowing all through the ceremony. The medicine men present raised this pipe and prayed to the Great Spirit in their own languages which I could not understand. But, on another level, I understood them well. That pipe gave us a common language and a common mind. Some reporters tried to take pictures, but not one of them came out. Wherever the pipe should have shown up, you could see only a white blur, something like a fog. That old pipe didn't want to be photographed at that time. Many men on our reservations have their own peace pipe. I won't be satisfied until there's one in each family. A Sioux without his pipe is only a half Indian, only half a man.

From the last person named Elk Head the keeping of our two most sacred pipes passed to Stanley Looking Horse and his son Orval, who are a part of the Elk Head clan. Orval is the nineteenth in the line of pipe keepers in that family. Very few people, even among our own tribe, have ever seen these two pipes unwrapped. Only once in a lifetime, if that often, can these two sacred heirlooms be seen. I was one of the few men privileged to hold these two pipes and to pray with them. It really changed my life.

One winter, many years ago, when I was a young man, I went north to Green Grass, where I heard the

Buffalo Calf Pipe was kept. Something within me urged me to do this, voices that told me I had to pray with this holy pipe. It was as if some power had taken hold of me, not bothering to ask me, "Do you want to do this?" I was like a car; someone was in the driver's seat making me go. The going was hard. There was a Cayuse wind, blizzards, an icy cold. The snow was hard and shiny, like glass. I thought that a man would be keeping that pipe but found out that a woman was in charge of it, Mrs. Elk Head, the older sister of Chief Elk Head, who had been the keeper before her. Some people told me, "If you want to see that woman you better hurry up, because she is dying."

I made my way through a snowstorm to her log cabin. I found the old lady sitting on the floor in the middle of the room. She was all skin and bone, so frail that a gust of wind could have blown her away. Her lips had receded and were so dry I had to wet them with a damp cloth. Seeing her like this, I didn't think she could live longer than another day or two.

I saw that her cabin was all prepared for a ceremony —sage on the ground, cedar, sweetgrass and all that. I asked her, "Who is doing a ceremony here?" She said, "You are. I had a vision that a young man from the south would come and cure me. I don't know you. I have never set eyes upon you before, but you are the one. All my grandchildren have turned Christians and no longer practice the old ways. Tomorrow, the snows will stop falling and the sun will come out full blast. There won't be any storm and the whole country, the whole earth, will be sparkling. If that happens tomorrow, you come over here. I will show you the sacred Buffalo Calf Bone Pipe. You will pray with it, and you will cure me. Be here tomorrow as soon as the sun is up."

I went to a house in Green Grass where I knew some people who let me sleep there. They told me, "You are making a fool of yourself. The radio has forecast blizzards to go on without a let-up. This storm will last a week or more." That wind sure was howling. It went around the house like a spy, testing doors and windows.

I suddenly woke up in the darkness before dawn. I wondered what had roused me. Then I knew that it was the stillness. The storm had died down; everything was quiet. I couldn't hear a sound. I got up, had a drink of water and went outside. Nothing stirred. It was as if the earth had come to a standstill. I noticed that the air had turned warm. The sun came up. It was big and red and glowing so brightly that I had to close my eyes. Even if I looked away from the sun, I still had to squint. The snow turned bright red, reflecting the sun. It sparkled, millions and millions of crystals glistening, a sun in every one of them. When I started walking, the snow made a noise like breaking eggshells. That was the only sound I could hear.

When I arrived at Mrs. Elk Head's log house she was again sitting in the middle of the room, waiting for me. There was a fragrance in the place, smoke from burning sweetgrass and cedar. That house had already been made holy. I sat down at the west side. I noticed a big canvas bundle, about the size of a man, tied up like a *yuwipi*. The old lady asked me to unwrap it. The bundle consisted of seven rawhides, buffalo skin, deer skin, red and blue flannel. I came to the last layer and there was the pipe—*Ptehincala Huhu Canunpa*—the Buffalo Calf Pipe, the most sacred thing in the world for me. There was a second bundle and I unwrapped that, too. It contained the other holy, tribal pipe of red pipestone. This one was very large. The Buffalo Calf Pipe was small.

Mrs. Elk Head instructed me to take both pipes in my hands, the big one at the bottom and the small one on top. *"Takoja,* Grandson," she said, "pray with these. I had a vision that you would come, and you are here. Always pass the pipe to your left. Always take it with the right. Give it from your heart, keep the head close to your heart. Let the spirit come to you." The old woman talked to me in Indian, in a secret language only I could understand.

I held the pipes. Their bowls were my flesh. The stem stood for all the generations. I felt my blood going into the pipe, I felt it coming back, I felt it circling in my mind like some spirit. I felt the pipes come alive in my hands, felt them move. I felt a power surging from them into my body, filling all of me. Tears were streaming down my face. And in my mind I got a glimpse of what that pipe meant. That Buffalo Calf Pipe made me know myself, made me know the earth around me. It healed the blindness of my heart and made me see another world beyond the everyday world of the green frog skin. I saw that the pipe was my church, a little piece of stone and wood, but I would need nothing more as long as I had this. I knew that within this pipe were all the powers of nature, that within this pipe was me. I knew that when I smoked the pipe I was at the center of all things, giving myself to the Great Spirit, and that every other Indian praying with his pipe would, at one time or other, feel the same. I knew that releasing the smoke to rise up to the sky, I also released something of myself that wanted to be free and that thereby I gladdened all the plants and animals on earth. All this I could understand only with my heart and blood, I guess in the same way an animal understands things, not with my mind, and I thought about this for many years. Even now, after so much time has passed since that moment, the memory of it keeps me awake at night.

It suddenly came to me that if I mingled my breath with the sacred smoke, I would also mingle it with the breath of every living creature on this earth, and I also realized that the glow in the pipe was the sacred fire of the Great Spirit, the same fire that is in the sun. I knew that in this pipe all small things were fused into one, making an entirety. The thought came to me that if I ever learned to understand all that the pipe meant, understand all the symbols hidden within it, only then would I fully know what it meant to be an Indian, what it meant to be me. Well, I still don't know it. I am still learning. Maybe I'll be getting near to it one day. It is hard to find words for the thoughts that came to me then, insight and confusion, sadness and happiness all mixed together. Nor can I describe the power which flowed into me from the pipe, shaking me up. I can't do it. All I knew when I was holding these pipes in my hand was that this was changing my life.

My prayers must have helped Mrs. Elk Head, because she recovered and lived for a number of years more. Before I left her she told me that some white Government people had taken one of the pipe bundles away from her but had become frightened and brought it back. She said, "Maybe I will have to bury them in order to keep them out of the wrong hands." She also told me: "The time will come when the Indians will rise again with this sacred pipe, when it will be smoked by all." More than thirty years later, when fifty-four tribes were praying with my own pipe, it came back into my memory what the old woman had told me. She really was *wakan* and had the power to see ahead. She also gave me a tattoo and a secret name that went with it.

From old Mrs. Elk Head the pipe bundles passed to Stanley Looking Horse, still among the Without Bows people. But to my thinking the Buffalo Calf Pipe belongs to all the Sioux. It belongs to the Hunkpapa at Standing Rock, where a woman turned into a stone, to the people of Sitting Bull, and to the Ogallalas at Pine Ridge, Crazy Horse's tribe. It belongs to the Oohenunpa—the Two Kettles—who share our reservation with us and who got their name when, starving and near death, they found a rawhide bundle full of meat, enough for "two kettles." It belongs to the Sihasapa—the Sioux Black Feet—who got their moccasins blackened a long time ago when they had to walk over miles of earth charred by prairie fires. It belongs to the Sicangu—the Burned Thigh people of

Rosebud—who had their legs scorched by flames when Pawnee enemies fired the grass around their campsite. It belongs to my own people, the Mnikowoju—the Planters by the Water. And, in a larger sense, it belongs to all Indians on this turtle continent.

It is a great task to keep the pipe bundle. It should be housed in a fine, old-style tipi. During the day it should be put up on a three-legged stand, and twice daily it should be faced in a different direction according to where the sun stands. It was not always possible to observe all the right ways in which the sacred pipe should be honored every day of our lives. I heard that for a time, when no other place could be found, the pipes were kept in a shed. I wished we could put up a tipi again for our sacred things. There have also been rumors that the big pipe has been lost or broken. I hope this is not true. I remember how upset the northern Cheyennes in Montana were when they found out that the keeper of their sacred Buffalo Hat was driving around with it, taking it out of the reservation, going toward Sheridan, where maybe some white anthropologist could have gotten hold of it. They didn't like it when this sacred hat left their land, and a big chase was on until they got it back. And they were right. Too many of our holy things wind up in museums, where people who don't know what they are stare at them, where their power can't work.

The sacred pipes have not been shown to the people for some years now. In the summer of 1969 we Sioux medicine men thought that the time had come to open up these bundles. But when word got around and there were rumors of TV crews coming in, offering us money for "exclusive rights" as they called it, we changed our minds. We have become like a strange horse: If you get too close to him, he takes off. I guess we have good reasons for this. We returned the bundles to their hiding places and everybody went home without having seen the pipes. The day will come when we will open them again, but it must be the right day, and those who come must do so for the right reason. When the day comes, we will know it.

We Indians hold the pipe of peace, but the white man's religious book speaks of war, and we have stood by while the white man supposedly improved the world. Now we Indians must show how to live with our brothers, not use them, kill them or maim them. With the pipe, which is a living part of us, we shall be praying for peace, peace in Vietnam and in our own country. We Indians say "our country" because it is still ours even if all other races are now in physical possession of it, for land does not belong to any single man but to all people and to the future generations.

We must try to use the pipe for mankind, which is on the road to self-destruction. We must try to get back on the red road of the pipe, the road of life. We must try to save the white man from himself. This can be done only if all of us, Indians and non-Indians alike, can again see ourselves as part of this earth, not as an enemy from the outside who tries to impose its will on it. Because we, who know the meaning of the pipe, also know that, being a living part of the earth, we cannot harm any part of her without hurting ourselves. Maybe through this sacred pipe we can teach each other again to see through that cloud of pollution which politicians, industrialists and technical experts hold up to us as "reality." Through this pipe, maybe, we can make peace with our greatest enemy who dwells deep within ourselves. With this pipe we could all form again the circle without end.

When an Indian prays he doesn't read a lot of words out of a book. He just says a very short prayer. If you say a long one you won't understand yourself what you are saying. And so the last thing I can teach you, if you want to be taught by an old man living in a dilapidated shack, a man who went to the third grade for eight years, is this prayer, which I use when I am crying for a vision:

"Wakan Tanka, Tunkashila, *onshimala* . . . Grandfather Spirit, pity me, so that my people may live."

# EPILOGUE
# Inyan Wasicun, the White Man with the Rocks

We were sitting on the floor in a large, empty room, I, my wife Jean, my two teenage sons, my little daughter and about forty Indians. Some of them were old and close friends; others I had never seen before. The walls against which we leaned our backs were made of bits and pieces, logs, parts of an old railroad car, anything that the Indian, who had built this house many years ago, had been able to lay his hands on. A huge tree trunk propped up a sagging ceiling. A kerosene lamp cast a timid light on the many-colored patchwork of the blankets which covered the walls. Next to me stood a large kettle with dog meat, the dog's head floating at the top, grinning at me. There were the many sacred things used for a *yuwipi* ceremony— colored flags, eagles' heads, oddly shaped stones, rattling gourds, the sacred pipe.

The light was extinguished and we were left with our thoughts—human islands in a sea of darkness. The drums throbbed as many voices rose in a quavering chant. The steady rhythm of the drums transmitted itself to the walls from where I absorbed it into my body through the shoulder blades. I not only heard the drums; I felt them physically. Lights appeared out of nowhere like so many fireflies. They came floating up out of the darkness for a fraction of a second and were gone almost before eye and brain had been able to register them. The spirits were coming in.

It was a familiar scene that I had witnessed a dozen times before, yet it was also strange and utterly improbable that I, an ex-Viennese, born in the old

Austro-Hungarian Empire, should be sitting here, in the Dakota prairie, with a bunch of Indian friends who happened to be medicine men.

I had been brought up in baroque cities, in the shadow of gargoyled cathedrals, among half-timbered houses. I had traveled all over Europe on foot, with a knapsack, at the rate of thirty kilometers a day, soaking up culture through my soles. Never, even in my wildest dreams, had I ever imagined myself in America, a country of skyscrapers and super-technocracy whose time-is-money philosophy had always frightened me. Nor had it seemed likely that I would ever meet real Indians, much less have them for friends. The medicine men, on the other hand, who look upon existence as a long sequence of symbols, symbols which have to be lived, which determine a man's past, his present, and his future, tell me that there was no way in which I could have avoided coming to South Dakota, that the symbolic road which I had to travel inevitably led to the place where the Austro-Hungarian would meet the Sioux.

Like most European children I was predisposed to love Indians. Together with my pals I used to go to the "blood opera," a movie house in Vienna which specialized in American Westerns. We cheered on the Indians and vehemently booed the cowboys and the cavalry. The reason for our acting this way was a man named Karl May.

May had started out in life as a pickpocket and petty thief in the petty state of Saxony, one of the lesser kingdoms in the Kaiser's empire. He operated, however, with a certain style. He showed up in shops and grocery stores introducing himself as an under-cover agent of the royal Saxonian counterfeit squad. He examined the cash registers and, inevitably, dis-covered a few counterfeit bills which he seized in the name of the state. He always left signed receipts, impressive, official-looking documents surmounted by the Saxonian coat of arms. As May plied his trade

in a very small area—he didn't even own a bicycle
and had to get around in a horse-drawn bus—he was
speedily captured. The counterfeit ploy had not been
his first offense and he found himself sentenced to
spend a number of years in a forbidding, medieval
prison-fortress.

The prison library contained a number of books on
Indians and the American West. They inspired May to
begin writing penny-dreadfuls which soon became
huge successes. By the time May was released, he was
already famous and moderately wealthy. His favorite
hero was Winnetou, a young Indian chief of super-
human strength, courage and nobility. Winnetou had
a sidekick, a German trapper called Old Shatterhand,
a reversal of the Lone Ranger–Tonto situation. Noble
Winnetou certainly was, but anthropologically he was
a failure. He was supposed to be an Apache Indian,
but was described as living in dark, cool, lake-studded
forests, getting around in a birch-bark canoe, or riding
over the prairie to hunt buffalo astride his white
mustang. He went on the warpath wearing a war
bonnet with a long trail like a plains Indian, and in
one white man's film he even had a totem pole
standing before his wigwam. He never killed his
enemies, but only stunned them temporarily with a
blow from his mighty fists. I worshiped Winnetou
uncritically, I didn't know that Apaches and birch-
bark canoes didn't go together.

I am a living personification of the old, multiracial,
multilingual, Austro-Hungarian Empire. I was part
Catholic, Protestant, Jewish, part Austrian, Hungarian, Czech. I lived in Vienna, Berlin, Budapest, Frank-
furt, Paris, the Balkans and Italy. As my father died
four weeks before I was born I was brought up by a
number of different relatives. As a small boy, in the
twenties, when hunger and inflation gripped Vienna, I
was sent to a number of aunts and uncles who were in
a position to fatten me up. I wound up first with a
Catholic aunt in Austria who ran her own little farm.

She was so pious that she received regular visits from St. Joseph and St. Jude Thaddeus, her favorite saints. I could hear her talking to them on some dark nights. She once encountered Christ in full daylight on the Reichsbruecke, the large bridge spanning the Danube near Vienna. She pretended to stumble and fall in order to adore him. She did not dare do so openly for fear that people might consider her crazy and drag her off to an asylum. She reproached herself for the rest of her life for not having openly acknowledged *him*. She went every morning to early mass at 5 A.M. and always came back from church full of fleas. Within half an hour I had all her fleas. My aunt said this was because my blood was sweeter than hers.

The next fattening-up station was at Budapest with a Jewish grandfather. He took me to the synagogue with him and we always brought a poor *jeshive bocher* home with us for a free supper. This grandfather taught me many things, to play tarot, to share my food with the poor, and to stay away from ham. He had a brown-skinned, full-bosomed Hungarian peasant girl for a maid. She and I used to sneak off to have ourselves a slice of smoked bacon covered with a fine powder of red paprika, very sinful and very delicious.

After that I stayed with Protestant relatives who took me to Wittenberg to listen to a preachment in the old medieval Schlosskirche, the church upon the door of which Luther had once nailed his ninety-five theses, thereby starting a new religion. I was also taken to the Wartburg, the castle in which Luther had translated the Bible into German and where a pesky devil had frequently appeared to him, interrupting his work. They showed me the dark stain on the wall where Luther had hurled his inkwell at the devil, and another, yellowish spot (sulphur, no doubt) where the imp from hell had broken wind in his anxiety to get away from the enraged reformer.

I even spent some time with one aunt by marriage who was a Mohammedan girl from Sarajevo. A cousin of my mother, who had been building railroad bridges all over Bosnia and similar remote provinces of the Austro-Hungarian Empire, had met her in the old bazaar, married her and died. And here she was and here I was. This aunt made me fast from sunup to sundown during Ramadan, nightfall being the signal for gargantuan feasts. She ground her own coffee beans in a long, cylindrical handmill of burnished brass covered with Arabic inscriptions. A day always ended with a tiny cup of thick black coffee with a rose petal floating on top. This aunt sang sweet, haunting songs, half Turkish and half Slav, which she interrupted from time to time with wild, trilling ululations, not unlike Indian war whoops.

The different religions confused me. Which was the right one? I tried to figure it out but had no success. It worried me. The different Gods—Catholic, Jewish, Protestant, Mohammedan—seemed all very particular in the way in which they expected me to keep on good terms with them. I couldn't please one without offending the others. One kind soul solved my problem by taking me on my first trip to the planetarium. I contemplated the insignificant flyspeck called earth, the millions of suns and solar systems, and concluded that whoever was in charge of all this would not throw a fit if I ate ham, or meat on Friday, or did not fast in the daytime during Ramadan. I felt much better after this and was, for a while, keenly interested in astronomy.

For two years I went to the Odenwald Schule, an experimental, avant-garde boarding school where boys and girls took their exercises outdoors in the nude. This school had no teachers and no grades. Some young man or woman took us into the woods and showed us which mushrooms were good to eat and which were likely to kill us. This constituted a lesson. The man who ran the school, a biblical patriarch with a long white beard reaching down to his waist, resembled a grandfatherly hippie. He wore shorts, sandals and a blue, open-necked "migrating bird" shirt. He put me in charge of the school's aviary, a fenced-over piece of woodland populated with a variety of birds and animals.

I was ten years old, very shy and withdrawn. Wherever I had been so far, I had belonged to the wrong religion, spoken the wrong language and behaved in a strange and therefore wrong way. To the Germans I was a sloppy Austrian, to the Austrians a *"Sau-preuss"*—a swinish Prussian. To the Hungarians I was the son of Habsburg oppressors. The Bosnians called me a *"Schwob,"* a chauvinistic Hungarian overlord. Frenchmen called me the little Boche. Depending on where I happened to be I was a damn popist, a Lutheran heretic, a Jewboy, a little goy. None of this was intended as a compliment.

I was, at that stage, afraid of people, especially strangers, and took my refuge in my own dream world, among books and animals. I therefore spent lots of time in the aviary with a bunch of little owls to whom I fed raw hamburger and, inadvertently, small fragments of my own finger tips. I liked to climb up high into a tree, settling down in a crotch of branches, with a book and one of the tiny, sleepy-eyed owlets, reading Ernest Thompson Seton's animal stories. I attached myself to a young geologist couple, helping them to dig fossils from Jurassic chalk cliffs. I tried to tame a *kreuz*-otter, one of the small vipers inhabiting the moors and the heather, but had to return it to its native lair. Even in the permissive Odenwald school vipers were out as pets.

The aunt and uncle who were responsible for my upbringing moved to Berlin and put me in an old-fashioned, Spartan Prussian school. The rumor that I came from that ungodly, subversive institution, the Odenwald school, where depraved children of both sexes cavorted stark naked in the woods, where four-letter words went unpunished, where pupils were taught to pick edible mushrooms instead of geometry, preceded me wherever I went.

I tried to please. In history I volunteered the information that Frederick the Great spoke German only to his dogs, that he couldn't make it with women, that he had tried to bugger Voltaire, that he had told his soldiers: "If you weren't such dumb bastards, you would have run away a long time ago." This would have earned me an "A" in Vienna, where Frederick was regarded as a traitorous vassal who had stabbed his empress in the back. In Berlin it only got me a beating with a bamboo cane. The outraged teacher, who had a Kaiser Wilhelm mustache and yellow, tobacco-stained teeth, called me a new Herostratos, after the Greek who had burned down the temple of Diana at Ephesus, one of the Seven Wonders of the Ancient World, just for the hell of it. The teacher explained that, thus, I was trying to destroy and tear down all that was sacred and dear to the fatherland.

I was instantly dubbed the rottenest kid in school and treated accordingly. Nobody would have anything to do with me except those nearly as rotten as I. We outcasts stuck together, even after finishing high school in 1932, when a troop of brownshirts moved into our neighborhood, taking over a saloon as their headquarters. We were their natural quarry. We had to travel in groups in order to survive. The police no longer protected us. Hitlerism was in the air. When the Nazis came to power, we went underground. The father of one of my closest friends had a small printing shop. At night, after the old man went to bed, we turned out a clandestine paper. We were betrayed. Most of us were arrested and disappeared in concentration camps, some forever. My friend whose father owned the printing shop was eventually beheaded. Getting one's head chopped off was something few people could afford. The parents of the condemned boy had to pay the costs—about 800 dollars. This included the expenses of the executioner and his assistants, who had to rent tuxedos and white gloves for their job.

I led a charmed life. I was arrested by a brutish-looking policeman who took me to a lonely park, where he burst into tears. He told me that he had a kid my age who even resembled me, that he was an old Social Democrat, that he would be damned if he handed over mere children like myself to a bunch of bloodthirsty gangsters. He finally recovered himself enough to wipe away his tears. His face suddenly struck me as beautiful. He gave me enough money to buy a third-class ticket to Austria, telling me to go straight to the station, looking neither right nor left. He sent me off with an old-fashioned *"Gott befolgen, mein Junge,"* recommending me to the mercy of God.

I studied art in Vienna, fell a few times in and out of love, traveled to Italy and France. One day, in March 1938, I returned from spring skiing in the mountains to find the German Army, the SS, and the Gestapo in Vienna. I went underground again. I had added to my former sins by drawing funny caricatures for newspapers of un-Germanic-looking Hitlers, fat and blubbery Goerings and dwarfish Dr. Goebbelses. I was hiding out in various places, staying only a few days in one and the same spot. Twice I had nothing to eat for three days.

I was a good European, trying to maintain a toehold on the Continent, retreating only one border at a time, but in 1940 I found myself finally in the Atlantic Ocean, on a British ship bound for America. I arrived in New York late at night. Viennese friends, who had preceded me by two years, took me to their apartment near Inwood Park. At sunrise I rushed to the window to see the skyscrapers but saw only rocks, squirrels chasing each other around a tree, a few screeching bluejays. I was immensely relieved. I would get along in America.

As I said before, some of my Indian friends tend to look upon life as a long series of symbolic images forming definite, harmonic patterns. They see man not as a separate entity viewed against a background, but as part of the earth upon which he walks. They see him as a kind of plant, almost, which extends roots and fibers in a number of directions, taking nourishment from different sources, exchanging juices with other plants, being perhaps eaten by some other creature and thereby becoming something else in the process, a living organism gaining strength from his surroundings as well as from certain powers inherent in nature. They see man as a small but essential particle of the universe, linked to all other living things by a number of what—for lack of a better word—I would describe as unseen but strongly perceived umbilical cords. It is difficult to look in this way upon a white man living in a city apartment. The medicine men, however, have no trouble figuring me out when I swap stories with them.

Lame Deer will say: "At least you had an aunt who had visions. Never mind whether these occurred just in her imagination or whether she was plumb crazy. She believed in them. Or the people who showed you the place where *wakan-sica*, the old devil, had an inkwell thrown at him by Luther. They at least believed that there could be a bad spirit bothering a holy man. All religions, all good beliefs, rest upon some vision. The trouble with white religion in America is this: If I tell a preacher that I met Jesus standing next to me in the supermarket, he will say that this could not happen. He'll say: 'That's impossible; you are crazy.' By this he is denying his own religion. He has no place to go. Christians who no longer believe that they could bump into Christ at the next street corner, what are they? Jews who no longer think they could find God in a pillar of fire, why would they go on being Jews? You at least come from places where some white people still could have some awe of the super-natural, or feel that there was a world beyond the green frog-skin world."

He would try to analyze me and roughly sum it up like this: "You were chased from your own land, like us. You are an artist and therefore can look beyond what is peddled to us as 'reality.' You were confused by the white man's religion as we were. When, as a boy, you spent hours dreaming in the crotch of a tree, or when you felt more at home with animals than with people, that was a kind of vision quest. Maybe it wasn't much, but it was something. Also you are always picking up odd-shaped stones, pebbles and fossils, saying that you do this because it pleases you, but I know better. Deep inside you there must be an awareness of the rock power, of the spirits in them, otherwise you would not pick them up and fondle them as you do. I always wanted somebody to help me write a book about Indian religion and medicine, and when I first met you I knew that you were the man I had been waiting for. Your coming was no accident."

Whether I was foreordained to meet Lame Deer or not, I did not think about Winnetou or Indians during my first years in America. A little to my own surprise, I liked New York, I liked my work as an illustrator. I married an American girl, an artist like myself, and raised three children. I was glad that I was not running anymore, that life gave me a new feeling of perma-nence, that a noise at four o'clock in the morning indicated the arrival of the milkman or the garbage collector, not the Gestapo.

But after a dozen years of settling down and grow-ing roots, I experienced a new restlessness, an uneasy feeling that I was turning into a barnacle. I managed to get a number of travel assignments from various publications and bought a large station wagon, which I filled with camping gear and kids, not only my own, but also usually a little friend or two who wanted to come along. Wanderlust, the urge to roam, transmitted itself to my wife, Jean, a nature girl, who is quite unruffled and comfortable in a blizzard or desert storm, which is probably one of the reasons we got married.

My first encounter with the American West was a strangely emotional experience. Naturally, it took place in South Dakota. We had been driving all day through corn country, flat and rather monotonous— widely spaced farms with white picket fences, each house surrounded by enormous cornfields. We crossed the Missouri and the old highway began to undulate, dip and rise, dip and rise, roller-coaster fashion. We drove over one dip and suddenly found ourselves in a different world. Except for the road, there was no sign of man. Before me stretched an endless ocean of hills, covered with sage and prairie grass in shades of silver, subtle browns and ochers, pale yellows and oranges. Above all this stretched the most enormous sky I had ever seen. Nothing in my previous life had prepared me for this scene of utter emptiness which had come upon me without warning.

I stopped the car and we all got out. There was emptiness of sound, too. The calls of a few unseen birds only accentuated it. I found myself over-whelmed by a tremendous, surging sensation of free-dom, of liberation from space, I experienced a moment of complete happiness. The children felt it, too—even Jean, who had seen all this before. For the rest of the day the excitement stayed with us. Jean later told me that I kept singing all the way until we hit our campsite.

That night, drinking coffee around the open fire, I talked to Jean about the emotional impact the land-scape had on me. It was not beautiful in the accepted sense of the word. It was not even pretty. Yet it had made more of an impact upon me than the stained-glass windows of the Sainte Chapelle, the hills of Rome, the Austrian Alps or the Loire Valley, which are all, by common consent, called "beautiful." I think it was a sense of being completely swallowed up by nature that gave the prairie its powerful attraction. There is nothing like it in all of Europe. Even high up on a Swiss glacier one is still conscious of the toy villages below, the carefully groomed landscape of multicolored fields, the faraway ringing of a church bell. It is all very beautiful, but it does not convey the prairie's sense of liberation, of losing oneself, of utmost escape. I believe, with the Indians, that a landscape influences and forms the people living on it and that one cannot understand them and make friends with them without also understanding, and making friends with, the earth from which they came.

My first Western trips did not bring me into immediate contact with Indians. I did illustrated stories on ghost towns, wildlife, wilderness camping. In 1952 one of my editors, a railroad buff, sent me to do a story on an old mining railroad. Working on it, we accidentally found ourselves on an Indian reservation. The Indians treated us with hostility and suspicion, especially one woman who plainly had no use for white people. Seeing the misery in which the Indians lived, and knowing the treatment they had been subjected to, I found their attitude toward us understandable but hard to take personally. We stood it for a day and were ready to pack up and leave, when the same woman who had treated us like poison up to this moment suddenly approached us with a big smile, hugged us and invited us into her house to share their supper. It all happened a long time ago, and she and her family have since become dear friends, but I never received a satisfactory answer from her when I asked what had brought on the sudden, to me unexplainable, reversal of attitude toward us. The only answer I ever got was a charming but enigmatic smile.

On nearer acquaintance my ideas about frowning, stoic, dead-pan, unsmiling Indians were thoroughly shattered. I had never before met people so gregarious, eager for company and fond of visiting, people with such a sense of wry, instant humor, people who laughed and cried as easily as my newfound friends.

We had such a good time staying with them that we were reluctant to depart and invited them to come to New York with us. What impressed them most was the Atlantic Ocean, which left them speechless. They lived in an arid, desertlike country, and any body of water was a thing contemplated by them with awe and wonder. We made it a habit to visit this family whenever we found ourselves within 500 miles of them. Our children played with theirs and we grown-ups enjoyed one another's company.

We used to travel together to neighboring tribes where this family had friends, who then became our friends, too. In this way we were being handed on from tribe to tribe and by 1964 wound up among the Sioux. A few times I tried to interest magazine editors in a story about Indians and their problems. I met a blank wall. At that time I was always told that Indians were box-office poison, that nobody wanted to read about them and that they sold no magazines. So I did stories on earth science, a wild-horse round-up, a float trip down the Green and Yampa rivers, anything that would get us back to our Indian friends.

In 1967 we fed about sixty Indians in our New York apartment. Twenty-six Sioux had come to New York to join Martin Luther King's peace march, to establish contact with the outside and to "break through the buckskin curtain." They decided, on the spur of the moment, to come to us for dinner afterward. As word got around it seemed that every Indian within fifty miles of New York was converging upon our place. A group of "white Indians," six boys and girls with long hair, beaded headbands and necklaces, simply trailed the Sioux into our apartment. I discovered them accidentally in our bedroom, smoking pot, in various attitudes of Kama Sutra. There were so many people there that I walked around in a daze. Lame Deer was there. He had a drum and he was singing the Sioux national anthem. Another group was busy singing Omaha songs in the studio. There was no chance really to get acquainted or even to remember all the faces. Whenever we are at Rosebud or Pine Ridge, strangers will walk up to us, shake our hands and say, "Remember me? I had dinner at your home." They also started calling our place on 89th Street "Sioux East" and began visiting us unannounced and spontaneously. One old man stayed for three months. I would also get mysterious collect calls from strange places. A disembodied voice in broken English would speak to me from a distance of 2,000 miles: "Hey, friend, remember me? I'm stuck between Upper Cut Meat and Wanblee. I'm out of gas money. I need six dollars and fifty cents to get home. Wire it to me."

I'd point out that it was four o'clock in the morning on a Sunday and that it was a damn nuisance to find an open Western Union office at a time like this. And please couldn't he find someone closer to him to help out? The unanswerable rejoinder usually was: "You are the only guy I know in the whole world who has got a phone."

Lame Deer had invited me to the sun dance he was organizing in his home town, Winner, South Dakota. He introduced me to a number of other medicine men. I was surprised at taking part in rites that I thought were long extinct. John made me a present of the buffalo skull which had been used in the sun dance. He said, "Come back." We visited back and forth many times, traveling together, spending whole days doing nothing but talking. The idea of writing a book occurred to us spontaneously, without argument, as if we had planned it all the time. I had, by then, already filled many notebooks of our conversations over a period of four years and recorded a great number of tapes. Yet I felt that I should visit as many medicine men as possible, together with Lame Deer, in order to round out the story and to gain a wider perspective. So I went out to the Dakotas for one more long trip, taking my family.

One day we were sitting in the house of a young medicine man, Leonard Crow Dog. John and he talked about how bad they felt seeing the sun dance being commercialized, the ticket-selling, the circus atmosphere, the desecration. Lame Deer said, "A few of us medicine men should get together and change all this." Leonard suggested, "Charlie Kills Enemy and John Strike don't live very far away. Somebody should go and get them in on this now." In no time we had a gathering of seven medicine men discussing the sun dance. It was a good occasion for holding a *yuwipi* ceremony. I was invited to have a sweat bath with them. Afterward I drove to Mission to get food for all the participants. When I got back to the Crow Dog place, I saw that word had already gotten around about the ceremony. People were arriving in cars, among them one old lady who said, "I know they don't put on this ceremony for me, but maybe the *yuwipi* will cure me all the same."

I knew all but two of the medicine men. Four had visited me in New York. They told me to bring my family and that it was all right to take pictures and tape the whole ceremony. They had heard about John and myself writing the book and were happy about it. "We are with you on this all the way. These things should be written down for our grandchildren."

And that was why I, an ex-Viennese turned New Yorker, was now sitting in the dark with a kettle of dog meat by my side. When the ceremony was at its height I got myself into trouble. For two years now I had been allowed to tape and photograph the ceremonies at will. This permission was based on the fact that I could be trusted not to transgress any of the unwritten laws pertaining to the ceremonies. It was all right for me to photograph a *yuwipi* meeting before the lights were extinguished, but once they were out I was under no circumstances to interfere with the spirits or try to take their picture.

There are times when I resent cameras and tape recorders. I am a mechanical idiot to begin with, engaged in a never-ending, losing battle with gadgets of all kinds. I suspect that they know how I feel about them and therefore try to get back at me. We were in the middle of the ceremony, the little lights had appeared, rattles were flying through the air. The *yuwipi* had come.

One of my electronic flash units chose this particular moment to go berserk. It began flashing of its own accord. At once there was a chorus of angry voices: "Shut off that damn light, no pictures!" I frantically tried to yank out all connections between battery and strobe, groping around in total darkness, and only made things worse. The strobe went off into a long series of brilliant flashes at intervals of 1/1000th of a second. I was in a cold sweat. If anybody believed that I was taking advantage of the situation by taking sneak photographs, I would no longer be trusted as a friend. I decided that I had to interrupt the ceremony. I said in a very loud voice: "This light has gone wild. I'm trying to disconnect it. I have already put my jacket over it. I'm not trying to take pictures."

There was an immediate response: "It's O.K. It doesn't matter. We'll wait. This is a good meeting. The spirits are here. They know you." Someone pushed a blanket over to me. "There, cover it all up." At the mention of a blanket the strobe finally gave in and stopped flashing. The ceremony resumed.

When it was finally over and the kerosene lamp was lit again, everybody said that it had been a great meeting, that all present had felt the spirits, the power of the stones. The sick lady thought that she was feeling better. When it was my turn to speak a few words I apologized for the disturbance I had caused. I also said that the strobe light had been like the spirits, like the Indian religion—hard to extinguish. Everybody smiled. Somebody named Bill, one of the medicine men, rolled a good-sized round, grayish rock toward me with his foot. To me it looked like one of the fossile concretions which one can find in the Badlands. I had broken many of them open to find 200-million-years-old opalescent seashells in them. Bill said, "Do you want to ask me a question about this rock?"

"Is it a very special rock?"

Bill insisted it was just an ordinary rock, like thousands of others. Yet I had seen it before, carefully wrapped in red flannel, in somebody's medicine bundle.

"Does this rock carry a special message?"

Bill answered that some rocks had a message written on them by nature. He didn't know about this one.

"Does this rock have something to do with me?"

Bill pretended not to know. I couldn't think of another question to ask him. Bill seemed disappointed, as if he expected something more from me. I felt stupid.

Suddenly the medicine men grabbed hold of me and pulled me into the center of the room where the altar had been set up. Two were holding my arms, while Lame Deer was placing the head of a bald eagle upon my head, saying, "The spirits have told us to give you a name, the name of a human being. You'll be known from now on as Inyan Wasicun." Somebody was burning sweetgrass, "smoking me up." I was also being fanned with an eagle feather. I was led back to my seat. Charlie Kills Enemy came over to me and shook my hand, giving me a big smile. "You got a good name there, not one of those phony names they give to a big-shot politician for money—something like 'Big White Eagle,' 'Proud Eagle,' Eagle something or other, that's phony. But Inyan Wasicun, that's a real name, a good one."

I knew that *inyan* meant rock and that *wasicun*

meant "white man." My name could therefore be interpreted as "Rock White Man," or "White Man with the Rock." The Sioux name for Moses, for instance, is Inyan Wasicun Wakan—Rock White Man Holy, because Moses went up on the mountain, had a vision and brought back an inscribed stone, which would make him into something of a *yuwipi* medicine man. But things are never quite so simple when it comes to Sioux symbolism. *Inyan* is not only a stone but also the spirit of the stone, its hidden message, the name of an ancient god. And *wasicun* does not mean only "white man." A modern Sioux dictionary defines *wasicun* as follows:

A) The white man, as used disparagingly.

B) Any person or thing that is *waken*. (Holy, supernatural, spiritual.)

C) Also a person or thing having, or characterized by, special powers resident in the universe and looked upon as a container or carrier of *"Ton"* (a spiritual power, any object into which has been put *"Ton"* by a holy man for his ceremonies and carried about him in a bag).

I asked my friends in what way I should interpret my new name but got no clear-cut answer except the repeated assurance that it was a good one. Leonard Crow Dog said, "I put it like this, the way I understand it. Inyan—that's the mind in your body. Inyan Wasicun can make a transaction, bring a dead body back. It's a spirit that helps. What you are doing there is being done in the Indian way. It makes you a spokesman. Up to now you spoke only for yourself. Now you are standing on that rock. It won't break. It will go into your boys.

"When you have grown old, when you are dead and gone, the younger ones among us will remember you. At a powwow somebody will give a donation to the drummers, go to the announcer stand and tell the people they'll sing a song for you, for Inyan Wasicun."

I was very touched but told him I was in no special hurry to be honored in this way. Johnny Strike was grinning. "That book John and you are doing, we're behind you on that. If it turns out to be a good book, then you'll be Inyan Wasicun the Interpreter of Mysteries. If the book turns out badly, then you'll just be a white man with rocks in your head." After that we had some dog meat and berry soup.

*Richard Erdoes*
New York

# GLOSSARY

*alowan:* singing a song of praise
*anpo wicahpi:* the morning star
*ate:* father
*bloka:* the male of animals
*blota hunka:* a war leader
*čan:* a tree, wood; prefix for anything made of wood
*čan cega:* drum
*čan gleska:* a hoop, the sacred circle
*čanku wicasa:* road man, he who presides over a
    peyote meeting
*čanshasha:* the red willow-bark tobacco
*čante:* the heart
*čanunpa:* the sacred pipe
*hanblečeya (hanblechia):* vision quest
*hanhepi:* night
*hanhepi wi:* the night-sun (moon)
*hehaka:* elk
*heyoka:* a sacred clown
*hokši (hokshi):* a child
*hokši cala:* baby
*hokšila:* boy
*hunka:* ancestor
*hunka lowanpi:* the making-of-relatives ceremony
*hupa gluza:* raising one's pipe in prayer
*ikce wičaša:* the people, the common wild men, the
    Indians
*iktomé (unktomi):* spider, the tricky spider-man
*ina:* mother
*inipi:* a sweat bath
*iňyaň:* a stone, rock, pebble
*išnati (ishnati):* to menstruate, dwelling apart
*išta (ishta):* the eye
*kaňkakpa:* opening a vein to bleed a patient
*kinnickinnick:* Indian tobacco

303

*kola:* friend

*kunshi, unči:* grandmother

*Lakota:* Indian name for the Western Sioux

*lekši:* uncle

*luta:* red

*mahpiya:* the clouds, the sky, heaven

*maka:* the earth

*maka sitomni:* the world, the world over, the universe

*mato:* bear

*maza:* metal; prefix for anything made of metal

*mazaska:* money (white metal)

*mitakuye oyasin:* all my relatives; words spoken after many Sioux ceremonies

*mni (mini):* water

*mni sha:* wine

*mni wakan:* whiskey, hard liquor

*nagi:* the spirit, soul, essence

*nape:* hand

*ohitika:* brave

*oinikaga tipi:* sweat lodge

*olowan:* song

*owanka wakan:* a holy place, altar

*peji:* herb, grass

*pejuta:* medicine

*pejuta wičaša:* medicine man

*peta:* fire

*peta owihankeshni:* the fire without end, the sacred fire

*pte:* the female buffalo, buffalo cow

*ptehinčala:* buffalo calf

*ptehinčala huhu canunpa:* buffalo-calf-bone pipe, the sacred pipe of the Western Sioux

*ša (sha):* red

*sapa:* black (Paha Sapa—Black Hills)

*šiča (shica):* bad

*siyotanka:* flute

*ska:* white

*šunka wakan:* horse

*tahca:* deer

*Tahca Ushte:* Lame Deer
*takoja:* grandchild
*tatanka:* buffalo bull
*tate:* wind
*tate topa:* the four directions of the universe
*tunka:* a sacred stone
*tunkashila:* grandfather
*unčela:* peyote
*unči kunshi:* grandmother
*wačanga:* sweet grass (incense)
*wagmuha:* a rattle, a sacred gourd
*wakan:* holy, sacred, supernatural, mysterious
*Wakan Tanka:* the Great Spirit, the great mystery
*wakinyan:* the thunderbirds, thunder beings
*wanagi:* ghost
*wanagi wačipi:* the ghost dance
*wanblee, wanbli:* eagle
*wasicun:* the white man
*wašte (washtay):* good
*waziya:* the power of nature, the great mystery of the
    north; also the modern word for Santa Claus; a
    prehistoric old-man god
*we:* blood
*wi:* the sun
*wičaśa (wichasha):* man, mankind, human being
*wičinča:* a girl
*wičinčala:* a little girl, but commonly used for pretty
    girl
*win:* female (adj.)
*winyañ:* woman
*wiwanyank wačipi:* the sun dance
*wolakota:* peace, friendship
*woniya:* spirit, life, breath
*wopila:* a thanksgiving ceremony
*wotawe:* a personal good-luck charm, a palladium,
    war charm
*wotuhañ, otuhan:* give-away feast
*wowakan:* something supernatural
*yuwipi:* small, translucent stones found on anthills

305

and put into a sacred gourd; a ceremony in which the medicine man is tied and wrapped up like a mummy

*yuwipi wašičuñ:* a sacred stone which has magic powers in the hands of a medicine man during *yuwipi* ceremony

In spelling I follow the usage of the current, modern Sioux dictionaries. The pronunciation is as follows:

č   as in "chase," "chaste"
ḣ   as in the German "ich," "ach"
ñ   not completely pronounced, as in the French "enfant," "allons"
s   as in "sit"
ś   as in "sure," "shade"

# SUGGESTIONS FOR FURTHER READING

Charles Bowden. *Killing the Hidden Waters*. Austen: University of Texas Press, 1977.

John Epes Brown, ed. *The Sacred Pipe*. Norman: University of Oklahoma Press, 1953.

Joseph Bruchac, ed. *Survival This Way: Interviews with American Indian Poets*. Tucson: University of Arizona Press, 1987.

Laura Coltelli, ed. *Winged Words: American Indian Writers Speak*. Lincoln: University of Nebraska Press, 1990.

Raymond J. DeMallie. *The Sixth Grandfather: Black Elk's Teachings Given to John G. Neihardt*. Lincoln: University of Nebraska Press, 1984.

Raymond J. DeMallie and Douglas R. Parks, eds. *Sioux Indian Religion*. Norman: University of Oklahoma Press, 1987.

Melvin A. Gilmore. *Uses of Plants by Indians of the Missouri River Region*. Lincoln: University of Nebraska Press, 1977.

Archie Fire Lame Deer and Richard Erdoes. *Gift of Power: The Life and Teachings of a Lakota Medicine Man*. Santa Fe, N.M.: Bear & Co., 1992.

Edward Lazarus. *Black Hills, White Justice: The Sioux Nation versus the United States, 1775 to the Present*. New York: HarperCollins, 1991.

Kenneth Lincoln. *Indi'n Humor: Bicultural Play in Native America*. New York: Oxford University Press, 1993.

Peter Matthiessen. *In the Spirit of Crazy Horse*. New York: Viking, 1991.

————. *Indian Country*. New York: Penguin, 1984.

James Mooney. *The Ghost Dance Religion and the Sioux Outbreak of 1890* (1896 reprint). Chicago: University of Chicago Press, 1976.

Marla N. Powers. *Oglala Women: Myth, Ritual, and Reality*. Chicago: University of Chicago Press, 1986.

William K. Powers. *Beyond the Vision: Essays on American Indian Culture*. Norman: University of Oklahoma Press, 1987.

Geoff Sanborn. "Unfencing the Range: History, Identity, Property, and Apocalypse in *Lame Deer, Seeker of Visions.*" In *American Indian Culture and Research Journal,* vol. 14, no. 4, 1990.

Virgil J. Vogel. *American Indian Medicine*. Norman: University of Oklahoma Press, 1970.

James R. Walker. *Lakota Belief and Ritual*. Lincoln: University of Nebraska Press, 1980.

# INDEX

Alcohol
  arrest for, 60, 69–70
  moonshine, 51, 68, 81
  reasons for drinking,
    73–75, 76
  treatment of drunks,
    67–70, 71, 75
  two-day drunk, 63
All my relatives, 4,
  189–90, 207, 268
  *see also* tribal unity;
    universal family
  *see also* insert
Allotments, 31
Animal understanding, 278
Ant power, 5, 57, 135, 162,
  193
Anthropologists, 3, 41, 64,
  154, 186, 280
Army, 9, 63, 245
Atom bomb, 65, 249

Badger power, 134–35,
  172, 179
Badlands, 2, 177, 247,
  251–52, 299
  *see also* insert
Bear power, 86, 104,
  128–31, 170, 201, 252
Big Foot, xvii, xxiii, 247
Binding
  between children and
    parents, 268–69

between humans and
  Great Spirit, 203
between men and
  women, 268
during *yuwipi* ceremony,
  192, 202–06
of *hunkas* and *kolas,* 203
of tobacco ties, 197, 203
Bird power, 5, 137–39,
  169, 288
  *see also* eagle power
Birth control, 157, 180
Black Elk, xi, xv, xvii, 154,
  226
Black Hills, xx, xxii–xxv,
  36, 90–93, 97, 230
  *see also* insert
Brightman, Lee, 97–100
Bucket dance, 257
Buffalo
  brotherhood with, 131,
    269–70
  fat as offering, 215
  fight with bull, 132–34
  hair as symbol, 115
  humor of, 132
  hunting, 4, 9, 215
  power and wisdom, 120,
    131, 169
  riding, 45
  robe, 214, 269–70
  sacredness of, 122–23,
    131, 238–39